AF657214

Buddhism, Reflection on Religious Conversion

Buddhism, Reflection on Religious Conversion

Sameer Das Gupta

CYBER TECH PUBLICATIONS
4264/3, Ansari Road, Daryaganj, New Delhi-110002 (India)
Ph.: 011-23244078, 011-43559448 Fax: 011-23280028
E-Mail: cyberpublicationsdelhi@yahoo.com
Website: www.cybertechpublications.com

BUDDHISM, REFLECTION ON RELIGIOUS CONVERSION

Sameer Das Gupta

© Reserved

First Edition 2010

All rights reserved. No part of this publication may be reproduced, stored in a retrieval system or transmitted, in any form or by any means, electronic, mechanical, photo copying, recording or otherwise, without the prior permission of the publisher.

Published by : Asian Offset Printers

G.S. Rawat for **Cyber Tech Publications**
4264/3, Ansari Road, Daryaganj, New Delhi-110002 (India)
Ph.: 011-23244078, 011-43559448 Fax: 011-23280028
E-Mail: cyberpublicationsdelhi@yahoo.com
Website: www.cybertechpublications.com

Preface

In the past many scholars and thinkers have sought to discover some deep-rooted factor common to all of medieval Japanese Buddhism, especially in the case of the "Kamakura Neo-Buddhist" sects. For example, Suzuki Daisetsu (1870-1966), who made an outstanding contribution to the introduction in the West of Oriental thought--particularly Zen--termed this common factor "Japanese spirituality" and has provided the following comment: When with the advent of Kamakura times government and culture lost their distinctively aristocratic and conceptual conventions and took on the qualities of the earth, Japanese spirituality awakened to itself.

Buddhism is also a belief system which is tolerant of all other beliefs or religions. Buddhism agrees with the moral teachings of other religions but Buddhism goes further by providing a long term purpose within our existence, through wisdom and true understanding. Real Buddhism is very tolerant and not concerned with labels like 'Christian', 'Moslem', 'Hindu' or 'Buddhist'; that is why there have never been any wars fought in the name of Buddhism. That is why Buddhists do not preach and try to convert, only explain if an explanation is sought.

With a history spanning more' than two and a half millennia and over 300 million adherents worldwide, Buddhism is one of humankind's most interesting and populous religions. While a historical dictionary of Buddhism must consider the various periods, events, individuals, circumstances, texts, and concepts from which the history of Buddhism takes its shape, it must also consider the sacred sites in Buddhist geography, the festivals, rites, and rituals that configure Buddhist religious practice, the manifestation of Buddhist religiosity as witnessed in biography, art, and mythology, and the soteriological methods employed by Buddhists throughout their history.

— *Author*

Contents

1

Introduction

A well known missionary of Peking, China, was invited one day by a Buddhist acquaintance to attend the ceremony of initiation for a class of one hundred and eighty priests and some twenty laity who had been undergoing preparatory instruction at the stately and important Buddhist monastery. The beautiful courts of the temple were filled by a throng of invited guests and spectators, waiting to watch the impressive procession of candidates, acolytes, attendants and high officials, all in their appropriate vestments. No outsider was privileged to witness the solemn taking by each candidate for the priesthood of the vow to "keep the Ten Laws," followed by the indelible branding of his scalp, truly a "baptism of fire." Less private was the initiation of the lay brethren and sisters, more lightly branded on the right wrist, while all about intoned "Na Mah Pen Shih Shih Chia Mou Ni Fo." (I put my trust in my original Teacher, SùJamuni, Buddha.)

The missionary was deeply impressed by the serenity and devotion of the worshipers and by the dignity and solemnity of the service. The last candidate to rise and receive the baptism of branding was a young married woman of refined appearance, attended by an elderly lady, evidently her mother, who watched with an expression of mingled devotion, insight and pride her daughter's initiation and welcomed her at the end of the process with radiant face, as a daughter, now, in a spiritual as well as a physical sense. At that moment an attendant, noting the keen interest of the missionary, said to him rather flippantly, "Would you not like to have your arm branded, too?" "I might," he replied, "just out of curiosity, but I could not receive the branding as a believer in the Buddha. I am a Christian believer. To be branded without inward faith would be an insult to your religion as well as treachery to my own, would it not? Is not real religion a matter of the heart?"

The old lady, who had overheard with evident disapproval the remark of the attendant, turned to the missionary at once and said, "Is that the way you Westerners, you Christians, speak of your faith? Is the reality of religion for you also an inward experience of the heart?" And with that began an interesting interchange of conversation, each party discovering that in the heart of the other was a genuine longing for God that overwhelmed all the artificial, material distinctions and the human devices through which men have limited to particular and exclusive paths their way of search, and drew these two pilgrims on the way toward God into a common and very real fellowship of the spirit. A Buddhist monk was passing by a mission building in another city' of China when his attention was suddenly drawn to the Svastika and other Buddhist symbols which the architect had skilfully used in decorating the building. His face brightened as he said to his companion: "I did not know that Christians had any appreciation of beauty in their religion."

These incidents reveal aspects of the alchemy of the soul by which the real devotee of one religion perceives values which are dear to him in another religion. The good which he has attained in his old religion enables him to appropriate the better in the new religion. A converted monk, explaining his acceptance of Christianity, said: "I found in Jesus Christ the great Bodhisattva, my Saviour, who brings to fruition the aspirations awakened in me by Buddhism."

Just as it has been said that they do not know England who know England only, so it may be said with equal truth that they do not know Christianity who know it and no other faith. There are many in China like the old lady at the temple, who have found in Buddhism something of that spiritual satisfaction and stimulus which true Christianity affords, in fuller measure. The recognition of such religious values by the student or the missionary furnishes a sound foundation for the building of a truer spirituality among such devotees.

As will be seen in what follows, religion in China is at first sight a mixed affair. From the standpoint of cruder household superstitions an average Chinese family may be regarded as Taoists; the principles by which its members seek to guide their lives individually and socially may be called Confucian; their attitude of worship and their hopes for the future make them Buddhists. The student would not be far afield when he credits the religious aspirations of the Chinese today to Buddhism, regarding Confucianism as furnishing the ethical system to which they submit and Taoism as responsible for many superstitious practices. But the Buddhism found in China differs radically from that of Southern Asia, as will be made clear by the following sketch of its introduction into the Flowery Kingdom and its subsequent history.

THE ENTRANCE OF BUDDHISM INTO CHINA

Buddhism was not an indigenous religion of China. Its, founder was Gautama of India in the sixth century B.C. Some centuries later it found its way into China by way of central Asia. There is a tradition that as early as 142 B.C. Chang Ch'ien, an ambassador of the Chinese emperor, Wu Ti, visited the countries of central Asia, where he first learned about the new religion which was making such headway and reported concerning it to his master. A few years later the generals of Wu Ti captured a gold image of the Buddha which the emperor set up in his palace and worshiped, but he took no further steps.

According to Chinese historians Buddhism was officially recognized in China about 67 A.D. A few years before that date, the emperor, Ming-Ti, saw in a dream a large golden image with a halo hovering above his palace. His advisers, some of whom were no doubt already favorable to the new religion, interpreted the image of the dream to be that of Buddha, the great sage of India, who was inviting his adhesion. Following their advice the emperor sent an embassy to study into Buddhism. It brought back two Indian monks and a quantity of Buddhist classics. These were carried on a white horse and so the monastery which the emperor built for the monks and those who came after them was called the White Horse Monastery. Its tablet is said to have survived to this day.

This dream story is worth repeating because it goes to show that Buddhism was not only known at an early date, but was favored at the court of China. In fact, the same history which relates the dream contains the biography of an official who became an adherent of Buddhism a few years before the dream took place. This is not at all surprising, because an acquaintance with Buddhism was the inevitable concomitant of the military campaigning, the many embassies and the wide-ranging trade of those centuries. But the introduction of Buddhism into China was especially promoted by reason of the current policy of the Chinese government of moving conquered populations in countries west of China into China proper, The vanquished peoples brought their own religion along with them. At one time what is now the province of Shansi was populated in this way by the Hsiung-nu, many of whom were Buddhists.

The introduction and spread of Buddhism were hastened by the decline of Confucianism and Taoism. The Han dynasty (206 B. C.-221 A. D.) established a government founded on Confucianism. It reproduced the classics destroyed in the previous dynasty and encouraged their study; it established the state worship of Confucius; it based its laws and regulations upon the ideals and principles advocated by Confucius. The great increase of wealth and power under this dynasty led to a gradual deterioration in the character of the rulers and officials. The sigid Confucian regulations became burdensome to the people who ceased to respect their leaders. Confucianism lost its hold as the complete solution of the problems of life. At the same time Taoism had become a veritable jumble of meaningless and superstitious rites which served to support a horde of ignorant, selfish priests. The high religious ideals of the earlier Taoist mystics were abandoned for a search after the elixir of life during fruitless journeys to the isles of the Immortals which were supposed to be in the Eastern Sea.

At this juncture there arose in North China a sect of men called the Purists who advocated a return from the vagaries of Taoism and the irritating rules of Confucianism to the simple life practised by the Taoist mystics. When these thoughtful and earnest minded men came into contact with Buddhism they were captivated by it. It had all they were claiming for Taoist mysticism and more. They devoted their literary ability and religious fervor to the spreading of the new religion and its success was in no small measure due to their efforts. As a result of this early association the tenets of the two religions seemed so much alike that various emperors called assemblies of Buddhists and Taoists with the intention of effecting a union of the two religions into one. If the emperor was under the influence of Buddhism he tried to force all Taoists to become Buddhists. If he was favorable to Taoism he tried to make all Buddhists become Taoists.

But such mandates were as unsuccessful as other similar schemes have been. In the third century A. D. after the Han dynasty had ended, China was broken up into several small kingdoms which contended for supremacy, so that for about four hundred years the whole country was in a state of disunion. One of the strong dynasties of this period, the Northern Wei (386-535 A. D.), was distinctly loyal to Buddhism. During its continuance Buddhism prospered greatly. Although Chinese were not permitted to become monks until 335 A. D., still Buddhism made rapid advances and in the fourth century, when that restriction was removed, about nine-tenths of the people of northwestern China had become Buddhists. Since then Buddhism has been an established factor in Chinese life.

THE ESTABLISHMENT OF BUDDHISM AS THE PREDOMINATING RELIGION OF CHINA

Even the historical influences noted above do not account entirely for the spread of Buddhism in China. In order to understand this and the place which Buddhism occupies, we need to review briefly the different forms which religion takes in China and to note how Buddhism has related itself to them.

The World of Invisible Spirits

The Chinese believe in a surrounding-world of spirits, whose origin is exceedingly various. They touch life at every point. There are spirits which are guardians of the soil, tree spirits, mountain demons, fire gods, the spirits of animals, of mountains, of rivers, seas and stars, of the heavenly bodies and of many forms of active life. These spirits to the Chinese mind, of today are a projection, a sort of spiritual counterpart, of the many sided interests, practical or otherwise, of the groups and communities by whom they are worshipped. There are other spirits which mirror the ideals of the groups by which they are worshipped. Some of them may have been incarnated in the lives of great leaders. There are spirits which are mere animations, occasional spirits, associated with objects crossing the interests of men, but not constant enough to attain a definite, independent life as spiritual beings. Thus surrounding the average Chinese peasant there is a densely populated spirit world affecting in all kinds of ways his, daily existence.

This other world is the background which must be kept in mind by one who would understand or attempt to guide Chinese religious experience. It is the basis on which all organized forms of religious activity are built. The nearest of these to his heart is the proper regard for his ancestors.

The Universal Sense of Ancestor Control

The ancestral control of family life occupies so large and important a place in Chinese thought and practice that ancestor worship has been called the original religion of the Chinese. It is certain that the earliest Confucian records recognize ancestor worship; but doubtless it antedated them, growing up out of the general religious consciousness of the people.

The discussion of that origin in detail cannot be taken up here. It may be followed in the literature noted in the appendix or in the volume of this series entitled "Present-Day Confucianism." Ancestor worship is active today, however, because the Chinese as a people believe that these ancestors control in a very real way the good or evil fortunes of their descendants, because this recognition of ancestors furnishes a potent means of promoting family unity and social ethics, and, most of all, because a happy future life is supposed to be dependent upon descendants who will faithfully minister to the dead. Since each one desires such a future he is faithful in promoting the observance of the obligation.

Consequently, ancestor worship, like the previously mentioned belief in the invisible spiritual world, underlies all other religious developments. No family is so obscure or poor that it does not submit to the ritual or discipline which is supposed to ensure the favor of the spirits belonging to the community. Likewise, every such family is loyal to the supposed needs of its deceased ancestors. In a very intimate way these beliefs are interwoven with the private and social morality of every family or group in Chinese society, and must be taken into account by any one who seeks to bring a religious message to the Chinese people.

Degenerate Taoism

Taoism is that system of Chinese religious thought and practice, beginning about the fifth century B. C., which was originally based on the teachings of Lao Tzu and developed in the writings of Lieh Tzu and Chuang Tzu and found in the Tao T'hing. It is really in this original form a philosophy of some merit. According to its teaching the Tao is the great impersonal background of the world from which all things proceed as beams from the sun, and to which all beings return. In contrast to the present, transient, changing world the Tao is unchangeable and quiet. Originally the Taoists emphasized quiescence, a life in accordance with nature, as a means of assimilating themselves to the Tao, believing that in this way they would obtain length of days, eternal life and especially the power to become superior to natural conditions.

There is a movement today among Chinese scholars in favor of a return to this original highest form of Taoism. It appeals to them as a philosophy of life; an answer to its riddles. Among the masses of the people, however, Taoism manifests itself in a ritual of extreme superstition. It recommends magic tricks and curious superstitions as a means of prolonging life. It expresses itself very largely in these degrading practices which few Chinese will defend, but which are yet very commonly practiced.

The Organizing Value of Confucianism

Confucianism brought organization into these hazy conceptions of life and duty. It took for granted this spiritual-unspiritual background of animism, ancestor-worship and Taoism, but reshaped and adapted it as a whole so that it might fit into that proper organization of the state and nation which was one of its great objectives. Just as Confucianism related the family to the village, the village to the district, and the district to the state, so it organized the spiritual world into a hierarchy with Shang Ti as its head. This hierarchy was developed along the lines of the organization mentioned above. Under Shang Ti were the five cosmic emperors, one for each of the four quarters and one for heaven above, under whom were the gods of the soil, the mountains, rivers, seas, stars, the sun and moon, the ancestors and the gods of special groups. Each of the deities in the various ranks had duties to those above and rights with reference to those below. These duties and rights, as they affected the individual, were not only expressed in law but were embodied in ceremony and music, in daily religious life and practice in such a way that each individual had reason to feel that he was a functioning agent in this grand Confucian universe. If any one failed to do his part, the whole universe would suffer. So thoroughly has this idea been adopted by the Chinese people that every one joins in forcing an individual, however reluctant or careless, to perform his part of each ceremony as it has been ordered from high antiquity.

The emperor alone worshipped the supreme deity, Shang Ti; the great officers of state, according to the dignity of their office, were related to subordinate gods and required to show them adequate respect and reverence. Confucius and a long line of noted men following him were semi-deified [Footnote: Confucius was by imperial decree deified in 1908.] and highly reverenced by the literati, the class from which the officers of state were as a rule obtained, in connection with their duties, and as an expression of their ideals. To the common people were left the ordinary local deities, while all classes, of course, each in its own fashion reverenced, cherished and obeyed their ancestors. It should be remarked at this point that Confucianism of this official character has broken down, not only under the impact of modern ideas, but under the longing of the Chinese for a universal deity. The people turn to Heaven and to the Pearly Emperor, the popular counterpart of Shang Ti.

Viewed from another angle, Confucianism is an elaborate system of ethics. In writings which are virtually the scriptures of the Chinese people Confucius and his successors have set forth the principles which should govern the life of a people who recognize this spiritual universe and system. These ethics have grown out of a long and, in some respects, a sound experience. Much can be said in their favor. The essential weaknesses of the Confucian system of ethics lie in its sectional and personal loyalties and its monarchical basis. The spirit of democracy is a deadly foe to Confucianism. Another element of weakness is its excessive dependence upon the past. Confucius reached ultimate wisdom by the study of the best that had been attained before his day. He looked backward rather than forward. Consequently a modern, broadly educated Confucianist finds himself in an anomalous position. He does not need absolutely to reject the wisdom which Confucianism embodies, but he can no longer accept it as a sound, reliable and indisputable scheme of thought and action. Yet its simple ethical principles and its social relationships are basal in the lives of the vast masses of the Chinese.

Buddhism an. Inclusive Religion

Upon this, confused jumble of spiritism, superstition, loyalty to ancestors and submission to a divine hierarchy Buddhism was superimposed. It quickly dominated all because of its superior excellence. The form of Buddhism which became established in China was not, to be sure, like the Buddhism preached by Gautama and his disciples, or like that form of Buddhism which had taken root in Burma or Ceylon. Except in name, the Buddhism of Southern Asia and the Buddhism which developed in China were virtually two distinct types of religion. The Buddhism of Burma and Ceylon was of the conservative H?y¡+ ("Little Vehicle" of salvation) school, while that of China was of the progressive Mahb.na ("Great Vehicle" of salvation) school. Their differences are so marked as to be worthy of a careful statement.

The Hinayana, which is today the type of Buddhism in Ceylon, Burma and Siam, has always clung closely to tradition as expressed in the original Buddhist scriptures. Its basic ideas were that life is on the whole a time of suffering, that the cause of this sorrow is desire or ignorance, and that there is a possible deliverance from it. This deliverance or salvation is to be attained by following the eightfold path, namely, right knowledge, aspiration, speech, conduct, means of livelihood, endeavor, mindfulness and meditation. To the beatific state to be ultimately attained Gautama gave the name Nirvana, explained by his followers variously either as an utter extinction of personality or as a passionless peace, a general state of well-being free from all evil desire or clinging to life and released from the chain of transmigration. Hinayana Buddhism appeals to the individual as affording a way of escape from evil desire and its consequences by acquiring knowledge, by constant discipline, and by a devotedness of the life to religious ends through membership in the monastic order which Buddha established. It encourages, however, a personal salvation worked out by the individual alone. The Mahb.na school of Buddhists accept the general ideas of the Hinayana regarding life and salvation, but so change the spirit and objectives as to make Buddhism into what is virtually another religion. It does not confine salvation to the few who can retire from the world and give themselves wholly to good works, but opens Buddhahood to all. The "saint" of Hinayana Buddhism is the arhat who is intent on saving himself. The saint of Mahb.na Buddhism is the candidate for Buddhahood (Bodhisattva) who defers his entrance into the bliss of deliverance in order to save others. Mahb.na Buddhism is progressive. It encourages missionary enterprise and was a secret of the remarkable spread of Buddhism over Asia. Moreover, while the H?y¡+ school recognizes no god or being to whom worship is given, the Maha.n#(ame to regard Gautama himself as a god and salvation as life in a heavenly world of pure souls. Thus the Mahb.na type of thinking constitutes a bridge between H?y¡+ Buddhism and Christianity. In fact, a recent writer has declared that H?y¡+ Buddhists are verging toward these more spiritual conceptions. [Footnote: See Saunders, Buddhism and Buddhists in Southern Asia, pp. 10, 20.]

After the death of Sù*amuni [Footnote: Sù*amuni is the name by which Gautama, the Buddha, is familiarly known in China.] Buddhism broke up into a number of sects usually said to be eighteen in number. When Buddhism came to China some of these sects were introduced, but they assumed new forms in their Chinese environment. Besides the sects brought, from India the Chinese developed several strong sects of their own. Usually they speak of ten sects although the number is far larger, if the various subdivisions are included.

To indicate the manifold differences between these groups in Buddhism would take us far afield and would not be profitable. It will be of interest, however, to consider some of the chief sects. One of the sects introduced from India is the Pure Land or the Ching T'u which holds before the believer the "Western Paradise" gained through faith in Amit¨(a. Any one, no matter what his life may have been, may enter the Western Paradise by repeating the name of Amit¨(a. This sect is widespread in China. In Japan there are two branches of it known as the Nishi-Hongwanji and the Higashi-Hongwanji with their head monasteries in Kyoto. They are the most progressive sects in Japan and are carrying on missionary work in China, the Hawaiian Islands and in the United States.

Another strong sect is the Meditative sect or the Ch'an Men (Zen in Japan). This was introduced by Bodhidharma, or Tamo, who arrived in the capital of China in the year 520 A.D. On his arrival the emperor Wu Ti tried to impress the sage with his greatness saying: "We have built temples, multiplied the Scriptures, encouraged many to join the Order: is not there much merit in all this?" "None," was the blunt reply. "But what say the holy books? Do they not promise rewards for such deeds?" "There is nothing holy." "But you, yourself, are you not one of the holy ones?" "I don't know." "Who are you?" "I don't know." Thus introduced, the great man proceeded to open his missionary-labors by sitting down opposite a wall arid gazing at it for the next nine years. From this he has been called the "wall-gazer." He and his successors promulgated the doctrine that neither the scriptures, the ritual nor the organization, in fact nothing outward had any value in the attainment of enlightenment. They held that the heart of the universe is Buddha and that apart from the heart or the thought all is unreal. They thought themselves back into the universal Buddha and then found the Buddha heart in all nature. Thus they awakened the spirit which permeated nature, art and literature and made the whole world kin with the spirit of the Buddha.

"The golden light upon the sunkist peaks,

The water murmuring in the pebbly creeks,

Are Buddha. In the stillness, hark, he speaks!"

Such pantheism and quietism often lead to a confusion in moral relations, but these mystics were quite correct in their morals because they checked up their mysticism with the moral system of the Buddha. Still another important sect originated in the sixth century A. D. on Chinese soil, namely, the T'ien

T'ai (Japanese Tendai), so called because it started in a monastery situated on the beautiful T'ien T'ai mountains south of Ningpo. Chih K'ai, the founder, realized that Buddhism contained a great mass of contradictory teachings and practice, all attributed to the Buddha. He sought for a harmonizing principle and found it in the arbitrary theory that these teachings were given to different people on five different occasions and hence the discrepancies. The practical message of this sect has been that all beings have the Buddha heart and that the Buddha loves all beings, so that all beings may attain salvation, which consists in the full realization of the Buddha heart latent in them.

There was a time when these sects were very active and flourishing in China. At the present time the various tendencies for which they stood have been adopted by Buddhism as a whole and the various sectaries, though still keeping the name of the sect, live peacefully in the same monastery. All the monasteries practice meditation, believe in the paradise of Amit¨(a, and are enjoying the ironic calm advocated by the T'ien T'ai. While the struggle among the sects of China has been followed by a calm which resembles stagnation, those in Japan are very active and the reader is referred to the volume of this series on Japanese Buddhism for further treatment of the subject.

When Buddhism entered China it brought with it a new world. It was new practical and new spiritually. It brought a knowledge unknown before regarding the heavenly bodies, regarding nature and regarding medicine, and a practice vastly above the realm of magical arts. In addition to these practical benefits, Buddhism proclaimed a new spiritual universe far more real and extensive than any of which the Chinese had dreamed, and peopled with spiritual beings having characteristics entirely novel. In comparison with this new universe or series of universes which Indian imagination had created, the Chinese universe was wooden and geometric. Since it was an organized system and a greater rather than a different one, the Chinese people readily accepted it and made it their own.

Buddhism not only enlarged the universe and gave the individual a range of opportunity hitherto unsuspected, but it introduced a scheme of religious practice, or rather several of them, enabling the individual devotee to attain a place in this spiritual universe through his own efforts. These "ways" of salvation were quite in harmony with Chinese ideas. They resembled what had already been a part of the national practice and so were readily adopted and adapted by the Chinese.

Buddhism rendered a great service to the Chinese through its new estimate of the individual. Ancient China scarcely recognized the individual. He was merged in the family and the clan. Taoists, to be sure, talked of "immortals" and Confucianism exhibited its typical personality, or "princely man," but these were thought of as supermen, as ideals. The classics of China had very little to say about the common people. The great common crowd was submerged. Buddhism, on the other hand, gave every individual a distinct place in the great wheel dharma, the law, and made it possible for him to reach the very highest goal of salvation. This introduced a genuinely new element into the social and family life of the Chinese people.

Buddhism was so markedly superior to any one of the four other methods of expressing the religious life, that it quickly won practical recognition as the real religion of China. Confucianism may be called the doctrine of the learned classes. It formulates their principles of life, but it is in no strict sense a popular religion. It is rather a state ritual, or a scheme of personal and social ethics. Taoism recognizes the immediate influence of the spirit world, but it ministers only to local ideals and needs. In the usages of family and community life, ancestor worship has a definite place, but an occasional one. Buddhism was able to leave untouched each of these expressions of Chinese personal and social life, and yet it went far beyond them in ministering to religious development. Its ideas of being, of moral responsibility and of religious relationships furnished a new psychology which with all its imperfections far surpassed that of the Chinese. Buddhism's organization was so satisfying and adaptable that not only was it taken over readily by the Chinese, but it has also persisted in China without marked changes since its introduction. Most of all it stressed personal salvation and promised an escape from the impersonal world of distress and hunger which surrounds the average Chinese into a heaven ruled by Amit¨(a [Footnote: Amit¨(a, meaning "infinite light," is the Sanskrit name of one of the Buddhas moat highly revered in China. The usual Chinese equivalent is Omi-To-Fo.] the Merciful. The obligations of Buddhism are very definite and universally recognized. It enforces high standards of living, but has added significance because it draws each devotee into a sort of fellowship with the divine, and mates not this life alone, but this life plus a future life, the end of human activity. Buddhism, therefore, really expresses the deepest religious life of the people of China.

It will be worth while to note some illustrations of the conviction of the Chinese people that there are three religions to which they owe allegiance and yet that these are essentially one. They often say, "The three teachings are the whole teaching." An old scholar is reported to have remarked, "The three roads are different, but they lead to the same source." A common story reports that Confucius was asked in the other world about drinking wine, which Buddhists forbid but Taoists permit. Confucius replied: "If I do not drink I become a Buddha. If I drink I become an Immortal. Well, if there is wine, I shall drink; if there is none, I shall abstain." This expresses characteristically the Chinese habit of adaptation. Such a decision sounds quite up to date.

The Ethical Culture Society of Peking, recently organized, has upon its walls pictures of Buddha, Lao Tzu, Confucius and Christ. Its members claim to worship Shang Ti as the god of all religions. An offshoot of this society, the T'ung Shan She, associates the three founders very closely with Christ. It claims to have a deeper revelation of Christ than the Christians themselves. A new organization, the Tao Yuan, plans to harmonize the three old religions with Mohammedanism and Christianity.

Buddhism has consistently and continually striven to bring about a unity of religion in China by interpenetrating Confucianism and Taoism. Quite early the Buddhists invented the story that the Bodhisattva Ju T'ung was really Confucius incarnate. There was at one time a Buddhist temple to Confucius in the province of Shantung. The Buddhists also gave out the story that Bodhisattva Kas'yapa was the incarnation of Lao Tzu, the founder of Taoism. An artist painted Lao Tzu transformed into a Buddha, seated in a lotus bud with a halo about his head. In front of the Buddha was Confucius doing reverence. A Chinese scholar, asked for his opinion about the picture, said: "Buddha should be seated; Lao Tzu should be standing at the side looking askance at Buddha; and Confucius should be grovelling on the floor."

A monument dating from 543 A. D., illustrates this tendency of Buddhism to represent its own superiority in Chinese religious life. At the top of the monument is Brahma, lower down is Sù*amuni with his disciples, Ananda and Kas'yapa on one face, and on the other Sù*amuni again, conversing with Buddha Prabhutaratna and worshipped by monks and Bodhisattvas. On the pedestal are Confucian and Taoist deities, ten in number. Thus Buddhism sought to rank itself clearly above the other two religions. From the early days Buddhism regarded itself as their superior and began the processes of interpenetration and absorption. In consequence the values originally inherent in Buddhism have come to be regarded as the natural possession of the Chinese. It does express their religious life, especially in South China, where outward manifestations of religion are perhaps more marked than in the north.

BUDDHISM AND THE PEASANT

In order that, one may realize the place that Buddhism holds in the religious life of the Chinese people as a whole, he must turn to the organizations through which it functions. It is sometimes difficult to estimate the place of Buddhism in China, because it so interpenetrates the whole cultural and social life of the people. It becomes their "way." To see how it touches the life of the average man or woman in various ways will, therefore, be illuminating. The most outstanding evidence of devotion are the many monasteries which dot the land in all Buddhist countries. China is less dominated by them than other lands, yet they form a very important reason for the persistence and strength of Buddhism there. One of the famous old shrines will represent them as a class and give evidence of their importance.

The Monastery of Kushan

Kushan Monastery, located about four hours' ride by sedan-chair from Foochow, is a famous shrine of South China. It occupies a large amphitheater about fifteen hundred feet above the plain, part way up Kushan, the "Drum Mountain," some three thousand feet high. From the top of the mountain on clear days with the help of a glass the blue shores of Formosa may be seen on the eastern horizon. The spacious monastery buildings are surrounded by a grove of noble trees, in which squirrels, pheasants, chipmunks and snakes enjoy an undisturbed life.

The ascent to the monastery begins on the bank of the Min River. At the foot of the mountain in a large temple the traveler may obtain mountain chairs carried by two or more coolies. The road, paved with granite slabs cut from the mountain side, consists of a series of stone stairs, which zig-zag up the mountain under the shadow of ancient pine trees. Every turn brings to view a bit of landscape carpeted with rice, or a distant view where mountains and sky meet. A brook rushes by the side of the road. Here it breaks into a beautiful waterfall. There it gurgles' in a deep ravine. The sides of the road are covered with large granite blocks which, loosened from the mountain side by earthquakes, have disposed themselves promiscuously. Their blackened, weather-beaten sides are incised with Chinese characters. One of them bears the words: "We put our trust in Amit¨(a." Another immortalizes the sentiments of some great official who has made the pilgrimage to the mountain. Near the monastery stand the sombre dagobas where repose the ashes of former abbots and monastery officials. Not far away on the other side of the road, hidden by trees, is the crematory where the last remains of the brethren are consumed by the flames.

As one approaches the monastery he hears the regular sounds of a bell tolled by a water-wheel, reminding the faithful of Buddha's law. He sees monks strolling leisurely about and lay brethren carrying wood, cultivating the gardens, or tending the animals released by pious devotees to heap up merit for themselves in the next world. Just inside the main gate is a large fish pond, where goldfish of great size struggle with one another, and with the lazy turtles, for the round hard cakes purchased from the monks by the merit-seeking devotee.

The monastery itself consists of a large group of buildings erected about stone-paved courts, rising in terraces on the mountain side. The large court at the entrance leads to the "Hall of the Four Kings." As one enters the spacious door, he is faced by a jolly, almost naked image of the "Laughing Buddha." This is Maitra®, the Mea siah of the Buddhists, who will return to the world five thousand years after the departure of Sù*amuni. In the northern monasteries Maitra® is often represented as reaching a height when standing of seventy feet or more, which indicates the stature to which man will attain when he returns to earth. On each side of the visitor are two immense images of the Deva kings. In Brahman cosmogony they were the guardians of the world. In this entrance hall of the Buddhist monastery they stand as guardians of the Buddhist faith. In the same hall looking toward the open court beyond is Wei To, another guardian deity of Buddhism. Somewhere near by is Kuan Ti, the god worshipped by the soldiers and merchants. Although a Confucian god, he was early adopted by Buddhist monks into their pantheon and made the guardian of their Order.

Beyond this entrance hall is a large stone-paved court. On the right side is a bell-tower whose bell is tolled by a monk who has kept the vow of silence for fourteen years. On the left is a drum-tower. On the right one finds a series of small shrines. A passage way leads to the library where numerous Buddhist writings repose in lacquered cases, some of them written in their own blood by devout monks. On the same side are guest halls, the dining room for three hundred monks, and the spacious, well equipped kitchen with running water piped from a reservoir in the hills above. A store where books, images and the simple requirements of the monks can be obtained is just above the dining room. On the left side of the court are large buildings used as dormitories far the monks, storerooms, and for housing the great printing establishment with its thousands of wooden blocks on which are carved passages from the Buddhist scriptures. Here also are kept the coffins in which the monks are to be burned.

On a terrace above the north side of the court rises the main hall, called the "Hall of the Triratna," the Buddhist Trinity, where three gilded images are seated on a lotus flower with halos covering their backs and heads. The center image is that of Sù*amuni, the Buddha. On his right is Yao Shih, the Buddha of medicine, and on the left, Amit¨(a. Quite often these images are said to represent the Buddha, the Law and the Community of Monks. On the altar are candlesticks and a fine incense burner from which curls of smoke arise. An immense lamp hangs from the ceiling. In the rear are banners with praises to Buddha given by pious devotees. The floor is tiled and covered with round mats made of palm fiber on which the monks kneel during worship. Before the mats are low stands for books. On each side of this main hall are the images of nine Buddhist saints (arhats), eighteen in all. Behind this large temple opens another court and on a terrace above it stands the hall of the Law with the images of Kuan Yin, the goddess of Mercy, and the twenty-four devas. Here also are small images of viceroys and patrons of the monastery.

The hillsides are dotted with numerous temples and shrines. There is one to Chu-Hsi, the great philosopher of the Sung dynasty, who was born in Fukien. In it are preserved a few characters indited by his hand. On the west side of the monastery are large buildings for the housing of animals released by merit-seeking devotees. Here cows, hogs, goats, chickens, geese and ducks spend their old age without fear of beginning their transmigration by forming the main portion of a Chinese feast.

The monastery is governed by an abbot, usually a man of good business ability, elected by the monks. Under him are the officers of the two wings or groups of attendants. One set looks after the spiritual interests, of the monks; the-other takes care of their material needs: The monks have worship about two o'clock in the morning and again at about four in the afternoon. The rest of the long day they spend in meditation, or study, in strolling about the mountain side or in sleep. Their life is separated from all stirring contact with the life of the world.

Monasteries Control F§«-shui

This monastery with its appointments is a good type of the monasteries all over China. It was founded at the request of the inhabitants of the neighborhood, because the dragons of the region used to cause much damage to the crops in the surrounding country. A holy monk came, founded the monastery, and by his good influence so curbed the dragons that the country-side has enjoyed peace ever since and the monastery has prospered. Since the fourth century of our era records show that by the building of monasteries in strategic place's holy monks brought rains and prosperity to various regions, or prevented floods and calamities from damaging the villages. In other words the monasteries are regarded as the controllers of f§«-shui (wind and water). According to the Chinese philosophy winds and water are spiritual forces and may be so controlled by other spiritual forces that instead of bringing harm they will confer benefit upon the people. Floods and dry seasons are so frequent in China that any institution holding out the promise of regulating them would become firmly established in the affection of the people. The monasteries have taken this place.

One of the picturesque features of a Chinese landscape is the pagoda. These structures were introduced in the early stages of Buddhism to enshrine the relics of Buddha. It was said that Buddha's body consisted of eighty thousand parts, hence numerous pagodas were erected to shelter these relics. Inasmuch as a pagoda contained the relics of Buddha, it possessed magic power and so came to play a great part in the control of the winds and the rains. The pagoda in China has an odd number of stories varying from three to thirteen. The odd numbers belong to the positive principle in nature which is superior to the negative principle. The pagoda plays quite a part in the festivals of the people. On certain occasions the stories are hung with lanterns and the pagodas are visited by numerous throngs.

Prayer for Rain

Prayers for rain afford such a common illustration of the relation of Buddhism to the life of the peasant that a detailed presentation of such a service may be of seal value.

During a prolonged drought in some district of China, when the heat opens gaping cracks in the fields and the grain is drying up, the populace may visit their highest official and apprise him of the dire situation. He often forbids the slaughter of all animals for three days and, in case rain has not thereby come, he goes in person or sends a deputy to the nearest monastery to direct the monks to pray for rain.

(a) The Altar.—On such an occasion the great hall of the Law may be used for the ceremony. Quite often a special altar is erected in an enclosure near the monastery on a platform one foot high and twenty-five feet on each side, overspread by a tent of green cloth. In the center seats are arranged for the presiding monk and his assistants. On each of the four sides of the altar is placed an image of the Dragon King who is supposed to control the rain. If an image is not obtainable a piece of paper inscribed with the name of the dragon may be used. Flowers, fruits and incense are spread before the images. On the doors of the tent are painted dragons with clouds. The tent and altar are green and the monks wear green garments, because green belongs to the spring and suggests rain. For this ceremony the monks prepare themselves by abstinence and cleansing. The presiding monk is one of high moral character and religious fervor. While some monks recite appropriate sutras, two others look after the offerings, the incense, and the sprinkling of water during the ceremony to suggest the coming of rain. The services continue day and night, being conducted by groups of monks in succession.

(b) The Prayer Service.—The ceremonial is opened by a chant as follows: "Pearly dew of the jade heavens, golden waves of Buddha's ocean, scatter the lotus flowers on a thousand thôusand worlds of suffering, that the heart of mercy may wash away great calamity, that a drop may become a flood, that a drop may purify mountains and rivers.

"We put our trust in the Bodhisattvas and Mahá,ttvas that purify the earth."

The chant ended, a monk takes a bowl of water and repeats thrice: "We put our trust in the great merciful Kuan Yin Bodhisattva." Then follows the chant:

"The Bodhisattva's sweet dew of the willow is able to make one drop spread over the ten directions. It washes away the rank odors and dirt. It keeps the altars clean and pure. The mysterious words of the doctrine will be reverently repeated."

This chant ended, the monks intone incantations of Kuan Yin, quite unintelligible even to them, but of magical value. While these are being uttered, the presiding monk and his attendants walk around the altar, while one of them with a branch sprinkles water on the floor. This symbolizes the cleansing of the altar and of the monks from all impurities which might render the ritual ineffective. When the perambulating monks have returned to their place, while the sprinkler continues his duties, the monks repeat the words: "We put our trust in the sweet dew kings, Bodhisattvas and Mahá,ttvas."

The Bodhisattvas have now come to the purified altar and while the abbot offers incense to them, the monks repeat the words:

"The fields are destroyed so that they resemble the back of a tortoise. The demons of drought produce calamity. The dark people [Footnote: A term denoting the Chinese.] pray earnestly while crops are being destroyed. We pray that abundant, limpid liquid may descend to purify and refresh the whole world. The clouds of incense rise."

This plaint is repeated thrice and is followed by an invocation:

"Wholeheartedly we cast ourselves to the earth, O Triratna, who dost exist eternally in the realm of dharma of the ten directions."

The leader remains quiet a long time with his eyes closed, visualizing the Buddhas, the Bodhisattvas, the dragon kings, and the saints, all with their heavenly eyes and ears knowing that this region is afflicted with drought, that an altar has been constructed and that all have come to make petition. This meditation is regarded as of chief importance. It is followed by an announcement to the effect that the sutra praying for rain was given by the Buddha, that a drought is afflicting the land, that the altar has been erected in accordance with the regulations and that prayer is being made for rain. But fearing that something may have been overlooked, the magic formula of "the king of light who turns the wheel" is read seven times so as to remedy such oversight.

The altar having thus been cleansed of all impurities, the rain sutra is opened and the one hundred and eighty-eight dragon kings are urged by name in groups of ten to take action. The formula is as follows:

"We with our whole heart invite such and such dragon kings to come. We desire that the heart and wisdom which knows others intuitively will move the spirits above to obey the Buddha, to take pity on the people below and to come to our province and send down sweet rain."

When the dragons have all been duly invited, the monks chant suitable magical formulas, while the leader sits in meditation visualizing these dragon kings and their tender solicitude for the people in distress. The monastery bell is sounded and the wooden fish is beaten, while drums and cymbals add their effect. The whole is intended to draw the attention of the dragon kings to the drought. Then the fifty-four Buddhas are invited in a similar manner in groups of ten, the sixth group consisting of four. A similar form of address is used and similar magical formulas are recited with the noisy accompaniment. The ceremony concludes by the expression of the hope that the three jewels (Buddha, the Law and the Community of Monks) and the dragon kings will grant the rain.

Upon the altar are four copies of an announcement to the dragon kings and Buddhas. On the first day three copies are sent to them through the flames, one to the Buddhas, one to the dragon kings and one to the devas. One copy is read daily and then sent up at the thanksgiving ceremony. The announcement is as follows:

"We put our trust in the limitless, reverent ocean clouds, the dragons of august virtue and all their host, all dragon kings and holy saints. Their august virtue is difficult to measure. In accord with the command of Buddha they send liquid rain. May their quiet mercy descend to the altar; may they send down purity and freshness, spreading over the ten directions. We put our trust in the company of dragon kings of the clouds, the saints and the Bodhisattvas."

The offerings are made only in the morning inasmuch as the Buddhas, following ancient custom, are not supposed to eat after the noonday meal. Great care is taken that the altar shall not be desecrated by any one who eats meat or drinks wine. The magic formulas of great mercy are uttered or the name of Kuan Yin is repeated a thousand times. The monks, take turn in these services which continue day and night until rain comes.

(c) Its Meaning.—In the religious consciousness of the people is the idea that the drought is a punishment for sin. The altar is made pure and acceptable and sin is removed in various symbolic ways. This fits in with the idea that man is an intimate part of the world order. His sin disturbs the order of nature.

Heaven manifests displeasures by sending down calamities upon men. Men should cease their wrongdoing which disturbs the natural order and should also wash away the effects of their sins. The services for rain with their magic formulas help to clear away the consequences of sin and to predispose Heaven to grant its blessings again.

Monasteries Are Supported Because They Control F§«-shui

The prayers for rain are an important part of the Chinese peasant's world order. Drought is the manifestation of Heaven's displeasure at the infraction of Heaven's laws. It calls for self-examination and repentance. Thus the monastery opens up the windows of the universal order as this touches the humble tiller of the soil.

The Buddhist monasteries not only hold services in time of drought, but also in time of flood and at times when plagues of grasshoppers afflict the land, or when diseases afflict human beings. Their adoption of Chinese customs led them to have special ceremonies at the eclipse of the sun and moon, although they knew the cause of the eclipse. Peasants and officials support the monastery because of these services regulating the wind and water influences and through them bringing the people into harmonious relation with the great world of spirits.

BUDDHISM AND THE FAMILY

One of the criticisms of the Chinese against Buddhism is that it is opposed to filial piety. According to Mencius the greatest unfilial act is to leave no progeny. In spite of this charge Buddhism has done much for the family. It has taken over the ethics of the family, filial piety, obedience and respect for elders, and has made them a part of its system. Transgression of these fundamental duties is visited by dire punishments in the next world. The faithful observance is followed not only by the rewards of the Confucian system, but results in the greatest rewards in the future life.

Kuan Yin, the Giver of Children and Protector of Women

Buddhism has done more. Out of its atmosphere of love and mercy toward all beings has developed Kuan Yin, the ideal of

Chinese womanhood, the goddess of Mercy, who embodies the Chinese ideal of beauty, filial piety and compassion toward the weak and suffering. She is especially the goddess of women, being interested in all their affairs. Her image is found in almost every household and her temples have a place in every part of China.

A brief history of this deity will enable us to understand the significance of the cult. Kuan Yin started as a male god in India, called Aval?ö¬ara, who was worshipped from the third to the seventh century of our era. He was the protector of sailors and people in danger. In the course of time, either in China or in India, the god became a goddess. Some think that this was due to the influence of Christianity. In China both forms survive, though the goddess is better known. A Buddhist once said that a Bodhisattva is neither male nor female and appears in whatever form is convenient.

Kuan Yin is a very popular goddess. Her experiences in Hades are dramatically presented by traveling theatrical companies. Her deeds of mercy are portrayed in art. Her well known story runs as follows:

Kuan Yin was the daughter of the ruler of a prosperous kingdom located somewhere near the island of Sumatra. Her birth was announced to the queen by a dream. The little girl ate no meat nor milk. Her disposition was very good. Her intelligence was most extraordinary. Once she read anything she never forgot it.

At the age of sixteen her father tried to betroth her to a young prince. She refused and decided to give herself to a life of fasting and abstinence. Angered b-v her obstinacy the father ordered her to take off her court dress and jewels, to put on the garb of a servant and to carry water for the garden. The garden never looked so beautiful. The daughter also looked well and showed no signs of weariness, because the gods assisted her in her work.

Relenting a little the king sent an older sister to urge Kuan Yin to accept the husband he had found for her. When she refused, he sent her to a monastery and charged the abbess to treat her harshly, so that she might be forced to return home. Expecting to win the king's favor, the abbess put the most unpleasant tasks on the girl. But again the gods assisted her and made her work light, so that her tasks were always well done and the young woman was cheerful.

One day the report came to the king that his daughter was associating with a young monk discussing heterodox doctrines and that she had given birth to a child. This news so enraged the king that he burned the monastery, killing many monks. The princess was captured and brought before him. Inasmuch as she was obdurate, the king ordered her to be executed. The executioner's sword, however, broke into a thousand pieces without doing her any injury. The king then ordered her to be strangled. A golden image sixteen feet high appeared on the spot. The princess laughed and cried: "Where there was no image, an image appeared. I see the real form. When body flesh is strangled, then appear the lights of ten thousand roads." She went to purgatory and purgatory at once changed into paradise. Yama, in order to save his purgatory, sent her back to the world. She appeared at Puto, an island off the coast of Chekiang near Ningpo. Here she rescued sailors and performed many miracles for people in distress.

In the meantime the father, who had committed many sins, became sick. His allotted time of life had been shortened by twenty years. Moreover, an ulcer grew on his body for every one of the five hundred monks he had killed when he burned the monastery. A miserable, loathsome old man, he came to an old monk, who was really the princess in disguise, and asked for help. The monk told him that an eye and an arm of a blood relative made into medicine was the only cure for his trouble. The two living daughters were willing to make such an offering, but their husbands would not permit them to do so.

The old monk urged the monarch to take up a life of abstinence, to rebuild the monastery he had burned, and to provide money for services to take the five hundred monks whom he had killed through purgatory. He also said that a nun in the convent would offer an arm and an eye. When the monarch entered the monastery, he found hanging before the incense burner an arm and an eye. These were boiled, mixed with medicine and rubbed on the king's body. He soon became well. Further inquiry revealed that these members belonged to his daughter.

This is the story of the most popular goddess in China. She is worshipped by her devotees on the first and fifteenth of every month, on the nineteenth of the sixth month, when she became a Bodhisattva, and on the nineteenth of the ninth month, when she put on the necklace. A month after marriage every young bride is presented with an image of the Goddess of Mercy, an incense-burner and candlesticks.

This goddess is worshipped whenever trouble comes to man or woman. Her names signify her willingness to listen to all prayers. She is the "one who regards the voice," i.e., prayer; "one who hears the prayers of the world;" "one who regards and exists by himself as sovereign;" "the ancestor of Buddha who regards prayer;" "one who frees from fear;" "Buddha the august king;" "the great white robed scholar;" "great compassion and mercy."

Kuan Yin, the Model of Local Mother-Goddesses

This conception is the creation of the social and religious consciousness of the women in China. It reveals their aspirations for mercy, compassion, filial piety and for the beauty that crowns a well developed character. Such an ideal does not mean that these have been realized in all the numerous homes of the Chinese, but it manifests their sense of such an ideal to be realized in life and their ardent longing for its realization.

Mother-goddesses are found all over China and they have all of them been influenced by Kuan Yin. Some of them have originated with actual women who were deified after death. Here is the story of one of these goddesses who presides over the censer in a small temple in Formosa. She was born in the province of Kuangtung. At the age of seven she was adopted by a family as the future wife of their eighteen-year-old son. One day while crossing a river he was drowned. This was a great blow to her. When she was fourteen years old the father of the family died. The two women, thus left alone, wept bitterly day and night. The comfort of relatives was of little avail. The mother was becoming emaciated with grief. The daughter, unable to bear the strain any longer, washed herself, burned incense before the ancestral tablet of her betrothed, and then took this vow: "I am willing to remain a virgin, to apply myself to carrying water and working at the mortar and to serve my mother-in-law. If I cherish any other purpose and change my chastity and obedience, may Heaven slay me and earth annihilate me."

When the mother heard this vow she stopped her weeping. Inasmuch as they had no uncle to look after them, they worked day and night. A relative of her future husband gave her one of his sons as an adopted son. The child died after a few months. This was a great grief. Then the mother died. The daughter sold her possessions to obtain money for a proper burial. She had only a coarse mourning cloth for her dress. After a while she adopted a child as her son. When he grew up she found him a wife who served her as faithfully as she had served her mother-in-law. When she was eighty years old, she dreamed that the golden maid and jade messenger of Kuan Yin stood beside her saying: "The court of Heaven has ordered you to become a god (sh©«." She died soon after this. She said of herself:

"Shang Ti took compassion upon me during my life, because with a firm heart I kept my chastity and served my mother-in-law with complete obedience. Therefore he gave me the office of Kuan Pin. I have performed my duties in several places. Now I am transferred to Formosa."

This story and many others like it mirror the moral ideals of the women of China in the midst of their struggles for help and light and guidance.

Exhortations on Family Virtues

The Buddhists issue a large number of tracts. These are very commonly paid for by devotees who make a vow that, if their parent becomes well, they will pay for the printing of several hundred or thousand of these tracts for free distribution. In these tracts are usually many stories illustrating the rewards of filial piety. The story is told in one of them about a Mrs. Chin whose father-in-law being ill was unable to sleep for sixty days. His condition grew worse. Mrs. Chin knelt before Kuan Yin's altar, cut out a piece of flesh from her arm and cooked it with the father's food. His health at once improved and he lived to the age of seventy-seven. Another story is told in the same tract of a woman who cut out a piece of her liver and gave it as medicine to her mother-in-law.

These Buddhist tracts take up all the moral habits which make the family and clan strong and stable and surround them by the highest sanctions. A tract picked up in a Buddhist temple at Hangchow purports to be the revelation of the will of Buddha. It urges sixteen virtues. The first is filial piety. The tract says:

"Filial piety is the chief of all virtues. Heaven and Earth honor filial piety. There is no greater sin than to cherish unfilial thoughts. The spirits know the beginning of such thoughts. Heaven openly rewards a heart that is filial."

The second one mentioned is another important family virtue, namely, reverence:

"The saints, sages, immortals and Buddhas are the outgrowth of reverence. The greatest sin is to lack reverence for father and mother. When brothers lack reverence for one another, they harm the hands and feet. When husband and wife lack reverence, the harmony of the household is ruined. When friends do not have reverence, they bring about calamity."

Then follow similar exhortations on sincerity, justice, self-restraint, forbearance, benevolence, generosity, absence of pride, covetousness, lying, adultery, mutual love, self-denial, hope for the consolations of religion and for an undivided heart ruled by peace. These are virtues quite essential to the integrity of the family. They are taught, not in the abstract but by the exhibition of shining examples, by vivid representations of the rewards both here and hereafter, and by pictures of awful punishments. So by precept and example, by threat of punishment here and hereafter and by declaration of reward in the future Buddhism has tried to maintain the family virtues of the Confucian system and has attempted to permeate them by the spirit of sacrifice. Still it has always been the sacrifice of the weak for the strong, of the young for the aged, of the low for the high, of women for men.

Services for the Dead

Buddhism very early took over the relatively simple services for the dead and developed them into an elaborate ritual which made very vivid the spiritual universe which Buddhism introduced. In the sixth century a service was held in behalf of the father-in-law of Emperor Ning Ti (516-528 A. D.) for seven times every seven days. He feasted a thousand monks every day, and caused seven persons to become monks. On the hundredth day after the death he feasted ten thousand monks and caused twenty-seven persons to become monks.

Since that time services on every seventh day after the decease until the forty-ninth day, when a grand finale ends the ceremonies, have been very popular.

The object of such services is to conduct the soul of the dead through purgatory, in order that it may return to life or enter the Western Paradise. This is done by making a pleasing offering to the guardians and officers of purgatory, and to the gods and Bodhisattvas whose mercy saves people. Numerous missives are consigned to the flames, informing the rulers of the nether world about the soul of the dead; offerings of gold and silver, of various articles of apparel, of trunks, houses, and servants are made, all, however, made out of bamboo frames covered with paper. Various powerful incantations are recited which force open the gates of purgatory and let the soul out.

The services may be crowded into one day or they may be held on every seventh day until the forty-ninth day, i.e., seven sevens. Various explanations are given' for these services.

During the first week the soul of the dead arrives at the "Demon Gate Barrier." Here money is demanded by the demons on the ground that in his last transmigration the deceased borrowed money. Accordingly large quantities of silver shoes [Footnote: The silver used for this purpose is molded, in accordance with ancient usage, in the shape of shoes and carried about in that form by merchants.] must be sent to the dead so that he may settle all claims and avoid beating and inconvenience. During the second week the soul arrives at a place where he is weighed. If the evil outweighs the good, the soul is sawn asunder and ground to powder. In the third week he comes to the "Bad Dog" village. Here good people pass unharmed, but the evil are torn by the fierce beasts until the blood flows. In the fourth week the soul is confronted with a large mirror in which he sees his evil deeds and their consequences, seeing himself degraded in the next transmigration to a beast. In the fifth week the soul views the scenes in his own village.

In the sixth week he reaches the bridge which spans the "Inevitable River." This bridge is 100,000 feet high and one and three-tenths of an inch wide. It is crossed by riding astride as on a horse. Beneath rushes the whirl-pool filled with serpents darting their heads to and fro. At the foot of the bridge lictors force unwilling travelers to ascend. The good do not cross this bridge, but are led by "golden youth" to gold and silver bridges which cross the stream on either side of this "Bridge of Sighs."

In the seventh week the soul is taken first to Mrs. Wang who dispenses a drink which blots out all memories of the earthly life. Then the individual enters the great wheel of transmigration. This is divided into eighty-one sections from which one hundred and eight thousand small and tortuous paths radiate out into the four continents of the world. The soul is directed along one of these paths and is duly reborn in the world as an animal or as a human being or passes on into the Western Paradise.

In imitation of this bridge a bridge is built of tables in front of the home of the dead. At the end the tables are placed upside down and a lantern placed on each table-leg. At night this bridge is illuminated. A company of monks repeat their prayers and incantations, while others mount upon the bridge to impersonate devils. The pious son with the tablet of his deceased parent comes to take his father over the bridge. When his way is disputed by the demons, he falls on his knees and begs and gives them money, negotiating the passage at last with the aid of a large quantity of silver.

Another ceremony is the breaking through purgatory. Five supplications duly signed are addressed to the proper authorities, four being suspended at each of the four sides of the table and one at the center. Tiles are then placed over the table or on the ground. After incantations have been repeated to the accompaniment of the sounding of the bell and the wooden fish, the supplications are burned and the tiles are broken as a symbol of breaking through purgatory and of releasing the soul.

Thus Buddhism has taken over the most important function of ancestor worship, has extended it and made it more significant to each individual as well as to the family.

BUDDHISM AND SOCIAL LIFE

How the Laity is Trained in Buddhist Ideas

A common way of emphasizing moral ideas among the people by Buddhist teachers is the use of tracts purporting to have a divine origin. The following gives the substance of such a tract:

Not long ago in the province of Shantung, there was a sharp and sudden clap of thunder. After the frightened people had collected their wits, they discovered a small book written in red in front of the house of a certain Mr. Li. Mr. Li picked up the book, copied it and read it reverently. He gave a copy to Mr. Ma, the prefect, but Mr. Ma did not believe in the book. Thereupon Maitra®, the Messiah of the Buddhists, spoke from the sky as follows:

"These are the years of the final age. The people under heaven do not reverence Heaven and Earth, they are not filial to father and mother, they do not respect their superiors. They cheat the fatherless, impose upon the widow, oppress the weak; they use large weights for themselves and small measures for others. They injure the good.

They covet for their own profit. They cheat men of money, use the five grains carelessly, kill the cow that draws the plow. This volume is sent for their special benefit. If they recite it they will avoid trouble. If they disbelieve, the years with the cyclical character Ping and Ting will have fields without men to plant them and houses without men to live in them. In the fifth month of these years evil serpents will infest the whole country. In the eighth and ninth months the bodies of evil men will fill the land.

*"Those who believe this book and propagate its teachings will not encounter the ten sorrows of the age: war, fire, no peace day and night, separation of man and wife, the scattering of the sons and daughters, evil men spread over the country, dead bones unburied, clothing with no one to wear it, rice with no one to eat it, and the difficulty of ever seeing a peaceful year. Sù*amuni foreseeing this final age sent down this volume in Shan-*

tung. The Goddess of Mercy saw the sorrows of all living beings.

Maitra® commanded the two runners of T'ai Shan, the god of the Eastern Mountain, to investigate the conduct of men and as a first punishment to increase the price of rice, and then besides the ten sorrows already mentioned above, to inflict the punishments of flood, fire, wind, thunder, tigers, snakes, sword, disease, famine and cold.

*The rule of Sù*amuni which has lasted twelve thousand years is now fulfilled, and Maitra® succeeds to his place."*

These sorrows may be escaped by reciting this sutra whose substance we find above. If it is repeated three times the person will escape the calamity of fire and water. If one man passes it on to ten men and ten men pass it on to a hundred, they will escape the calamities of sword, disease and imprisonment, and receive blessings which cannot be measured. He who in addition to repeating the sutra practices abstinence will insure peace for himself. He who presents one hundred copies to others will insure his personal peace. He who presents a thousand copies will insure the peace of his family. He who is attacked by disease, may escape it by taking five cash of the reign of Shun Chih (1644-1661 A. D.), the first emperor of the Ch'ing dynasty, one mace of the seed of cypress, one mace of the bark of mulberry, boil in one bowl of water until only eight-tenths of the water remain, drink and he will become well.

In this way the five Buddhist commandments for the laity not to kill any living creature, not to steal, not to commit adultery, not to lie, and not to use intoxicating liquor are propagated and made real to the common man. The method is quite efficient. Whole provinces have been put into a panic by such prophecies.

Effect of Ideals of Mercy and Universal Love

The command not to kill any living being has had considerable influence in China. There are volumes of stories telling of the punishments which will be visited upon those who disobey and of the rewards of those who release living animals.

Every monastery has a special place for animals thus released by pious devotees.

There is a popular story about a fishmonger of the T'ang dynasty who was taken sick and during his illness dreamed that he was taken to purgatory. His body was aflame with fire and pained him as though he were being roasted. Flying fiery chariots with darting flames swept around him and burned his body. Ten thousand fish strove with one another to get a bite of his flesh. The ruler of the lower regions accused him of killing many fish and hence his punishment. For a number of days he was hanging between life and death. His relatives were urged to perform some works of penance. They had his fishing implements burned. With reverent hearts they made two images of Kuan Yin, presented offerings and repented. The whole family performed abstinence, stopped killing living things, printed and gave away over a hundred copies of the Diamond Sutra, and ferried over a large number of souls through purgatory. As a result of their efforts the sick man became well.

The following comment was made on the above story by a scholar. If its premises are granted, the conclusion is inevitable:

> *"If the fiery chariots are seal, why does not man see them? If they are false, how is it that man feels the pain? But where do the fiery chariots come from? They come from the heart and head of the one who kills fish. The fire in the heart (heart belongs to the element fire) causes destruction. The chariot fire also causes destruction."*

This attitude of mercy has been extended to human beings. There are numerous tracts against the drowning of little girls in those regions where this custom is prevalent. One tells the following story: In the province of Kwangtung there lived a Mrs. Chang who daily burned incense and repeated Buddha's name. One day she and her husband died. Much to their surprise and consternation Yama (the potentate of hell) decided that Mr. Chang must become a pig and Mrs. Chang a dog. Mrs. Chang accordingly went to Yama and said, "During life we honored Buddha and so why should we become animals after death?" Yama said, "What use is it to honor Buddha? During life you drowned three girls whom I sent into life. People with the face of a man and the heart of a beast, should they not be punished?" The husband accordingly took on a pig's skin and the wife a dog's. Then by a dream they revealed to their brother Chang number two that, although they repeated Buddha's name, they were not permitted to be reborn as men, because they had drowned little girls.

Perhaps the extent of this spirit, of mercy and its possibilities may be illustrated by the reverence for the ox. While there is a great deal of cruelty in China to animals and men, it is rarely that one sees an ox abused. Up to the advent of the foreigner an ox was not killed for meat. In many places in China today the slaughter of an ox would bring the punishments of the law upon the butcher. No doubt this reverence is due to the great Indian reverence for the cow. The law of kindness has been extended to other animals, taking the rather spectacular form of releasing a few decrepit animals and allowing them to spend their last days in a monastery compound. There are many kindly things done in China. The dead are buried, the sick are provided with medicine. Every year numerous wadded garments are given away to poor people. Various groups carrying on a humble ministry of helpfulness have found a real inspiration in the ideals held before them in Buddhism, the rewards promised and punishments threatened.

Relation to Confucian Ideals

Why have not these ideals exercised a larger influence in China? The answer is quite simple. The activities of the monks have been strenuously opposed by the Confucian state system. The philosopher, Chang Nan-hsiian, a contemporary of Chu-Hsi, states concisely for us the differences betwen Confucianism and Buddhism in his comment on a passage in the Book of Records. "Strong drink is a thing intended to be-used in offering sacrifices and entertaining guests,—such employment of it is what Heaven has prescribed. But men by their abuse of such drink come to lose their virtue and destroy their persons—such employment of it is what Heaven has annexed its terrors to. The Buddhists, hating the use of things where Heaven sends down its terrors, put away as well the use of them which Heaven has prescribed.

"For instance, in the use of meats and drinks, there is such a thing as wildly abusing and destroying the creatures of Heaven.

The Buddhists, disliking this, confine themselves to a vegetable diet, while we only abjure wild abuse and destruction. In the use of clothes, again, there is such a thing as wasteful extravagance. The Buddhists, disliking this, will have no clothes but those of a dark and sad color, while we only condemn extravagance. They, further, through dislike of criminal connection between the sexes, would abolish the relation between husband and wife, while we denounce only the criminal connection.

"The Buddhists, disliking the excesses to which the evil desires of men lead, would put away, along with them, the actions which are in accordance with the justice of heavenly principles, while we, the orthodox, put away the evil desires of men, whereupon what are called heavenly principles are the more brightly seen.

Suppose the case of a stream of water. The Buddhists, through dislike of its being foul with mud, proceed to dam it up with earth. They do not consider that when the earth has dammed up the stream, the supply of water will be cut off. It is not so with us, the orthodox. We seek only to cleanse away the mud and sand, so that the pure water may be available for use. This is the difference between the Buddhists and the Learned School." [Footnote: Shu King, Pt. V, Bk. X, p. 122.]

This statement reveals at once the opposition of the sect of the Learned and the influence which Buddhism exerted upon its members.

Buddhism while enjoying occasional favor from the state was often zealously persecuted. In 819 Han Yii issued his celebrated act of accusation. In 845 the emperor Wu Tsung issued his decree of secularization. At that time 4600 monasteries and 40,000 smaller establishments were pulled down and 265,000 monks and nuns were sent back to lay life. Their rich lands were confiscated.

Under the Ming dynasty, as well as under the Ch'ing dynasty, Buddhism enjoyed a precarious existence. Whether Buddhism would have improved the moral conditions of the Chinese; if it had been given a free hand, is difficult to affirm. Still its failure is at least partly due to the opposition of Confucian orthodoxy.

The Embodiment of Buddhist Ideals in the Vegetarian sects

The state persecutions of Buddhism forced it to leave temporarily its institutional life and trust itself to the people. These persecutions were usually followed by a revival of piety and religion among the people. The Buddhist teachers gathered about themselves a large number of lay devotees who formed societies which practice religious rites in secret. These sects have preserved the genuine Buddhist piety, not only in times of persecution, but at times when the Buddhist organization under imperial favor was departing from its simplicity.

A number of these sects have continued under different names for several centuries. For example, the Tsai Li, a society now enjoying a quiet existence in North China, is successor to the White Lotus society. The latter started in the fifth century. Its members sought salvation in the Pure Land of Amitabha. In the eleventh century it enjoyed imperial favor. During the Mongol dynasty it fought against the throne with rebels and placed one of its leaders, Chu Y?ang, a monk, on the throne, who became the founder of the Ming dynasty. The sect was soon proscribed and its members persecuted by the government. During the Ch'ing dynasty it took part in a rebellion and was ruthlessly exterminated. At present it goes under the name of Tsai Li, i.e., within the Li or principles of the three religions. It is a mediator among the three religions. There are thirty-one organizations of this sect in Peking and branches throughout North China. The society forbids the use of wine and opium, though it does not forbid the use of meat. It usually has a Buddhist image, Kuan Yin or some other. It uses Buddhist prayers and incantations. The outstanding doctrines held during its long history have been the hope of salvation in the Western Heaven of Amit¨(a, the early coming of Maitra®, the Buddhist Messiah, and the large use of magic formulas and incantations.

Another sect which embodies Buddhist ideals is the Chin Tan, the sect of the philosopher's stone or pill of immortality. Its founder was the writer of the Nestorian tablet and so the sect is related to Christianity. It exalts the teaching of universal love. This is one of several examples of a supposed contact between Buddhism and Christianity.

These sects of which the two above are examples are present in all parts of China. They obey the five Buddhist commandments for laymen. The members spend much time in fasting and prayer, and in the repetition of Buddhist books. Their lives as a rule are simple and sincere. They are preparing for rebirth in the land of Amit¨(a, or are expecting the early coming of the Buddhist Messiah to set this world right. In the meantime, by means of incantations, personal regimen and cooperative action they are doing all they can to usher in a better state.

Pilgrimages

Pilgrimages are very popular in China. The famous Buddhist shrines are Wu T'ai Shan in Shansi, Puto on the coast of Chekiang, Chiu Hua Shan in Anhwei, and Omei Shan in Szechuan. These, one on each side of China, represent the four elements of Buddhist science, wind, water, fire and earth. They are also the centers of the worship of the four great Bodhisattvas, Wenshu, Kuan Yin, Titsang and Puhsien. Besides these large centers there are many others to which pilgrims direct their footsteps.

In the spring of the year, when the god of spring covers the earth with a green mantle, when the sky and winds call, many start on their pilgrimage. Many go singly and laboriously, kneeling and bowing every few steps. Others go in happy companies, chaperoned by a pious, village dame, who has organized the group. Some go because their turn has come. They are members of a guild which has a fund devoted to pilgrimages by its members. Some go for the performance of a vow made to Kuan Yin, when the father was sick unto death and the goddess prolonged his life. To others it is the culmination of a pious life. All go for the joy which travel in the spring gives.

Puto, an island off the coast of Chekiang, is the goal of many pilgrims from all parts of China. In, the monasteries on the island are about two thousand monks. In the pilgrim season this number is increased to ten thousand monks and thousands of lay pilgrims.

A group of pilgrims was going along merrily. The sun was bright, lighting up the white caps on the deep blue sea. Spring was rioting all about. One member was an abbot from Hangchow. A small, humble-looking man with a few straggling long hairs where the mustache usually grows, was a lay Buddhist from Wuchang. One was a bright young monk from Tientsin. Last, but almost omnipresent and always bubbling over, was a servant of the abbot from Hangchow. He was in the presence of divinity and his whole life was heightened for the time being. "Why did you come!" they were asked. "We came to worship the holy mother, Kuan Yin." When they entered a shrine each purchased three sticks, of incense and two candles and reverently placed them before the image of the goddess, kneeling and bowing. Then they sat and partook of the tea offered by the attendant. After paying a small gratuity, they went on to the next shrine.

On the way a large black snake as thick as an arm lazily crossed over the road. They stood, reverent and awestruck, until he disappeared in the grass, remarking that this was a good omen. When crossing a sand dune piled up by the winds the abbot from Hangchow remarked that this was called the flying sand, wafted there by the goddess who took pity on some travelers who had been compelled to cross a narrow strait in order to come to a cave.

This cave, called Fan Yin Tung, is one of the rifts made by an earthquake and washed out by wind and waves. Below it rushes the tide; from above the sun sends down a few rays. Each pilgrim after offering incense looks into the darkness to see whether he can behold in the dark cavern an image of some Buddha. One sees Kuan Yin and is acclaimed as having had a good vision. Another sees the Laughing Buddha. All exclaim that he has been the most fortunate of all, for this Buddha is the Messiah to come and he who beholds him will be blessed. So from place to place they wander, chatting and seeing the sights of the island. Thus thousands are doing in various parts of China, and in this way strengthening the hold of Buddhism upon themselves and their communities.

BUDDHISM AND THE FUTURE LIFE

Before the advent of Buddhism the Chinese had only a vague idea regarding life after death. The Land and Water Classic mentions the Tu Shuo mountain in the Eastern Sea, under which spirits of the dead live, the entrance guarded by two spirits, Sh «Tu and Y? who are in general control of the demons. In some parts of China the names or pictures, of these spirits are placed on the doors of a house to guard it. The Taoists early developed the idea of a western paradise presided over by the Queen of the West, located at first in the K'un Lun mountains and later in the islands of the Eastern Sea. This heaven, however, was limited to Taoist hermits and mystics. Buddhism made a complete purgatory and heaven known to every one in China.

The Buddhist Purgatory

This is really Buddhism's most noteworthy addition to China's religious equipment; Buddhism lays much stress upon the experiences of a soul immediately after death. Its punishments are well known to every individual. The temple of the City Guardian found in every walled city has a replica of the court in purgatory over which he presides. In the temples of T'ai Shan there is an elaborate exhibit of the tortures inflicted on culprits in purgatory. Every funeral service conducted by Buddhists or Taoists is intended to conduct the soul of the dead through purgatory and pictures vividly the progressive experiences from the first seventh day to the seventh seventh day. On the the seventh month, on the fifteenth day [about August] a special service is held for the souls of the dead in purgatory. Furthermore, every community has a general service [about October] for the souls of those who died a violent death or who have no one to look after them. During the war many services were thus held for those who died on the battlefields of Europe. At such services the scenes in purgatory are vividly portrayed by pictures and figures. The temples distribute tracts with pictures of purgatory so that women may see them and understand. On the stage are often acted powerful plays whose scenes are laid in Hades. This propaganda is perhaps the most efficient of its kind.

Purgatory is depicted as consisting of ten courts each surrounded by small hells, where the soul undergoes punishment and cleansing. The fifth court, which may be taken as an example of the other courts, is in charge of Yen Lo or Yama. Yama was once in charge of the first court, but his tender heart pitied the souls who came before him and sent them back to earth. Because of this leniency he was placed in charge of the fifth court.

When a soul has passed through the first four courts and it has been discovered that there is no good conduct to its credit, it is led to the fifth court and examined every seven days regarding past conduct. In order to get back to the world of men, it eagerly promises to complete various unfinished vows, such as to repair monasteries, schools, bridges, or roads, to clean wells, to deepen rivers, to distribute good books, to release animals, to take care of aged parents, or to bury them suitably. But it is plainly told that the gods know its artifices, and that now these unfinished tasks can never be completed. The gods have reached the unanimous opinion that no injustice is being done. Accordingly there is no appeal, but each soul is led by attendants with bulls' heads and horses' faces to a tower whence they may see their native village. Its front is in the shape of a bow with a perimeter of twenty-seven miles; its height is four hundred and ninety feet. It is guarded by walls of sword trees.

Good men, whose deeds of omission are balanced by the good they have done, return to life. Only souls judged to be evil see their village from this tower. These can see their own families moving about, and can hear their conversation. They realize how they disobeyed the teachings of their elders. They see that the earthly goods for which they have struggled are of no value. Their plottings rise up with lurid reality. They see how they planned a new marriage although already married, how they appropriated fields, state property, and falsified accounts, putting the blame on persons who were dead. While they observe their village they behold their erstwhile friends touch their coffin and inwardly rejoice. They hear themselves called selfish and insincere. But their punishment does not stop here. They behold their children punished by magistrates, their women afflicted with strange diseases, their daughters ravished, their sons led astray, their property taken away, the ancestral house burned and their business ruined. From this tower all passes before them as a lurid dream and they are stricken in heart.

About the fifth court are sixteen small hells where the soul is punished. In each one are stakes buried in the ground and fierce animals. The hands and feet of the guilty one are bound to a stake, his body is opened with small knives, and his heart and intestines quickly devoured.

In each of these sixteen hells is a certain type of sinner: (1) Those who do not reverence the gods and demons and who doubt the existence of rewards and punishments; (2) those who hurt and kill living beings; (3) those who break their vows to do good; (4) those who resort to heterodox practices and vainly hope to attain eternal life; (5) those who upbraid good men, fear the wicked and hate men because they do not die speedily; (6) those who strive with other people and then put the blame upon them; (7) men who force women; and women who seduce young men, and all who have libidinous desires; (8) those who gain profit for themselves by injuring others; (9) the stingy and those who absolutely disregard others, whether alive or dead, giving them no help in dire need, when they can do so without injury to themselves; (10) those who steal and put the crime upon others; (11) those who requite favors with hate; (12) those whose hearts are perverse and poisonous, who instigate others to do wrong even if they may not have carried out their suggestion; (13) those who tempt others by deceit; (14) those who involve others in their squabbles and in gambling and then themselves win out; (15) those who stubbornly persist in their false ideas, do not repent, and slander others; (16) those who hate good and virtuous men.

Besides these sixteen sorts of sinners the fifth court deals with other types of wicked people; those who do not believe in rewards and punishments after death, who hinder good causes, who burn incense without a sincere heart, speak of the sins of others, who burn books that urge men to be good and worship the Great Dipper, but persist in eating meat; those who hate men; who repeat sutras and incantations, and take part in religious ceremonies, but do not fast beforehand; who slander the Buddhist and Taoist religions; who know how to read, but refuse to read the ancient and modern exhortations regarding rewards and punishments; who dig into graves and destroy their marks, who purposely set fire to trees and underbrush, or are careless with fire in their own houses; who shoot arrows at animals with the intent, to kill; who urge and tempt the sick and weak to enter into contests of any kind with themselves; who throw tiles and stones over neighboring walls, poison fish in the river, fire guns, or make nets or traps for birds; who sow salt on the ground, who do not bury dead eats and snakes very deep and thus cause death to those who dig; who cause men to dig the frozen ground in winter or spring (the vapors of earth chill such diggers to death); who tear down adjoining walls and compel their neighbors to move the kitchen stove; who appropriate public highways, lands, close wells and stop gutters. Those who have committed any of the above sins are taken, to the tower whence they can see their own village and then are consigned to the great crying hell, Rr-ava, that is, the fourth of the Buddhist hot hells. [Footnote: Buddhism distinguishes hot and cold hells. In a country like India severe cold is a serious torture.] Thence they go to their respective small hells. When their time has expired, they are examined in order to see whether they have any other sins which need punishment.

Those who have committed any of the above sins may not only escape punishment, but may have their punishment in the sixth court lessened, if they fast regularly on the eighth day of the first month and take a vow not to commit these sins. Some sins, however, cannot be arranged for in such a way, such as the killing of living beings and hurting them; the associating with heretics; committing fornication with women and then poisoning them; committing adultery, violence, envy, or injuring the good name of others; stealing, requiting favors with hatred, and hearing exhortation but not repenting. These are major sins.

Its Social Value

The social value of purgatory is quite plain from the description of the fifth court and of the sinners who are punished therein. Purgatory is the social mirror of China, wherein the consequences of all unsocial acts are pictured in such a vivid way as to deter the individual from committing them. It is effective in China, not only because of the realistic presentation, but because the opinion of the community is against such acts and in favor of repressing them on every occasion.

The Buddhist Heaven

Buddhism brought into China not only a fully developed purgatory but also a heaven which all may enter. The sovereign of the western heaven is Amitäa (or in Chinese O-mi-to-fo), with whom Kuan Yin, the goddess of Mercy, is usually associated.

Amit¨(a is explained as meaning "boundless age." The original meaning is "boundless light," which suggests a Persian origin with Mannichean influences. The translations of the Amit¨(a sutras were wholly made by natives of central Asia.

Amit¨(a is one of the thousand Buddhas; he is regarded as the reflex of Sakyamuni and is connected also in his earthly incarnation with a monk called Dharmá*ra. This monk desired to become a Buddha. This wish he presented to L?'varar¡* asking him to teach him as to what a Buddha and a Buddha country ought to be. L?'varar¡* imparted this knowledge. Then the monk after meditation returned having made forty-eight vows that he would not become a Buddha, until all living beings should attain salvation in his heaven.

The eighteenth vow expresses his ideal:

"O Bhagavat, if those beings who have directed their thought towards the highest perfect knowledge in other worlds, and who, after having heard my name, when I have obtained Bodhi (knowledge), have meditated on me with serene thoughts; if at the moment of their death, after having approached them surrounded by an assembly of monks, I should not stand before them worshipped by them, that is, so that their thoughts should not be troubled, then may I not obtain the highest perfect knowledge."

A few extracts from the Amit¨(a Vy?? will illustrate the Buddhist idea of life in this Pure Land:

"In the western region beyond one hundred thousand myriads of Buddhist lands there is a world. Great Happiness by name. This land has a Buddha called Amit¨(a. The living beings there do not suffer any pain, but enjoy all happiness. Therefore, it is called the land of Pure Delight... the land of Pure Delight has seven precious fountains full of water containing the eight virtues. The bottom of these fountains is covered with golden sand. On four sides there are steps made of gold, silver, crystal and glass, precious stones, red pearls, and highly polished agates. In the pools are variously colored, light emitting lotus flowers as large as cart wheels, delicate, admirable, odorous and pure..."

"The Buddha of this land makes heavenly music. It is covered with gold. Morning and evening during six hours it rains the wonderful celestial flowers (Erythrina Indica). All the inhabitants of this land on clear mornings after dressing offer these celestial flowers to the hundred thousand myriads of Buddhas of the regions who return to their country at meal time. When they have eaten they go away again."

"This country possesses every kind of wonderful varicolored birds, the white egret, the peacock, the parrot, the s'rarika (a long legged bird), the Kalavingka (a sweet voiced bird)... All these birds, morning and evening during the six hours, utter forth a beautiful harmonious sound. Their song produces the five indrya (roots of faith, energy, memory, ecstatic meditation, wisdom), the five bala (the powers of faith, energy, memory, meditation and wisdom), the seven bodhyanga (the seven degrees of intelligence, memory, discrimination, energy, tranquillity, ecstatic contemplation, indifference), and the eight portions of the correct path marga, (the possession of correct views, decision and purity of thought and will, the ability of reproducing any sound uttered in the universe, vow of poverty, asceticism, attainment of meditative abstraction of self-control, religious recollectedness, honesty and virtue), and such doctrines. When all beings of this land have heard the music, they declare their faithfulness to the Buddha, Dharma and the Sangha (the Buddha, the Law and the community of monks)."

As to those who enter this land it says:

"All living beings who hear this should make a vow to be born in that land. How can they reach the Pure Land? All very good men will gather in that place... He whose blessedness and virtue are great can be born into that country. If there is a good man or woman who, on hearing of Amit¨(a, takes this name and holds it in his mind one, two, three, four, five, six, or seven days, and his whole heart is not distracted, to that man at death Amit¨(a will appear. His heart will not be disturbed. He

will at once enter into life in the land of Pure Delight of Amit¨(a. I see this blessing and hence utter these words. Those living beings who hear these words should make a vow to be born in that land."

The Harmonization of These Ideas with Ancestor Worship

The extension of life beyond the grave in purgatory, or in the Pure Land and through transmigration was readily accepted in China. Both the new ideas and the disciplines through which to realize them were eagerly adopted, and have held their place to this day. In other lands the creation of a heaven and a hades has weakened the grip of ancestor worship and ultimately displaced it.

In China the opposite result has obtained, due, no doubt, to the fact that the family system and along with it the supreme duty of filial piety were fostered by the state and Buddhism and its teachings were permitted only in so far as they bolstered it up. Another reason lies in the agricultural basis of China's civilization, reenforced by the great difficulty of communication, which tended to make the family system dominant in China. Today, the improvement of communication and the introduction of the industrial system of the West with the individual emphasis of modern education are factors which are weakening the family system and with it ancestral worship.

THE SPIRITUAL VALUES EMPHASIZED BY BUDDHISM IN CHINA

Near the House of Parliament in Peking is located a small monastery dedicated to the goddess of Mercy, Kuan Yin. Before her image the incense burners send forth curling clouds of smoke. The walls are decorated with old paintings of gods and goddesses. The temple with its courtyard has the appearance of prosperity. Its neat reception room, with its tables, chairs and clock, shows the influence of the modern world. Here a monk in the prime of life spent a few months recently lecturing on Buddhism to members of parliament and to scholars from various parts of China. Frequently the writer used to drop in of an afternoon to discuss Buddhism and its outlook. Usually a simple repast concluded these conversations, the substance of which forms the greater part of this section.

The Threefold Classification of Men Under Buddhism

"What does Buddhism do for men?" "There are in the world at least three classes of men. The lowest class live among material things, they are occupied with possessions. Their life is entangled in the crude and coarse materials which they regard as real. A second, higher class, regard ideas as realities. They are not entangled in the maze of things, but are confused by ideas, ascribing reality to them. The third and highest class are those who by meditation have freed themselves from the thraldom of ideas and can enter the sixteen heavens."

Salvation for the Common Man

"What can Buddhism do for the lowest class?"

"For this class Buddhism has the ten prohibitions. Every man has in him ten evils, which must be driven out. Three have to do with evil in the body, namely, not to steal, not to kill, not to commit adultery; four belong to the mouth, lying, exaggeration, abuse, and ambiguous talk; three belong to the mind, covetousness, malice, and unbelief."

"Is not this entirely negative?"

"Yes, but it is necessary, for during the process of eliminating these evil deeds, man acquires patience and equanimity. Buddhism does not stop with the prohibitions. The believer must practice the ten charitable deeds. Not only must he remove the desire to kill living beings, but he must cultivate the desire to save all beings. Not only must he not steal, but he must assist men with his money. Not only must he not give himself to lasciviousness, but he must treat all men with propriety. So each prohibition involves a positive impulse to virtue, which is quite as essential as the refraining from evil."

"What energizing power does Buddhism provide?"

"First, is purgatory with its terrors. The evil man, seeing the consequences of his acts upon himself, becomes afraid to do them and does that which is good. Then there is transmigration with the danger of transmigration into beasts and insects. Again, there are the rewards in the paradise of Amit¨(a. Moreover, there is even the possibility not only of saving one's self, but by accumulated merit of saving one's parents and relatives and shortening their stay in purgatory."

The Place of Faith

"Can any man enter the western paradise of Amit¨(a?"

"Yes, it is open to all men. The sutra says: 'If there be any one who commits evil deeds, and even completes the ten evil actions, the five deadly sins and the like; that man, being himself stupid and guilty of many crimes, deserves to fall into a miserable path of existence and suffer endless pains during many long ages. On the eve of death he may meet a good and learned teacher who, soothing and encouraging him in various ways, will preach to him the excellent Law and teach him the remembrance of Buddha, but being harassed by pains', he will have no time to think of Buddha.'"

"What hope has such a man?"

"Even such a man has hope. The sutra says: 'Some good friend will say to him: Even if thou canst not exercise the remembrance of Buddha, utter the name of Buddha Amitabha.' Let him do so serenely with his voice uninterrupted; let him be (continually) thinking of Buddha, until he has completed ten times the thought, repeating 'Namah O-mi-to-fo,' I put my trust in Buddha!

On the strength of (his merit of) uttering Buddha's name he will, during every repetition expiate the sins which involve him in births and deaths during eighty millions of long ages. He will, while dying, see a golden lotus-flower, like the disk of the sun, appearing before his eyes; in a moment he will be born in the world of highest happiness. After twelve greater ages the lotus-flower will unfold; thereupon the Bodhisattvas, Aval?ö¼aras and Mahasattva's, raising their voices in great compassion, will preach to him in detail the real state of all the elements of nature and the law of the expiation of sins."

"Does faith save such a man?"

"Yes, not his own faith, but the faith which prompted the vow of Amitabha. Amit¨(a's faith in the possibility of his salvation gives him supreme confidence that he will attain salvation. All he needs is to have the desire to be born in that paradise and to repeat the name of Amitabha."

Salvation of the Second Class

"How do those of the second class attain salvation?"

"The men of the second class regard ideas as realities. They are not entangled in the maze of things, but are confused by ideas, regarding them as real. These men do not need images and outward sanctions, but they need heaven and purgatory though regarding them as ideas. By performing the ten good deeds they will obtain a quiet heart, having no fear, and become saints and sages. Among men, saints and sages occupy a high rank, but not so among Buddhists. By merit of good works merely they enter the planes of sensuous desire, the six celestial worlds located immediately above the earth."

Salvation for the Highest Class

"And the third class?"

"This class has many ranks. There are those who by the practice of meditation (four dkyanas) [Footnote: Dhyana means contemplation. In later times under the influence of the idea of transmigration heavens were imagined which corresponded to the degrees of contemplation.] can enter the sixteen heavens conditioned by form.

By the practice of the four ar?hy¡+s [Footnote: That degree of abstract contemplation from which all sensations are absent.] they enter the four highest heavens free from all sensuous desires and not conditioned by form. These heavens are the anteroom of Nirvana."

"What is the driving power in all this?"

"It is v?a or energy."

Heaven and Purgatory

"Do heaven and purgatory exist?"

"Heaven and purgatory are in the minds and hearts of men. Really heaven is in the mind of Amit¨(a and purgatory exists in the illusioned brains of men."

"Does anything exist?"

"Nâ)rjuna says: 'There is no production, no destruction, no annihilation, no persistence, no unity, no plurality, no coming in and no going forth.'"

Sin

"Does sin exist?"

"In the mind of the real Buddhist sin and virtue are different aspects of the all. Sin is illusion; virtue is illusion, There is a higher unity in which they are reconciled."

Nirv¡+

"Do you know of any one who attained Nirv¡+?"

"Yes, I have experienced it. It is not a state beyond the grave. It is a state into which one can enter here."

"Can you express this experience in words?"

"Impossible. I can only indicate the shore of this great ocean. At first I was in great distress and agony, as though carrying the illusions of the world. Then came a great peace and calm, ineffable, serene, and surpassing the power of language to express."

The Philosophical Background

"What is behind this universe!"

"Underlying this universe of phenomena and change there is a unity. It is the basis of all being. It is within all being and all being rests in it. It is because of this common background that men are able to apprehend it. This universal basis we call dharma, or law. Its characteristics are that everything born grows old, is subject to disease and death; that the teachings of Buddha purify the mind and enable it to obtain supreme enlightenment; that all Buddhas by treading the same way of perfection will attain the highest freedom."

"You speak of the Buddhist Trinity."

"Yes, we have the Dharmaka.. This is the essence-body, the ground of all being, taking many forms, Buddhas, Bodhisattvas, spirits, angels, men and even demons. It is impersonal, all-pervasive. It may be called the first person. The second person is the Sambhogaka., the body of bliss. This is the heavenly manifestation of Buddha. The third person is the Nirm¡+ka.. This is the projection of the body of bliss on earth."

Some identify this trinity with that of the Christian faith. While there is a resemblance, we should note that the first person of the Buddhist trinity would correspond to God as the absolute or the impersonal background of universal Being. The second corresponds to the glorified Christ and the third to the historic Jesus. There is no counterpart either to God the Father or to the Holy Spirit.

"Do you believe in the salvation of all beings?"

"Yes, all have the Buddha heart. All living beings will finally become Buddhas."

Then turning to a friend of mine the speaker said: "What have you done in Buddhism?" The friend answered: "I have written and translated many books." "I do not mean that," he answered. "What work have you done?" The friend confessed that he had not done much else. Then he said: "Every morning when you awake, reflect deeply and profoundly upon your state before you were born. Think back to that state where your soul was merged with Buddha. Find yourself in that state and you will find ineffable enlightenment and joy."

The sun was setting behind the Western hills. The blare of trumpets sounded on the city wall. Outside of the door was the whirling sound of Peking returning home from its mundane tasks and joys. We joined the rushing, restless crowd and still we felt the calm of another world. Has not Christianity a message of balm and peace for these sons of the East who are so sensitive to the touch of the eternal and sublime?

What Buddhism Has to Give

An important government official obliged to deal with many vexatious requests and demands declared: "I could not get through my day's work, if I did not spend an hour every day in meditation, just as Buddha did when he became enlightened." He was asked what he did when he meditated or prayed. "Nothing at all." "Well, about what do you think?" "Of nothing at all. I stop thinking when I engage in religious meditation. Life makes me think tco much. I should lose my sanity, if I did not stop thinking and enter into the 'void', whence we all came and into which we all are going to drop back."

His Christian inquirer still was unsatisfied by the Buddhist's description of his prayer life, and pressed further for details. "What happens when you meditate or pray?"

"Nothing happens, I tell you, except, that I experience a peace which the passing world cannot give and which the passing world cannot altogether take away. The secret of religion is simply to realize that everything is passing away. When you accept that fact, then you become really free. The Christian world seemed to have been tremendously impressed by the slogan of the French soldiers at Verdun, 'They shall not pass!' Perhaps the German soldiers did not pass just then or there. But the French soldiers themselves are all passing away. And everything in the world is passing away. What our Buddhist religion teaches us is: 'Let it pass!' You cannot keep anything for very long. And prayer or meditation is simply to practice yourself in that thought deliberately. Oh, it is a wonderful peace when you fully believe that gospel, and enter into it every day. Vanity of vanities, everything is vanity! Why worry? We do altogether too much worrying. To pray means simply to quit worrying, to quit thinking, to enter into the indescribably passionless peace of Nirvana." Here seemed to be an ardent Buddhist. When asked what he thought as the difference between a Buddhist and a Christian, he answered promptly:

"Yes, there is my wife. She is a very good woman. All the neighbors come to her, when there is any one sick or in trouble. So I say to her: 'Wife, I should think you would make a first-class Christian.' But I think she lets herself be worried by altogether too many troubles. She is all the time thinking and fussing and planning. To be sure, it is mostly about other people, But then she does have the children and the house and the relatives and friends and neighbors to look after. Perhaps she really cannot be a Buddhist. Perhaps it is all a matter of temperament. Oh, but I tell you it is great to be a Buddhist, because it gives you such a wonderful peace."

PRESENT-DAY BUDDHISM:

Periods of Buddhist History

The history of Buddhism in China may be divided into four periods. Buddhism entered China, as we have seen, in the second century B.C. The first period, that of the translation and propagation of the faith, ended in 420 A.D. The second period, that of interpenetration, lasted to the beginning of the T'ang dynasty, 618 A.D. The third, the period of establishment, ended with the close of the five dynasties, in 960 A.D. The fourth period, that of decay, has extended to the present day.

The Progress of the Last Twenty-five Years

There are signs of a revival of Buddhism in China. Whether this is a tide, or a wave, only the future can reveal. In 1893 Dharmapala, an Indian monk, stopped in Shanghai on his way back from the Congress of Religions in Chicago. It was his purpose to make a tour of China, to arouse the Chinese Buddhists to send missionaries to India to restore Buddhism there, and then to start a propaganda throughout the whole world. He addressed the monks of Shanghai. Dr. Edkins, the veteran missionary, acted as his interpreter. Dharmapala was surrounded by a horde of curious monks who were more interested in his strange appearance and in the cost of his garments than they were in his great ideals. They were also feeling the iron heel of the Confucian government and at once inquired about the attitude of the government toward such an innovation. Dharmapala did not go beyond Shanghai.

Japanese Buddhists, especially the members of the Hongwanji sect, have taken a deep interest in Chinese Buddhists. Count Otani once visited the chief monasteries of China. Numerous Japanese Buddhists have made such visits. In 1902, the Empress Dowager, fired by a reforming zeal, decided to confiscate Buddhist property and to use the proceeds for the spread of modern education. The Buddhist monasteries put themselves under the protection of Japanese monks in order to hold their property. When by 1906 the Empress Dowager saw the consequences of her edict, she at once issued a new edict, reversing the former one, and the Japanese monks took their departure.

The Japanese Buddhists have been fired by missionary zeal for China. In many of the large cities of China are the temples of the Hongwanji sect. Established primarily for the Japanese, these temples are intended to serve as points of departure for a nation-wide missionary work. The twenty-one demands made upon China included two significant items in the last group which the Chinese refused to sign: "Art. 2: Japanese hospitals, churches and schools in the interior of China shall be granted the right of owning land." "Art. 7: China agrees that Japanese subjects shall have the right of missionary propaganda in China." Under Japanese influence there was established in 1907 at Nanking, under the leadership of Yang, a lay Buddhist devotee, a school for the training of Buddhist missionaries. The students were to go to Japan for further training, and the more promising ones were to study in India. This project was discontinued after the death of Yang on account of the lack of funds.

When the republic was established Buddhism felt a wave of reform. The monasteries established schools for monks and children. A magazine was published which appeared irregularly for several numbers and then stopped. A national organization was formed with headquarters at Peking. A survey of monasteries was begun. The activities in lecturing and propaganda were increased, but Yuan Shih-kai issued twenty-seven regulations for the control of Buddhist monasteries, which markedly dampened the ardor of the reformers. The world war which accentuated the spirit of nationalism had the added effect of stirring up Buddhist enthusiasm. There are at present signs of new activity among them in China.

Present Activities

While Buddhism may be standing still or even dying in certain parts of China, it is showing signs of new life in the provinces of Kiangsu and Chekiang and in the large cities. Such revival in centers subject to the influence of the modern world shows that Buddhism in China as in Japan has sufficient vitality to adjust itself to modern conditions. Let us consider some of these activities.

(a) The Reconstruction of Monasteries.—During the T'ai Ping rebellion, which devastated China in 1850-1865, the monasteries suffered with the towns. Not only were the monasteries burned to the ground, but their means of support were taken away and the monks were scattered. There are still many of these ruined monasteries in the Yangtze valley and in southern and western China. Quite a number of them have been rebuilt. Perhaps the most notable example is that at Changchow which was destroyed during the rebellion. Today it is the largest monastery in China, having about two thousand monks. In Fukien several new monasteries have been built in the last few decades. In the provinces of Chekiang and Kiangsu, in the large cities and about Peking there are building activities, showing that the monasteries are feeling a new wave of prosperity.

T'ai Hsu, one of the leaders' of modern Buddhism, is holding up an ideal program for Buddhism in this time of reconstruction. He proposes that there should be 576 central monasteries, 4608 preaching places, 72 Buddhist hospitals and 72 orphanages.

(b) Accessions.—Regarding the number of monks it is almost impossible to obtain any reliable figures. A conservative estimate, based upon partial returns, makes the number of monks about 400,000 and that of nuns about 10,000. The impression among the Buddhists is that the number of monks is increasing. That is quite probable in view of the rebuilding and repairing which is now in progress.

More significant is the number of accessions from the learned class. Many officials, disheartened by the present confused political situation, have sought refuge in the monasteries. Some of them are now abbots of monasteries and are using their influence to build them up. All over China there are Confucian scholars who are giving themselves to the study of Buddhism and to meditation. Some of the Chinese students who have studied in Buddhist universities in Japan are propagating Buddhism by lecture and pen.

(c) Publications.—Quite as significant is the increase in the publication of Buddhist literature of all kinds. Many of the monasteries have printing departments where they publish the sutras needed for their own use. In addition, there are eight or more publishing centers where Buddhist literature is printed. The most famous are Yang's establishment at Nanking, the Buddhist Press in Yangchow and that in Peking. In these establishments about nine hundred different works are being published. The most noteworthy recent publication has been that of the Chinese Buddhist Tripitaka in Shanghai.

Among these publications are a few modern issues. The Chung Hua Book Company has published several works on Buddhism. Other books have been issued for the sake of harmonizing Buddhism with western science and philosophy. In this enterprise Japanese influence is visible. In 1921 a Shanghai press published a dictionary of Buddhist terms containing 3302 pages, based on the Japanese Dictionary of Buddhism. Other works also show the influence of Japanese scholarship.

Among the publications have appeared two magazines. One published at Ningpo, is called "New Buddhism." This is struggling and may have to succumb. The other is known as the "Sound of the Sea Tide," now published in Hankow. Moreover, in all the large cities there are Buddhist bookshops where only Buddhist works are sold. These all report a good business. This literary activity reveals an interest among the reading classes of China. Few such books are purchased by the monks. The Chinese scholars read them for their style and for their deep philosophy, but also for light and for help in the present distracting political situation of their country.

(d) Lectures.—Along with publication goes the spread of Buddhism by lectures in the monasteries and the cities of China. A few years ago Buddhist sermons, however serious, were only listened to by monks and by a few pious devotees. Today such addresses are advertised and are usually well attended by the intellectuals. Often many women are found listening. Monks like T'ai Hs?Yuan Ying have a national reputation. Not only monks, but laymen trained in Japan are delivering lectures on the Buddhist sutras. The favorites are the Awakening of Faith and the Suddharma Pundarika sutra.

(e) Buddhist Societies.—With the lectures goes the organization of Buddhist societies for all sorts of purposes. There is a central society in Peking which has branches in every province. The connection is rather loose. Buddhism has never been in favor of centralization. Nor for that matter would the government have allowed it. The chief ends aimed at by these societies are fellowship, devotion, study, propagation, and service. Such societies, often short lived, are springing up in many quarters. They meet for lectures on Buddhism or to conduct a study class in some of the sutras. Occasionally the more ambitious conduct an institute for several months. Some spend part of the time in meditation together. Several schools for children are supported by these societies. They also encourage work of a religious nature among prisoners, distributing tracts and holding services. Such activities are especially appreciated by those who are to suffer the death penalty. The societies are also doing publishing work. The two magazines are supported by the members of the larger societies.

(f) Signs of Social Ambition.—Social work is a prominent feature of some of these Buddhist societies. They have raised money for famine stricken regions, have opened orphanages, and assist in Red Cross work. One of the largest Chinese institutions for ministering to people who are sick and in trouble is located at Hankow. Around a central Buddhist temple is a modern-built hospital, an orphanage and several schools for poor children. It may not maintain western standards of efficiency, but it certainly represents the outreach of modern Buddhism.

Perhaps their most far-reaching advance has been made because of the realization that leaders are needed and that they must be trained. Several schools for this purpose have sprung into existence. Such schools are necessarily very primitive and are struggling with the difficulties of finding an adequate staff and equipment and of obtaining the best type of students.

Another sign of new life has been the making of programs for the future development of Buddhism. One of the most comprehensive appeared a short time ago. For the individual it proposes the cultivation of love, mercy, equality, freedom, progressiveness, an established faith, patience and endurance. For all men it proposes (1) an education according to capacity; (2) a trade suited to ability; (3) an opportunity to develop one's powers; (4) a chance for enlightenment for all. For society it urges the cultivation of cooperation, social service, sacrifice for the social weal, and the social consciousness in the individual. On behalf of the country it urges patriotism, participation in the government, and cooperation in international movements. For the world it advocates universal progress. As to the universe it specifies as a goal the bringing of men into harmony with spiritual realities, the enlightenment of all and the realization of the spiritual universe.

A Buddhist writer sums up the aims of new Buddhism as follows:

> *"Formerly Buddhism desired to escape the sinful world. Today Buddhism not only desires to escape this world of sin, but longs to transform this world of sin into a new world dominated by the ideals of Buddhism. Formerly Buddhism was occupied with erecting and perfecting its doctrines and polity as an organization. Today it not only hopes to perfect the doctrines and polity, but desires to spread the doctrines and ideals abroad so as to help mankind to become truly cultured."*

The Attitude of Tibetan Lamas

Not only the Chinese Buddhists, but the Lamas of Mongolia and Tibet are feeling the impulses of the new age. Quite recently an exhibition was held in the Lama temple at Peking which attracted thousands of visitors. Its object was to obtain money to repair the temple, and thus to give its work a fresh impulse. That these impulses are not necessarily hostile to Christianity is shown by a letter written by the Kurung Tsering Lama of Kokonor district to the Rev. T. S?sen of Szechuan:

> *"I, your humble servant, have seen several copies of the Scriptures and, having read them carefully, they certainly made me believe in Christ. I understand a little of the outstanding principles and the doctrinal teaching of the One Son, but as to the Holy Spirit's nature and essence, and as to the origin of this religion, I am not at all clear, and it is therefore important that the doctrinal principles of this religion should be fully explained, so as to enlighten the unintelligent and people of small mental ability.*
>
> *"The teaching of the science of medicine and astrology is also very important. It is therefore evident if we want this blessing openly manifested, we must believe in the*

religion of the only Son of God. Being in earnest, I therefore pray you from my heart not to consider this letter lightly. With a hundred salutations."

Enclosed with this letter was a poem written in most elegant language.

"O thou Supreme God and most precious Father, The truth above all religions, The Ruler of all animate and inanimate worlds! Greater than wisdom, separated from birth and death, Is his son Christ the Lord shining in glory among endless beings. Incomprehensible wonder, miraculously made! In this teaching I myself also believe—As your spirit is with heaven united, My soul undivided is seeking the truth Jesus the Savior's desire fulfilling, For the coming of the Kingdom of Heaven I am praying. Happiness to all."

The Buddhist World Versus the Christian World

Looking back over the last twenty-five years we see rising quite distinctly a Buddhist world growing conscious of itself, of its past history and of its mission to the world. This Buddhist, world has much more of a program than it had twenty-five years ago. Its object is to unite the Mahay¡+ and the H?y¡+ branches of Buddhism and to spread Buddhist propaganda over the world. At present the leadership of this movement is in Japan. It is in part a political movement. There is no question that Christianity is not at all pleasing to the Japanese militarists. It is regarded by them as the advance post of western industrialism and political ambition. Quite naturally such leaders desire to make the Buddhist world a unit. It is also a social movement. The spirit of the Japanese Buddhist has been brought to consciousness by the new position of Japan. Japan is seeking to take its place in the world as a first rate power. By this not only will Japan's industry and commerce profit, but its spiritual values must also be adapted to the world. The movement then has its spiritual side. Japanese travelers and people are going to all parts of the world. They carry with them the religious ideals which have been shaped by Buddhism. Buddhism in the past was one of the great religions of salvation with an inspiring missionary message. It is again awakening to this task of evangelization. Under the leadership of Japanese scholars and religious statesmen the Japanese are seeking to unite the Buddhist world so that it shall become a force in the new world. Japan is thus trying to give back what it has received in the past.

At present in Buddhist countries there is a strong force working against this movement. Nationalism is a new force to be reckoned with. Still even with the spirit of nationalism permeating every group, the Buddhist world is getting together and will strive to make its contribution to the life of the whole world.

THE CHRISTIAN APPROACH TO BUDDHISTS

Questions Which Buddhists Ask

Buddhists are approaching Christianity. In many places a spirit of inquiry and interest in the Christian religion is met. It is not necessary that there should be a Buddhist world permanently over against a Christian world. The questions which Buddhists ask a missionary indicate an interest in vital themes. Some of them are as follows:

We put our trust in the three Precious Ones. In what do you trust? Is not your Shang Ti (name for God used in China) a being lower than Buddha and just a little higher than a Bodhisattva? Is not Shang Ti the tribal god of the Jews? Do you believe in the existence of purgatory? What sufferings will those endure who do not live a virtuous life? Do you believe in the reality of the Western Paradise? How can one enter it? There being three kinds of merit, by what method is the great merit accumulated? How is the middle and the small merit accumulated? What are the fruits of these proportions of merit and what are they like? Tell me how to believe Christ. What work of meditation do you perform? Is not Buddhism more democratic than Christianity, because it holds out the possibility of Buddhahood to all beings? Is not Buddhism more inclusive, because it provides for the salvation of all beings?

Knowledge and Sympathy

These questions make it plain that the worker who is to deal with Buddhists should have a broad background of general culture. He must be thoroughly humanized. He should have a good knowledge of the history of philosophy and religion, including the work of the modern philosophers. A knowledge of the life of Buddha and of the doctrines of the H?y¡+ or Southern Buddhism, as well as the tenets of the Mahay¡+ should be in his possession.

The psychology of religion should interpenetrate his historical learning; the best methods of pedagogy should guide his approach to men. Of course he must speak the language of the Buddhist, not only the spiritual language, but his everyday patois. He will find it an advantage to know some Sanskrit. While this requirement is not very urgent at present, it will rapidly become a necessity for doing the best work.

This knowledge should be interpenetrated by a genuine sympathy, that is, imagination tinged with emotion. The worker should be able to view doctrines, values and actions from the point of view of the Buddhist and his past history. He must have a genuine interest in and a great capacity for friendship. The Buddhists are very human, responding to friendship very quickly. Such friendship forms a link between the man and the larger friendship of Christ.

Emphasis on the Aesthetic in Christianity

A Chinese Christian leader described his idea of a church as a place removed from the din of the street, approached by a walk flanked with trees and flowers and adorned within by symbols speaking to the heart of the Chinese. He longed for the mystic silence and the beauty of holiness which would open the windows of the world of spiritual reality and throw its light upon the problems of life. He was asked, "Would you adapt some of the symbols of the Chinese religions?" He said, "Many of those symbols are neutral. They suggest religious emotion. Their character depends upon the content which the occasion puts into them. If the content is Christian then the symbols and emotions will become Christian."

Christianity is a religion of beauty. The beautiful in architecture, symbol and ritual, expressing the spiritual universe of the past, present and future, makes a strong appeal to the Chinese heart. It may well be emphasized in the future as never before.

Emphasis on the Mystical in Christianity

Not long ago a Buddhist in one of the large cities of China was converted. He found great joy in the experience which revived him and gathered into unity the broken fragments of his life. He attended church regularly and participated in the prayer meetings. Gradually he discovered that he was not being nourished. He felt his joy slipping away from him and his divided life reinstating itself. He went to Buddhism for consolation. He is not hostile to the church. He appreciates the help he received, but he said that he came for consolation and peace and found the same—hard orthodoxy and morality so familiar to him in Confucianism.

While the case of this man may have individual peculiarities, it may be made the starting point for a discussion of the situation in many churches in China. The early message to the Chinese was doctrinal. The false notion of many gods had to be displaced by the idea of the one true God. With this idea of the true God a few other tenets of the Christian religion are often held as dogmatic propositions to be repeated when questions are asked. The great sin preached is the worship of idols.

The second part of the Christian message is salvation by faith in Jesus Christ. This salvation is other-worldly to a large extent. The extreme emphasis upon it has made of the church an insurance society, membership in which insures bliss in the world beyond.

The third part of the message has been concerned with moral acts, abstinence from opium (liquor and tobacco in some churches), polygamy, and the gross sins. Attendance upon church services, contribution for the support of the church, and the refusal to contribute to idolatry have also been required.

The emphasis to a large extent was doctrinal, moral and individual. The result has been a body of people free from the gross sins, but also innocent of the great virtues and individualistic in their outlook upon this world and the next. This emphasis is needed, but in addition there should be the cultivation of the presence of God in the soul by appropriate means. The Christian Church of China should develop a technique of the spiritual life suited to the East.

The formation of habits of devotion should be emphasized. Intercessory prayer should be given a larger place. Contemplation and meditation should be regarded not merely as an escape from the turmoil and strife of the world, but as a preparation for the highest life of service and sacrifice. Buddhist mysticism united the whole universe and was the great foundation of Chinese art, literature and morality. The spiritual world of Christianity must likewise seep through into the very thought of Asia and inspire the new art, literature and morality which will be the world expression of a Christian universe.

Emphasis on the Social Elements in Christianity

To the aesthetic and mystical emphasis must be attached a social emphasis. Buddhism is often criticized as not being social. It is a highly socialized religion. It has had a large influence upon social life in the East. This social life is different from ours. We see its wrongs and weaknesses. Likewise do the Buddhists see the materialism and injustice of our social life. Christianity must relate itself to the modern world as it is rising in China and seek not merely to remedy a few wrongs or heal a few diseases, but must release the healing stream into the social life of the East. This will be done and is being done through the Church community which has become conscious of itself, realizing its needs and wants, seeking in an intelligent and systematic way to rehabilitate itself. It is not so much the external unrelated efforts that accomplish the thing needed, but it is rather the community life stirred by ideals and fired by a new dynamic which begins the work of reformation.

Emphasis on the Person of Jesus Christ

(a) As a Historical Character.—The great asset of the missionary among Buddhists is the historical person of Christ. In contrast to many of the Bodhisattvas, the saviours of the Buddhists, Jesus is a historical character. His life among men was the life of God among men.

(b) As the Revealer.—God is like Christ. Christ reveals God as the complete, the perfect person. He possessed the pure spiritual personality. The chief characteristic of this personality is love. This love conscious of itself finds its highest joy in the well-being of others. This love of God produced human life which, springing from the lowest form, broke through the material elements and is capable of attaining the highest development.

Christ reveals to man his heavenly relationship. Man created in the likeness of God stands in the highest relation of one person to another through love. He likens this relation to that of father and son. He lifts man to the fellowship with the divine. Yet such a fellowship that man preserves his personality.

Christ reveals man in his relation to men as a brother and the form of love which shall control the relation of man to God as well as man to man.

Christ revealed and founded the Kingdom, a society of the saved, dominated by the spirit of the founder and making this spirit of love and service the organizing power in the world.

(c) As the Saviour.—Mahay¡+ Buddhism emphasized saviourhood. Christ is the saviour of men. In Buddhism the stress is placed upon the merit of the saviour and the saved. There is no question that merit has some value. Yet Christ does not save us by merit, nor do we help to save one another by merit. Salvation is a moral and spiritual process. It is concerned with the biology of the soul. The salvation that we preach is not the salvation by knowledge, or meditation, or merit, but by the interpenetration of Christ's spirit in ours, by the mystic and moral union of our life with his. As Paul says: "That I may know Him and the power of His resurrection and the fellowship of His suffering." Yet He is not the saviour of the individual alone. He saves the community, the church. Only as His spirit permeates and dominates the community does he find his true self and the real salvation.

(d) As the Eternal Son, of God.—The Mahay¡+ system does not emphasize the historicity of Amitabha or of the Bodhisattvas. Spiritual truth is the development of the soul. It is not limited by time and place. Likewise Christianity must emphasize the eternal character of

Jesus Christ. "The Logos existed in the very beginning, the Logos was with God, the Logos was God." To the Mahb.nist this spiritual history is more real than any fact conditioned by time and place.

The Christian worker must learn to understand the import of the Gospel of John. He must see in Jesus Christ "The real Light, which enlightens every man." He must be able to convince himself that the Christ is the fulfillment of the highest aspirations of the Mahb.na system.

How Christianity Expresses Itself in Buddhist Minds

In 1920 a number of Buddhist monks, under the leadership of Rev. K. L. Reichelt formed a Christian brotherhood. The members of this small brotherhood decided that they must subscribe to vows and they took the four following: "I promise before the Almighty and Omniscient God, that I with my whole heart will surrender myself to the true Trinity, God the Father, the Son and the Holy Spirit. I will with my whole heart have faith in Jesus Christ as the Saviour of the world who gives completion to the profoundest and best objects of the higher Buddhism. I will live in this faith now and ever after.

"I promise solemnly before God with my whole heart to devote myself to the study of the true doctrine and break wholly with the evil manners of the world and show forth in my public and private life that I am truly united with Christ.

"I promise that I in every respect will try so to educate myself that I can be of use in the work of God on earth. I will with undivided heart devote myself to the great work; to lead my brethren in the Buddhist Association forward to the understanding of Christ as the only One, who gives completion to the highest and profoundest ideas of Higher Buddhism.

"I promise that until my last hour I will work so that out of our Christian Brotherhood there may grow forth a strong church of Christ among Buddhists. I will not permit any evil thing to grow in my heart, which could divide the brotherhood, but will always try to promote the progress of every member in the knowledge of the holy obligations laid down in these vows and our constitution."

Such men ought, to make choice Christians.

Christianity's Constructive Values

Buddhism in the course of its long history developed certain religious ideas and values which we find in Christianity. It faced the fact of sin and placed it in the heart. It diagnosed the fundamental instincts of men, sex-appetite, will-to-achieve, and pugnacity. These must be overcome. It regards them as delusions which must be eliminated. Christianity also deals with these instincts. It is under no delusion as to their strength. There are certain tendencies in Christianity which have tried to annihilate them. The central tendency of Christianity, however, recognizing their power for good, seeks to sublimate them and make them serve the individual and society. This attitude of the two religions toward these instincts is fundamentally different. The attitude of Christianity has been justified even in Buddhist lands where the religious life of the people has followed the same line that Christianity advocates.

Early Buddhism tried to dissolve man's personality. Later Buddhism corrected this and perhaps has appealed too much to the desire on the part of the individual to enter a heaven which is merely a replica of the earth. Christianity starts with a personal God and holds up before the believer the goal of perfection for his own personality. It finds man without a self and confers a real selfhood upon him.

Early Buddhism taught that salvation is accomplished by the individual alone. It denies the possibility and the necessity of help from a divine source. Subsequent history has proved this to have been wrong. In India, Buddhism has been displaced by Hinduism, and in China, and Japan, the Mahb.na has developed the idea of salvation through another. The great stream of Buddhism has recognized that man by himself is helpless. He must have the help of a divine power in order to obtain salvation. Christianity asserts that salvation is possible only through the intervention of God. The incarnation, the life, death and resurrection of Jesus and his work in the world through the Holy Spirit on the one hand are the expression of God's solicitude for man, and, on the other hand, correspond to the deep need which men of all ages have felt, for a power above themselves. From the early stages of magic to the highest reaches of religion we find this constant factor recognized by human groups all over the world. They bear witness to a power above themselves to whom they continually appeal. In Christianity we find this main tendency enunciated most clearly. The individual carnot save himself. Mankind cannot save itself. Both must rely upon the assistance of the divine power which started this universe on its way and which is the ever present creative force.

Christianity, moreover, has established the community of believers including all classes and conditions of men. Herein each one may realize him&if. Herein also he may realize the kind of community which is friendly to his highest aspirations for himself. Herein he has the opportunity to transmute the instincts above mentioned into forces which make for the larger development of his own person and the well-being of the community.

Accordingly, as Christians face Buddhists, they can do so with the consciousness that this great religion has been reaching out after the light which shines brightly in our Christian religion. They have the assurance not only that they have a message which brings fulfilment to the ideas of the Mahb.na, but also that it has prepared the way for the hearts of the Chinese to receive the highest message of Christianity.

2

INDIA AND THE BUDDHIST PEOPLE

It was a quiet, cool January dawn in the South-Indian city of Tiruchirapalli in the year 1964. A can in his hand, a man named Chinnasami left his home—leaving behind his aging mother, young wife, and infant daughter—and walked to the city's railway station. On reaching there, he doused himself with its contents and set himself on fire, shouting out aloud, *"inti ol1ika!tamil1 vâl1ka!"* (Death to Hindi! May Tamil flourish!). Chinnasami's example was not lost. A year later, to the date, history repeated itself but not necessarily as farce: five other men burned themselves alive "at the altar of Tamil." Three others died just as painfully—not in a raging blaze, but by swallowing insecticide—also for the sake of Tamil, they declared in their own last words.

These dramatic acts were reported by the mainstream news media in India, sometimes in a matter of fact fashion, sometimes with derision, but invariably as yet another example of the "frenzy" and "fanaticism" that speakers of Tamil habitually display when it comes to their language. American newsmagazines like *Time* and *Newsweek* briefly noted the acts, translating them for the benefit of their readers by reporting that "in the style of Vietnamese monks," these men had "turned [themselves] into human funeral pyre[s]." The Vietnam analogy came home to roost in South India: the monks immolated themselves for their religion, but no one had yet burned themselves for their language, it was suggested. That pride of place goes to speakers of Tamil. *Utòal manònòukku, uyir tamil1ukku,* "body to earth, life for Tamil": in stories and poems about these men which have circulated since, so is their "sacrifice" for their language commemorated.

How do I, a late-twentieth-century-historian, make sense of these deaths? Disciplined by history, I would naturally demand, What is it that led so many men and women to proclaim that they would live and die for their language? Why did they so passionately confess that a life without Tamil is not worth living, that they would forsake material gains and worldly pleasures, even the ambrosia of the gods, for its sake? Trained by my discipline to always historicize, these deaths—as indeed the lives of these women and men—have nonetheless taught me to appreciate the hubris of the historical will to elucidate, as they have laid bare the inadequacies of the very language of history itself to write about matters such as these. Yet historicize I must, if only to rescue these men and women from charges of "frenzy" and "fanaticism." And so I will return to their stories, later, but only after resorting to history.

And yet it would seem that history as a discipline has no place for acts such as Chinnasami's or, for that matter, for the language for which he sacrificed himself. While it is hardly news that languages have histories, "the odd thing about the *questione della lingua* [the language question] is how rarely historians ask it," Gramsci's attempt to theorize it notwithstanding (Steinberg 1987: 199). This is especially true for colonial and post-colonial India where the language question—that complex of issues relating to language, politics, and power—has hardly been interrogated by disciplinary history despite its obvious importance for the political cultures of the emergent nation-state.

The historian is a rare presence in scholarly debates on the national language crisis, the internal partitioning of the nation into linguistic states, or the pedagogical dilemmas of multilingualism. This is partly because of a (Orientalist) preoccupation with caste and religion, those two gatekeeping concerns of South Asian studies on identity politics (Ramaswamy 1993: 684-85). But just as clearly, it seems that because our historical conceptions come to us in and through language, historians have tended to treat it, the linguistic turn notwithstanding, as a transparent medium of communication of information rather than as an ideological formation that itself has a politics which has to be historicized.

Yet, even as I try to make a case in this study for (Indian) historians to take the language question seriously, I do so with the troubled knowledge that disciplinary history has been complicit in the Europeanization of alternate life-worlds and imaginations. For the knowledge procedures and institutional practices of history have universalized the European historical experience as the desirable norm, against which all other histories, Indian included, appear inadequate and incomplete (Chakrabarty 1992). Nevertheless, as Dipesh Chakrabarty insists, we cannot give up on history, for it is one of the fundamental modalities of our times, "in the establishment of meaning, in the creation of truth regimes, in deciding, as it were, whose and which 'universal' wins." What we can—and must—do instead, as Meaghan Morris recommends, is to resist the writing of histories of places like India "as a known history, something which has already happened elsewhere, and which is to be reproduced, mechanically or otherwise, with a local content" (quoted by Chakrabarty 1992: 17-20). Histories which seek to corrode the universalizing imperative of Europe's knowledge practices ought to heed all those "scandalous" moments of "difference" which "shock" and "disrupt" the homogenizing flow of history-as-usual:

Subaltern histories, thus conceived in relationship to the question of difference, will have a split running through them. On the one hand, they are "histories" in that they are constructed within the master code of secular History and use the academic codes of history-writing (and thereby perforce subordinate to themselves all other forms of memory). On the other hand, they cannot ever afford to grant this master-code its claim of being a mode of thought that comes to all human beings naturally, or even to be treated as something that exists out there in nature itself. Subaltern histories are therefore constructed within a particular kind of historicized memory, one that remembers History itself as a violation, an imperious code that accompanied the civilizing process that the European Enlightenment inaugurated in the eighteenth century as a world-historical task.

The "unassimilable," the "untranslatable," the "different"—these then are the stuff of histories written in a post-colonial moment. The goal is not the illusory quest for the authentic, but a narrative refusal to seek recognition through collapsing the "difference" of India's histories into the "sameness" of Europe's. And so, when I raise the *questione della lingua,* and demand that Indian historians heed it, I do so with the full realization of its European origins. And yet, the work of colonialism and modernity has ensured that this is no longer a question that just belongs to Europe but is also a dilemma for the worlds that it colonized. To ask the language question, but to answer it and write it differently for a colonial and post-colonial context—these then are the burdens of this book.

Language and Devotion

How then do I write *differently* the (hi)stories of Chinnasami and his fellow speakers who claimed a willingness to die for Tamil? Although Chinnasami's immolation by itself is a spectacularly singular act, defying easy translation into universal categories, the attitudes that produced it could be conveniently assimilated into the metanarrative of nationalism, as yet another instance of "linguistic nationalism." Indeed, this is typically how the few scholarly works that deal with the question of Tamil, if only tangentially, gloss it—as "Tamil nationalism," or its variant, "Tamil revivalism," and as such, an entity that is forged in the shadows of metropolitan Indian nationalism, itself declared a "derived" version of the normative European form (Chatterjee 1986). It would be hard to deny the importance of ideologies of nationalism, derived or not, for much that happens in late colonial and post-colonial India. We hear repeatedly in the words of many a speaker of Tamil, from at least the later decades of the nineteenth century, the logic of Herder, Fichte, and other prophets of (European) linguistic nationalism:

Language is breath;

Language is consciousness;

Language is life;

......

Language is the world;

Without language, who are we?

(Bharatidasan 1978: 132)

That the cunning of Europe ensures that Herder & Co. speak in such clear Tamil tones only reminds us of the regimes of repetition and mimicry that colonialism sparked among subject populations. Yet, as Homi Bhabha observes, colonial mimicry is marked by a profound ambivalence, for "in order to be effective, mimicry must continually produce its slippage, its excess, its difference." Mimicry in the colony, "on the margins of metropolitan desire," is always "a subject of difference that is almost the same, but not quite" (Bhabha 1994: 85-92). But how do we narrate the lives of those who lived in the colony so as to keep alive this ambivalence of mimicry, this tension between the "almost the same" but the "not quite," which dismembers European norms and forms, as Bhabha reminds us? Equally crucial, how may we write their stories so as to displace the universal narrative of nationalism, a narrative whose normative "silent referent" is always (western) Europe, that paradigmatic site of the modern nation-state (Chakrabarty 1992)? For inevitably in such a narrative, "Tamil" nationalism is a (distorted) variant of something that has already happened elsewhere, but reenacted with local content.

This is not the only problem with the analytic of nationalism for writing a different history. Even as the nation-state has become so ubiquitous in this century that, as Benedict Anderson (1983: 14) observes, "everyone can, should, will 'have' a nationality, as he or she 'has' a gender," there has been a tremendous surge in scholarly works on nationalism. Indeed, that single term, "nationalism," has become theoretically overburdened, rendering it incapable of capturing the many incommensurable differences that separate the story of one nation from another. And yet, nationalisms "do not work everywhere the same way: in a sense they must work everywhere in a *different* way, this is part of the national 'identity' " (Balibar 1989: 19). This is especially true when it comes to the complex nexus between linguistic identity and nationalism. Herder, Fichte, and others may have declared that "those who speak the same language...belong together and are by nature one and inseparable whole" (Kedourie 1961: 69). But nationalism is not everywhere predicated on linguistic passions, nor does language loyalty necessarily or always induce a singular nation-state, if we recall the Swiss in the very heart of Europe, modern Latin

America as it emerged from the former Spanish and Portuguese empires, or even Arabic in parts of its diaspora, to cite a few random examples (Seton Watson 1977). In other words, passions of the tongue do not readily map onto the passions of the nation. As Prasenjit Duara has recently suggested in his *Rescuing History from the Nation,* "although nationalism and its theory seek a privileged position within the representational network as the master identity that subsumes or organizes other identifications, *it exists only as one among others* and is changeable, interchangeable, conflicted, or harmonious with them" (1995: 8, emphasis mine). In this book, I hope to "rescue history from the nation" by displacing the latter as the locus of this particular history I write, and by refusing to subordinate, all too quickly, the sentiments and notions of all those who lived and died for Tamil under the rubric of "nationalism." Which is why I propose a new analytic to theorize the discourses of love, labor, and life that have coalesced around Tamil in this century, discourses which can only be partially contained within a metanarrative of nationalism, or even a singular conception of the nation, as we will see.

My access to this analytic—and hence to a different take on the language question—is through a Tamil word, *par1r1u,* which speakers of Tamil routinely use in their talk about the language. Typically, the term appears with the word *tamil1* in the compound *tamil1ppar1r1u,* the hinge on which hangs the structure of affect and sentiment that develops around Tamil. So, its speakers are told to cultivate *tamil1ppar1r1u,* to demonstrate *tamil1ppar1r1u,* and to not sacrifice *tamil1ppar1r1u* for worldly gains. Those who practice *tamil1ppar1r1u* are *tamil1ar,* "Tamilians" by the same token, anybody who does not show *tamil1ppar1r1u* is not a Tamilian. The lexical meanings of *par1r1u* include adherence, attachment, affection, support, love, and devotion. Out of these, I have chosen "devotion" to gloss *par1r1u,* and the term "Tamil devotion" to denote *tamil1ppar1r1u,* as well as other similar sentiments that Tamil speakers express for the language: *an1pu,* "affection" *pâcam,* "attachment" *kâtal,* "love" *ârvam,* "passion" and the like.

This then is a book about the poetics and politics of *tamil1ppar1r1u,* "Tamil devotion"—those networks of praise, passion, and practice centered on Tamil. And it is about the lives of those women and men who declare themselves to be *tamil1ppar1r1âlòar* or *tamil1an1par,* "devotees of Tamil." I analyze how the language has been transformed into an object of devotion in the course of the social mobilization and political empowerment of its speakers. I explore the consequences of this for the ontology of Tamil, as well as for the formulation of cultural policies around it. And I consider how language devotion produces the modern Tamil subject—*tamil1an1,* the "Tamilian"—an entity whose subjectivity merges into the imagined self of Tamil. *enkòum tamil1, etilum tamil1,* "Tamil everywhere, everything in Tamil": this is the leitmotif of *tamil1ppar1r1u* at its climactic moment. "If we live, we live for Tamil; if we die, we die for it," declared one of its devotees (Puthumai Vanan 1968: 7). Another insisted, "[Our] mind is Tamil; [our] entire body is Tamil; [our] life is Tamil; [our] pulse is Tamil; [our] veins are Tamil; [our] flesh, muscle, everything is Tamil; everything in [our] body is Tamil, Tamil, Tamil" (S. Subramanian 1939: 15-16).

Body, life, self: all these dissolve into Tamil. Devotion to Tamil, service to Tamil, the sacrifice of wealth and spirit to Tamil: these are the demands of *tamil1ppar1r1u* at its radical best.

As we will see, there are considerable differences among Tamil's devotees over the meaning of their language, and over how best to practice *tamil1ppar1r1u.* Nonetheless, I consider them as members of one singular community because they all agree upon one foundational certainty: the natural and inevitable attachment between Tamil and its speakers, an attachment that is repeatedly presented in devotional talk as inviolable, eternal, sacral. The goal of this study lies not so much in exposing the illusory nature of this certitude as in illustrating how, and in what manner, *tamil1ppar1r1u* is able to generate and sustain it in the first place. What ideological devices and strategies of persuasion are deployed by Tamil's devotees to convince their fellow speakers of the natural and unshakable bond(s) between themselves and their language? What are the institutional practices through which such a certitude is disseminated among Tamil speakers so as to appear self-evident and commonsensical? What are the ways in which its logic is used to mount resistance against putative foes, and to garner power? And finally, how is this certitude deployed to produce the modern Tamilian, whose subjectivity is anchored by Tamil and has no existence independent of it?

My use of *tamil1ppar1r1u* to interrogate the language question thus is not a nativist gesture, for I make the concept do theoretical work for me in ways which exceed the many tasks that speakers of Tamil have themselves assigned to it in their prolific discourses. Neither is it meant to alienate non-Tamil-speaking readers, despite its alterity (heightened no doubt by the diacritical marks that grace its English transliteration!). Nevertheless, its frequent presence in these pages marks the difference accompanying the ideologies of Tamil that cannot be readily assimilated into preexisting categories such as nationalism. By leaving it untranslated in many instances, and by glossing it in English in others, I seek to remind the reader (and me) of the ironies of writing about Tamil devotion in English, as I wish to draw attention to the inevitable hybridity that accompanies academic exercises like this one, which are conducted between cultures, between languages. But above all, following the cue of many who have written on the politics of translation, *tamil1ppar1r1u* allows me to "inscribe heterogeneity" in these pages, even as its assertions betray, as we will see, the colonial and post-colonial space which it inhabits (Niranjana 1992).

So, what kind of theoretical work does the analytic of devotion perform in this study? Most obviously, by hijacking it from the domain of religion to which it has been conventionally confined in South Asian studies, I wish of course to suggest that devotion is not solely directed towards deities and religious personages in India. Instead, piety, adoration, and reverence have routinely centered on sovereigns and parents; more recently, on politicians, movie stars, and other figures of popular culture; and most distinctively in our time, on the nation. Remarkably, through the intervention of its supporters, Tamil, too, joins their ranks, and even subversively displaces them—so much so that, as *tamil1ppar1r1u* gathers strength as the century wears on, it is increasingly asserted that Tamil alone ought to be the sole and legitimate focus of the unconditional devotion of its speakers. This indeed is the dream, and demand, of the most fervent of its adherents. The analytic of devotion allows me to demonstrate how sentiments that accumulate about Tamil among its speakers resonate with attitudes expressed towards deities, sovereigns, and parents. In fact, central to the work of *tamil1ppar1r1u* is the wholesale annexation of genres of praise, vocabularies of reverence, and habits of adulation which have been conventionally reserved for such notables.

Further, the analytic of devotion enables me to track the myriad micronetworks of statements and practices through which Tamil has been transformed, over time, in specific historical, political, and social circumstances, into an object of passionate attachment. Despite what its devotees might claim, Tamil (or for that matter, any language) does not have an inherent, natural, even God-given capacity to generate loyalty, love, longing; it is made to do so, and to serve specific ends. Such structures of sentiment that tie a language to its adherents are crucial to the politics of its empowerment. Yet they are too hastily passed over by a social science scholarship that has its sights set on demonstrating how languages have been used as agents of social and political mobilization, or as catalysts for nationalist activity. In such analyses, we learn little about how specific languages are transformed into sites of such loyalty, reverence, and love. How indeed do they acquire the capacity which *enable* them to act as symbols or catalysts, or, just as crucially, *disable* them from doing so? To remember Chinnasami, once again, *how* does Tamil acquire the power to move him to burn himself alive in its name?

The politics of language empowerment, however, are never independent of its poetics, those rhetorical norms and strategies of persuasion through which its adherents attempt to convince their fellow speakers about the glories of their language, the urgency of its cause, and the need to surrender their wealth, bodies, and souls for it. Such networks of talk are especially crucial for *tamil1ppar1r1u,* for the hold that Tamil appears to exercise over its devout follows not least from the deployment of the persuasive power(s) of the language itself. Its devotees repeatedly confess to the joys of hearing the very sound of Tamil, and comment on its *men1mai* (softness), *in1imai* (sweetness), *nunòmai* (fineness), and so on. The potency of

Tamil devotional talk lies not just in the scholarly breadth it displays or in the logic of its arguments, but just as crucially in its strategic use of alliterative phrases, affective figures of speech, catchy idioms, rhetorical flourishes, and the like. My analysis of Tamil devotion therefore follows the suggestion that "linguistic practice, rather than simply reflecting social reality, [is] actively...an instrument of...power....Words [do] not just reflect social and political reality; they [are] instruments for transforming reality" (Hunt 1989: 17).

Attention to linguistic practices is particularly necessary in colonial situations where new language hierarchies emerge to displace older ones, as European languages, linguistic forms, and literary genres capture prestige, profit, and power (Cohn 1985; Fabian 1986; Rafael 1988). As elsewhere in the British empire, Tamil devotion, too, paradoxically relies on English to stimulate *tamil1ppar1r1u,* a reliance that noticeably diminishes by the 1920s and can rightfully be seen as one of its more visible successes. The attitudes of Tamil's devotees towards English, the language of their colonial masters, are quite equivocal and contradictory. While many of them—as is typical of bilinguals spawned by colonial systems—are clearly at ease in going back and forth between the two languages, there are many differences in the structure and logic of arguments, the representational devices, and the strategies of persuasion they deploy in doing so. Rather than reflecting some essential qualities inherent to either language, such differences are themselves traces of the different ideological work performed by the two languages, Tamil and English, within *tamil1ppar1r1u.* All this of course only reminds us that linguistic practices such as these are never just about languages. Instead, our choice of languages and the myriad ways in which we use them are intimately reflective of our sense of selves and the worlds in which we live, the economies of prestige and power within which we function, and the politics of our beings.

Finally, I turn the lens of devotion on *tamil1ppar1r1u* itself, to reveal how despite the claims of Tamil's devotees, there is no singular, homogeneous language that consolidates itself as the focus of their love and adulation; there is no singular, homogeneous community that emerges in their imaginings; and there is no singular path to practicing what they praise and preach. Its apparent singularity as a sentiment notwithstanding, *tamil1ppar1r1u* itself is multiple, heterogeneous, and shot through with difference.

Language, Colonialism, and Modernity

Tamil's devout have been quick to assimilate Chinnasami and his fellow self-immolators into a pantheon of devotees which stretches back into the hoary mists of time and includes mythical sages, legendary kings, even the gods themselves. For like the nation, that other entity produced in modernity, *tamil1ppar1r1u,* too, is driven by the imperative to clothe itself in timeless antiquity, so that devotion to Tamil appears to be as ancient as the language itself. Yet Tamil devotion—in the sense in which I have identified it as networks of praise, passion, and practice through which the language is transformed into the primary site of attachment, love, and loyalty of its speakers—is a more recent phenomenon whose foundations were laid in the nineteenth century with the consolidation of colonial rule in what was then the multilingual Madras Presidency. Writing the Tamil question differently also therefore means a resistance to assimilation into a nativist antiquity. For, continuities with the past notwithstanding, Chinnasami's act, and the stories of his fellow devotees who proclaimed their willingness to place their life and limb at the service of the language, has to be located within new regimes of imagination, institutional practices, and technologies of meaning production that were ushered in, however skewed, with colonialism and modernity. And what were some of these?

First, although it has been transformed into a subject of sustained devotion fairly recently, Tamil attracted praise from at least the second half of the first millennium C.E. But much of this praise was episodic, scattered, even oblique. The language was rarely the primary subject of such eulogies, for the fundamental concern of even its most ardent admirer was with ensuring the literary worth of its poetry, or the salvational potential of its hymns, rather than with Tamil per se. Indeed, it is only in the latter half of the nineteenth century that Tamil emerges as an autonomous subject of praise (Krishnan 1984). Further, in the pre-nineteenth-century verses of praise, the power of the language was complexly entangled with the power(s) of divinities and extraordinary beings, rather than with the power of "the people." Tamil was eulogized, but not because it ensured communication between its speakers, enabled the schooling of the citizenry, or facilitated the governance of the populace. Instead, it was held in awe for its demonstrated ability to perform wondrous miracles and command the all-powerful gods (Ramaswamy 1996).

This is not to say, in a reworking of the old secularization argument, that an enchanted world in which Tamil was divine and salvational gave way, with modernity, to a disenchanted one in which it is bureaucratized and rationalized. On the contrary, the language continues to be assigned a salvational task within the regimes of Tamil devotion, as we will see. Yet the terms on which Tamil is rendered salvational vary, as does the logic. In *tamil1ppar1r1u,* the ideological work done on the language places the people who speak it at the very center of the project, as an imagined community. It is the task of ensuring that Tamil commands the adulation and veneration of its speakers, rather than the attention of the gods, which consumes its modern devotees. We get a glimpse of this new people-centered ideology in the Tamil-speaking region from around 1879:

Tamil gave birth to us; Tamil raised us; Tamil sang lullabies to us and put us to sleep; Tamil taught us our first words with which we brought joy to our mothers and fathers; Tamil is the first language we spoke when we were infants; Tamil is the language which our mothers and fathers fed us along with milk; Tamil is the language that our mother, father, and preceptor taught us.... [T]he language of our home is Tamil; the language of our land is Tamil.

As we will see later, the imagining of Tamil as the favorite of the gods lingers on well into this century, but it has to contend with a new sentiment ushered in with modernity in which languages are seen as the personal property of their speakers (Anderson 1983: 66-69). Hence the insistent use of collective pronouns, such as "our" and "their," in modern discourses on language. This people centered ideology of modernity inaugurates a *patrimonial* imagination in which language is constituted as a tangible, material possession that is transmitted from one generation of its speakers to another who relate to it as a property owning "collective individual" (Handler 1988: 140-58). Since it is their patrimony, its speakers are enjoined to ensure the well-being of their language, for in this lay the future of the community whose very existence is now predicated on its possession. Propelled by such a logic of possession—of language as personal property—*tamil1ppar1r1u,* too, declares that speakers of Tamil "have" a language; it renders them the new masters of Tamil, masters who are called upon, ironically, to "serve" the language with their body and life.

Chinnasami and his fellow devout also lived and operated in a world in which print culture had become normalized (Venkatachalapathy 1994). This was a hybrid culture; put in place in the seventeenth and eighteenth centuries by sundry European missions and colonial establishments, it then bloomed prodigiously after 1835 with the legalization of Indian ownership of presses. From around 1812, the College of Fort St. George in Madras, with its coterie of British administrator scholars and their Tamil-speaking subordinates, began to publish Tamil grammars, editions of ancient literary works, prose translations and commentaries, and so on (Zvelebil 1992: 159-64).

By the 1890s, when *tamil1ppar1r1u* began to manifest itself, it was quite clear that print and prose were fundamental technologies through which it would be practiced. Well into the next century, the devout struggled to find funds for their printing presses, subscribers for their journals, and readers for their books. But they did not give up their confidence in this new miraculous technology that allowed them to circulate their ideas about their language among the populace, however limited its literacy.

Speeches made in Tamil revival organizations and literary academies, at public rallies, even street poetry and processional songs, were invariably translated into print. Print helped in the standardization and homogenization of Tamil, and granted it a visible continuity with an ancient remote past that it resurrected. It ushered in new discursive styles, modes of punctuation and syntax, genres of literature, transformations in script, and new ways of relating to the language—as something seen and read, rather than merely heard. Like the modern nation, the devotional community was at its core a print community, a network of Tamil speakers who were also now readers and consumers of the language, "connected through print" (Anderson 1983: 47-49).

Finally, as Tamil emerges as a subject of devotion in the late nineteenth century, it also becomes a subject of history. In 1903, V. G. Suryanarayana Sastri (1870-1903) posed a novel question—"What is the history of a language?"—and then replied: "The emergence of sounds to express thought, and the formation of words; speech and its development into language; alphabets and their use in writing; grammatical conventions and language formation; word conventions and textual traditions—these are the contents of the history of a language" (Suryanarayana Sastri 1903: i-ii).

Recognizing the existence of such histories in Europe, Suryanarayana Sastri appropriated the new European sciences of comparative philology and historical linguistics to publish his *Tamil1mol1iyin1 Varalâr1u* (History of the Tamil language), arguably the first secular history of the language in Tamil. A little prior to this, M. Seshagiri Sastri had published a philological analysis of the language (1884). Indeed, comparative philology elicited much admiration among the devout. As one of them, D. Savariroyan (1859-1923), declared:

The science of Comparative Philology—the invention of German writers enables one to understand the secrets of languages, their points of resemblance or divergence. It discloses as in a mirror, the origin and growth of a language, its primary and secondary stages, its manifold transformations, its word-formation and its grammatical structure. The cultivation of such a study confers innumerable benefits on the languages and without doubt we also shall be partakers of these advantages according to the degree to which we cultivate it.

This fascination with comparative philology and historical linguistics was clearly compensatory, a response to colonial comments on the absence of "historical," "comparative," and "scientific" work in India prior to the arrival of European technologies of knowledge. So, the missionary Robert Caldwell (1814-1891), author of *A Comparative Grammar of the Dravidian or South-Indian Family of Languages* (1856), acknowledged the "earnestness" and "assiduity" with which "native" grammarians had hitherto studied their languages, but observed with regret that they did not have the "zeal for historic truth" that is the "special characteristic of the European mind":

> They have never attempted to compare their own languages with others—not even with other languages of the same family. They have never grasped the idea that such a thing as a family of languages existed. Consequently the interest they took in the study of their languages was not an intelligent, discriminating interest.... Their philology, if it can be called by that name, has remained up to our own time as rudimentary and fragmentary as it was ages ago. Not having become comparative, it has not become scientific and progressive.... If the natives of southern India began to take an interest in the comparative study of their own languages and in comparative philology in general... [t]hey would begin to discern the real aims and objects of language, and realise the fact that *language has a history of its own, throwing light upon all other history.*

The "comparative" study of languages, the genealogical links between languages of the same "family," the "history" of language, and the "progress" of language: these provided the agenda for the numerous linguistic studies carried out in colonial India, "the happy hunting ground of the philologist," from the late eighteenth century. Colonial ideologies were driven by the assumption that "mastery" of India's languages would secure the "mastery" of India; it would enable British "command" and "native" obedience; and it would ensure "the vast and noble project of the Europeanization of the Indian mind." The "grand work" of British rule was thus inevitably accompanied by the colonization of Indian languages, a project involving "descriptive appropriation" and "prescriptive imposition and control" (Cohn 1985; Fabian 1986: 76). India's numerous languages were collected, classified, standardized, enumerated, and thus dramatically transformed from "fuzzy" and "uncounted" entities into neatly bounded, counted, and mapped configurations (Kaviraj 1992). The result was an arsenal of grammars, manuals, dictionaries, and glossaries culminating in the grand, multivolume authoritative *Linguistic Survey of India* (1903-28). Caldwell's *Grammar*—the most cited English-language narrative in Tamil devotional discourse—belonged to this arsenal and authorized many of the founding assumptions of Tamil devotion. It popularized the key term "Dravidian" (based on the Sanskrit word *drâvidòa,* itself a transmutation of *tamil1*) as the umbrella category for Tamil and the other languages of South India whose origins and structure, as demonstrated using the "scientific" principles of comparative philology, were quite different from Sanskrit and its "Indo-European family of tongues" of the North. Partha Chatterjee (1993: 7) has recently suggested that the modernization and standardization of Bengali from the mid-nineteenth century was carried out by an emergent bilingual intelligentsia "*outside* the purview of the [colonial] state and European missionaries." Yet India's languages, Bengali included, were (re)appropriated by their speakers only after they had been incorporated into a colonial economy of distinctions, hierarchies, and meanings. Thus Tamil's devotees waged their battles on a colonial (and colonized) terrain where Sanskrit loomed loftily as a "classical" tongue, and Tamil was reduced to a mere "vernacular" where Sanskrit was the language of the "fair" and "noble" Aryans, Tamil the tongue of the "menial" and "dark skinned" Dravidians; and so on. Colonial knowledges of India were certainly "dialogically" produced through interactions with "native" categories, traditions, and informants. In the process, however, many a "native" notion was fundamentally altered in meaning as well as in use, the modern concept of "Dravidian" being an excellent case in point (Irschick 1994).

Above all, the colonization of language meant its historicization: language has a history of "its own," a history that, like many others in the nineteenth century, was imagined organically. So languages are born, grow, produce literatures, spawn civilizations, and even die, if not tended to appropriately. The histories of various languages were laid out in linear narratives which sequentially charted their evolution through time. Produced as they were in a colonial context, many such narratives about India's languages were steeped in the rhetoric of decline and degeneration. A glorious past was inevitably followed by the dismal present; under the aegis of the British and enlightened "natives," India's languages could be rescued, "revived," and "improved," paving the way to a bright future. This logic of decline and of improvement drives Tamil devotionalism as well, which attempts to historicize Tamil by locating its "origins," "development," and "spread." Such a historicization is invariably accompanied by a comparison of its "progress" with that of other languages; not surprisingly, it culminates in the lament that Tamil was utterly doomed, and that something had to be done to save it. When this historicizing imperative converges with the patrimonial imagination about Tamil, an entirely novel horizon of sensibilities crystallizes that I characterize as *modern*. The life of the language is now perceived as inextricably intertwined with the lives of its speakers as an imagined community: their pasts, present, and futures are inseparable. So declared one of Tamil's devotees in 1915: "O Tamil pandits! O Tamil people! Be warned! Guard your language. Language is the life of its community of people. If the Tamil language is destroyed, the excellence and glory of the Tamilians, too, will be destroyed....Let your tongues only speak Tamil; let your quills only write Tamil; let your hearts only desire Tamil" (Subramania Siva 1915: 202).

It is because Chinnasami and his fellow devout are subjects of such an imagination that their stories inevitably differ from those of any speaker of Tamil who loved and praised the language prior to modernity.

Language and Gender

The globalization of the nation form and its cultures of modernity enabled the universalization of the concept of language as "mother tongue," the site where culture becomes nature. The mother tongue is a construct that emerged at a particular historical moment in the complex transformation of Europe's linguistic landscape from the middle of the second millennium, as Latin was progressively withdrawn from the public domain and the "vernacular" was elevated as the language first of the state and then eventually, by the nineteenth century, of the nation (Seton Watson 1977). The historicity of the construct, however, has scarcely been explored. Consider the following statement by the American literary critic Walter Ong:

Why do we think so effortlessly of the first language we learn as our "mother" tongue?...The concept of "mother" tongue registers deeply the human feeling that the language in which we grow up, the language which introduces us as human beings to the human life-world, not only comes primarily from our mother, but belongs to some degree to our mother's feminine world. Our first language claims us not as a father does, with a certain distance that is bracing...but as a mother does, immediately, from the beginning, lovingly, possessively, participatorily, and incontrovertibly. Mother is closer than father: we were carried in her womb. In her and from her we were born. Our world is a fragment of hers.

Yet neither Ong nor other scholars who routinely use the term "mother tongue" interrogate the historical conditions under which the "first language" comes to be so "effortlessly" attached to "our mother's feminine world," from philology to pedagogy. Why in so many contemporary societies whose patriarchal foundations have been only further updated with modernity, and where everything from property inheritance to the generational transmission of one's very name is reckoned through the father, does the figure of the mother come to be associated with language? The association seems especially surprising given the importance accorded in modernity to language as the essence of the national spirit. Even for feminist theorists of language, this has not been a matter of concern (Cameron 1990), nor has it been one for scholars of South Asia. This is particularly striking because the category of the "mother tongue"—and its equivalent in Indian languages—appears to have gained salience only from the second half of the nineteenth century in the subcontinent, but has since become ubiquitous. Today, speakers of Tamil invariably use this term, and its Tamil gloss, *tâymolli* (lit., "mother language"), to refer to their language. Consider how one of its admirers defines Tamil as *tâymolli:* "Tamil is the *tâymolli* of the Tamil community. The newly born child calls the woman who gave birth to it, '*ammâ*' [mother]. She, too, coos over her child and calls it '*kanònòç*' [precious one]. So, because Tamil is the language with which the mother is hailed, and it is the language which the mother herself uses, it is our *tâymolli*" (Sivagnanam 1970: 2).

The echoes here of Ong's statement from the other side of the world are loud and clear. As we will see, Tamil's devotees, as indeed others in India, struggled to secure official recognition, from the colonial state, of their language(s) as "mother tongue." What was at stake in doing so? Why does the new people centered ideology of language and the patrimonial imagination ushered in with modernity resort to the figure of the mother? In attempting to answer such questions for Tamil, this study opens up for critical scrutiny the feminization of languages in modernity, a feminization that has been so naturalized as to have sealed off the "mother tongue" from history.

Tamil devotion would remain simply a rehearsal of Europe's linguistic history if all that happens to Tamil in the course of being drawn into various structures of modernity is its recasting as "mother tongue," *tâymol1i.* Yet this is not the only kind of feminization that the language undergoes within the regimes of *tamil1ppar1r1u.* For lurking in the shadows of the "mother tongue," but frequently disrupting its hegemonic claim on Tamil, is Tamil1ttây (lit., "Mother Tamil"), the apotheosis of the language as goddess, queen, mother, and maiden. Indeed, in the discourses of Tamil's devotees, there is a ready slippage between *tamil1* Tamil1ttây; *tâyppâl,* "mother's milk" *tây,* "mother" and *tâymol1i,* "mother tongue," all of which over time come to be synonymous with each other. Like other figures of difference, Tamil1ttây operates subversively to disrupt the flow of hegemonic discourses and ideologies, compelling the "mother tongue" to reveal the convergence between "language" and "motherhood" that has come to be so naturalized. The work of Tamil1ttây thus offers a striking illustration of the displacement and disarticulation of European notions at the very site of their colonial deployment.

My first introduction to Tamil1ttây came in 1988 when I chanced upon an anthology of poems called *Mol1iyaraci,* "Queen language." Its very first selection, drawn from an 1891 play, *Man1ôn1manòîyam,* by P. Sundaram Pillai (1855-97), represented the earth as a woman whose beautiful face is *paratak kanòtòam* (India) and whose radiant brow is the southern peninsula. The *tirâvitòa nâtòu* (Dravidian land) adorns that brow as an auspicious *tilakam* (sacred mark). The poem then declared:

- O great goddess Tamil (*tamil1 anòanku)!*
- Like the fragrance of that *tilakam,* your fame spreads in all directions, and delights the whole world.
- Spellbound in admiration of your splendid youth and power, we offer you our homage.

The poem went on in this vein for several more verses (Velayutam Pillai 1971: 1-3). My interest in it was further piqued when I discovered that its first verse was institutionalized in June 1970 as the Tamilnadu state's "prayer song." The government's reasons for doing this are telling:

It is observed by Government that many prayer songs are being sung at the commencement of functions organized by Government or attended by Ministers. In order to ensure uniformity in the singing of prayer songs, the Government have been for some time considering whether a theme might be chosen for being rendered as a prayer song, which will have no religious or sectarian association. After very careful consideration, the Government have decided that the piece containing six lines from Thiru. [Mr.] Sundaram Pillai's "Manonmaneeyam" which is an invocation to the Goddess of Tamil, would be an appropriate theme for being rendered as a prayer song.

In his reminiscences, M. Karunanidhi (b. 1924), the Tamilnadu chief minister who ordered the institution of the prayer song, observes that there were orthodox Tamilians who objected to this official recognition accorded by the state to the "Goddess of Tamil." Yet despite this, the government stood by its decision. Soon after, in April 1971, the adjoining union territory of Pondicherry, the predominantly Tamil-speaking former French colony, also instituted an anthem in praise of Tamil1ttây based on a 1939 poem by the well-known poet and native of Pondicherry, Bharatidasan (1891-1964) (Krishnamurthy 1991: 139-40).

Over the next couple of decades, both governments faced many problems in implementing their orders and getting their constituents to sing these songs correctly. Many Tamilians do not even realize that Tamil1ttây is the embodiment of the language they speak when they invoke her in these songs. Nevertheless, what intrigues me is that the governments of both these Tamil-speaking regions chose to make Tamil devotion into an everyday public and performative act in this way. Why personify the language, and why resort to the female figure? How is the female body deployed in devotional discourse(s), and to what ends? Why does the figure of the mother come to dominate from among a whole range of female subject-positions?

Just as intriguing to me has been the virtual lack of recognition accorded to Tamilttây by scholars. Elsewhere, I have suggested that this may be due to the many ambiguities that surround the figure in the intellectual and cultural discourses and practices of the region (Ramaswamy 1993: 687-90). But it is precisely because it is a figure—of speech, worship, and identity—which manifests itself episodically that I am intrigued by the cultural, political, and ideological work to which Tamilttây has been put by her devotees. How does one write the history of a concept that is not ubiquitous, consistent, or immediately apparent? Fellow scholars in Tamilnadu frequently expressed incredulity and even skepticism over my interest in Tamilttây. "There is no such thing as Tamilttây," one of them told me; "she is only a figment of our imagination," another assured me. I found it difficult to reconcile such statements with my innumerable encounters with her in essays, poems, songs, textbooks, newspaper reports, and public speeches. If Tamilttây is so inconsequential, why did these texts dwell in such loving detail and at such length on her various attributes, marvel over her many past achievements, and lament over her current state of decrepitude? If she is only a figment of the imagination, how would we account for the colorful posters and newspaper cartoons which have made visible what is arguably a mere metaphor? And what about her wooden and stone statues and metal images which have transformed literary imagination into material substance? Coming of age as a historian at a time when the clarion call of my discipline has been to make the hidden, the submerged, and the suppressed "visible," I asked myself how one writes the history of something that is visible but not seen.

For her devotees, Tamilttây is a singular figure with her own unique biography, a repertoire of deeds that cannot be reproduced, and a range of powers unfathomable. There is literally no one like her. Yet it is clear that she joins a pantheon of comparable female icons of the nation such as Bhârata Mâtâ, "Mother India" Britannia of England; Marianne of France; Guadalupe of Mexico, and the like (Agulhon 1980; Gutwirth 1992; Mosse 1985; Ryan 1990; Sarkar 1987; Warner 1985; Wolf 1958). Some other Indian languages have been similarly feminized (King 1992). Nevertheless, because she is a figure who cannot be easily assimilated or translated into a ready-made narrative of language-and-nationalism organized around the founding concept of "mother tongue," Tamil1ttây allows me to interrogate and write the language question differently. So, in spite of her interstitial and episodic presence in the narratives of her own devotees, Tamil1ttây emerges as one of the principal protagonists of this book.

Preview

Tamil's devotees tell numerous stories about their language. The many variations and differences in these stories are informed, however, by one foundational narrative, which goes like this. Once upon a time, long long ago, Tamil1ttây had reigned supreme, lavishly patronized by great Tamil kings. That had been an age of peace, prosperity, and happiness. There had been no inequities based on caste, creed, or gender. Learning, culturc, and civilization had flourished. Today, however, ignored by her "children," "Tamil1ttây has been cast into prison.... [S]he has several ailments. She languishes away, devoid of the fine food of poetry....How many wounds, how many scabs, how many boils, how many pustules, how many scars, plague our mother! Tamil1ttây's beautiful body—her glorious form—is now riddled with bloody wounds. And what of her heart?" (Kalyanasundaranar 1935: 30-31).

Her devotees identify their land and community with the body of Tamil1ttây: "O Mother! Your land shrinks! Your sons diminish! Your body, too, shrinks!" (Suddhananda Bharati 1936: 10). In turn, the salvation of the body politic lies in ridding the body of Tamil1ttây of its wounds, scars, and centuries of neglect. Her devotees repeatedly insist that if Tamil1ttây prospers, so too will Tamilians, and so too will their land and community. In the mystical poet Suddhananda Bharati's utopian vision of a new Tamil homeland restored to the reign of Tamil1ttây and Tamil learning:

Thre is gold and greenery everywhere;

The smile of our illustrious queen who reigns over the cool Tamil grove, is like the glow of the morning light that destroys darkness...[!]

Countless poets sing their songs!

The cuckoos fill the air with sweet Tamil music!

......

The land holds high its head; our own arts and sciences shoot up like mountains!...

The parched land is now a pleasant grove!

......

Holding her auspicious scepter, our mother reclines gloriously on her priceless throne of knowledges....

And celestials pray for her long life thus, "Long live Tamil sweeter than nectar!...

May you grace us so that Tamil learning flourishes and the entire world flourishes with it!"

(Velayutam Pillai 1971: 80-81)

This narrative of the golden past of Tamil, its degenerate present, and its utopian reign in the future provides the driving imperative for Tamil devotional practice, which draws its strength from the desire to restore Tamil and Tamil1ttây's lost honor and pride. This imperative manifests itself in the repeated plea that Tamil speakers should wake up from their centuries of "sleep" and, filled with a new consciousness (*unòarcci*), bring about the "improvement" (*valòarcci*) of Tamil. Only thus could they fulfill their filial debt to their language/mother and reestablish the rule of Tamil (*tamil1 âtòci*) (Kothandaraman 1986). Clear as this agenda may appear, it was constrained from the start by the multiple and often countervailing conceptions that prevailed about the language among its devotees, and it is these that I first detail in chapter 2. I follow this, in chapter 3, with an analysis of Tamil1ttây, a figure that appears on the surface to bring unity to the multiple imaginings about Tamil, but that on closer scrutiny dissolves into the contrary images of goddess, mother, and maiden. My aim in this chapter is to demonstrate that just as Tamil is multiply configured, and Tamil1ttây is multiply imagined, so too is language devotion multiply manifested, as religious, filial, and erotic, all struggling for prominence and domination.

From love, I move to questions of labor in chapter 4. Here, I explore how the differing agendas of the various imaginations about Tamil come into play in public policies and politics, and I track the many dilemmas that trouble its devotees as they translate their "talk" of *tamil1pparlr1u* into *tamil1ppanòi,* "service" and "work" for Tamil. And then at last in the penultimate chapter 5, I turn to the lives and stories of those devotees, which are offered as models of emulation for all good and loyal Tamil speakers. My concern here is to chart the production of what I characterize as the "devotional subject," an entity wrought in the cauldron of Tamil devotionalism whose history is the story of the language, and whose life cannot be imagined independently of Tamil. At the turn of this century, the devotional subject is one among a large number of possible subject-positions occupied by speakers of Tamil. By the middle of this century, not least because of the myriad activities of *tamil1pparlr1u,* there is a dramatic shift: the devotional subject is the only legitimate subject, for to be Tamilian meant that one *has* to be a devotee of Tamil; there is no other subject-position possible or desirable for its speaker, in the view of the ardent enthusiast. I explore this at some length in my concluding chapter 6, where I consider how the "Tamilian" becomes a subject of Tamil as the language itself becomes subject to *tamil1pparlr1u.*

Love, labor, and life as these are articulated in the discourses of Tamil devotion around the figure of Tamil1ttây: these, then, are the primary concerns of this study. It is with the help of Tamil1ttây and the practices of *tamil1pparlr1u* that coalesce around her that I set out to explore the language question in Tamil India differently—as a history that appears almost the same, but is not quite.

ONE LANGUAGE, MANY IMAGININGS

One Language, Many Imaginings

In his important reflections on language and nationalism, *Imagined Communities,* Benedict Anderson concludes evocatively: "What the eye is to the lover..., language—whatever language history has made his or her mother tongue—is to the patriot. Through that language, encountered at the mother's knee and parted with only at the grave, pasts are restored, fellowships are imagined, and futures dreamed" (1983: 140).

In this statement, as elsewhere in the vast scholarly literature on nationalism, languages are assumed to have singular, homogeneous, and stable identities that their speakers carry with them from mother's knee to the grave. Yet this in itself is perhaps one of nationalism's lasting myths, installed by its own strategies of rationalization and standardization of language. The many adventures of Tamil within the discourses of *tamil1ppar1r1u* suggest rather that attachment to a language is rarely singular, unanimous, and conflict-free. A language may carry a singular name—its "proper" name—but this does not necessarily translate into a singular body of sentiments that connect it to its speakers. Instead, as languages are subjected to the passions of all those interested in empowering them, they attract multiple, even contrary, imaginings. The power that they exercise over their speakers is correspondingly varied, multiplex, and historically contingent.

The putative unity suggested by the name "Tamil" notwithstanding, there is no monolithic presence which reigns in the regimes of Tamil devotion that so assiduously transform the language over time into an object of adulation, reverence, and allegiance. Instead, it is imagined in different ways in different contexts by different devotees. In four such regimes of imagination—the "religious," the "classicist," the "Indianist," and the "Dravidianist"—Tamil is variously conceived as a divine tongue, favored by the gods themselves; as a classical language, the harbinger of "civilization" as a mother tongue that enables participation in the Indian nation; and as a mother/tongue that is the essence of a nation of Tamil speakers in and of themselves. *Tamil1ppar1r1u* is thus not a static monolith, but evolves and shifts over time, entangled as it is in local, national, and global networks of notions and practices about language, culture, and community.

What follows in this chapter, then, is a discursive history of Tamil from the 1890s to the 1960s. By "discursive history" I mean the history of the discourses that gathered around Tamil as it became the focus of talk and practice. "Discourse" has become one of the most frequently used but casually understood terms of our times. My own sense of it has been influenced by Foucault's. Although I do not necessarily agree with many aspects of his work nor explore all its consequences,

I do follow his assumption that discourses are "practices that systematically form the objects of which they speak," and I agree with his insistence that production of discourses (= "knowledges") cannot be divorced from the work of power (Foucault 1972: 49). Accordingly, I focus on statements not primarily to analyze their truth-value, their accuracy, or the extent to which they correctly reflect the "beliefs" of their producers; instead, my concern is to consider how propositions are advanced and arguments built; to uncover the ideological devices used and conceptual moves made in this process; and to determine how certain notions about language, culture, community, and history acquire a hard materiality with the circulation and recirculation of such utterances through talk as well as institutional practices. For devotees of Tamil, undoubtedly, *tamil1ppar1r1u* is a state of mind, an exemplary habit, a way of life—indeed, the only possible condition of being. It may be all these, but I analyzc it as a network of discourses which forms, and reforms, the focus of its attention, the Tamil language.

Further, I also treat *tamil1ppar1r1u* as a network of competing "projects." The concept of "project," too, has been much-used but little defined in recent scholarship. Like Nicholas Thomas, I find the concept useful, for it draws our attention "not towards a totality such as a culture, nor to a period that can be defined independently of people's perceptions and strategies, but rather to a socially transformative endeavor that is localized, politicized, and partial, yet also engendered by longer historical developments and ways of narrating them" (1994: 105). As Thomas writes,

A project is neither a strictly discursive entity nor an exclusively practical one: because it is a willed creation of historically situated actors it cannot be dissociated from their interests and objectives, even if it also has roots and ramifications which were not or are not apparent to those involved. And a project is not narrowly instrumental: the actors no doubt have intentions, aims, and aspirations, but these presuppose a particular imagination of the social situation, with its history and projected future, and a diagnosis of what is lacking, that can be rectified....This imagination exists in relation to something to be acted upon...and in tension with competing...projects, yet it is also a self-fashioning exercise, that makes the maker as much as it does the made. And projects are of course often projected rather than realized.

Not least of the reasons I find such a notion of the project attractive is because it allows me to consider Tamil's devotees not as mute ciphers but as interested beings grappling with the many new ideas—and some old ones—about their language ushered in with modernity, even as it draws attention to the discursively situated contexts of their articulations and practices.

Religiously Tamil: The Language Divine

Through much of the nineteenth century in many parts of India, the quest for foundational principles for the "reform" of society in the aftermath of colonial conquest led to a retreat into "religion" and "tradition," imagined as sites outside the sphere of the colonial state, and hence pure and untouched. What followed was a fundamental redefinition of religious identities, the polarization of communities on religious principles, and the yoking of religious traditions to the various political and cultural projects of modernity (K. Jones 1989). These came to pass in the context of a colonial regime which singled out religiosity as the essential, inherent, and eternal trait of the Indian, just as materialism and science were the province of the West. For India, therefore, true modernity "would lie in combining the superior material qualities of Western cultures with the spiritual greatness of the East" (Chatterjee 1986: 51).

Living as they did in the crosswinds of colonial modernity, many of Tamil's devotees, too, fell victim to the assumption that religious fundamentals would provide salvation to a populace imagined in decline. The means to such a salvation lay in divine Tamil, "the tongue vouchsafed by God to fulfill his purpose in this world" (Devasikhamani 1919: 24). (Re)assertions of Tamil's divinity (*teyvattan1mai*) accompanied a wave of religious revivalism which surfaced in the Madras Presidency in the closing decades of the nineteenth century, primarily centered around a reworking of Shaivism, declared the most ancient and authentic religion of those Tamilians who were not Aryan Brahmans. Neo-Shaivism, as I shall refer to this reformulated religion, began to make its presence felt from around the 1880s through the publishing and organizational activities of some its principal exponents, such as P. Sundaram Pillai, J. M. Nallaswami Pillai (1864-1920), P. V. Manikkam Nayakar (1871-1931), K. Subramania Pillai (1888-1945), Nilambikai Ammai (1903-45), and, most prolific of all, Maraimalai Adigal (1876-1950). These reformers typically hailed from the ranks of the new elites spawned by colonialism everywhere in India: they were educated, urban, middle-class, upper-caste "non-Brahman" professionals and government employees. They may have disagreed with each other on finer points of terminology or doctrine, but they were unanimous in their demand for the removal of "polytheistic" religious practices, claimed to have been introduced into a pristine Shaivism by Aryan Brahmans from the North through their linguistic vehicle, Sanskrit. Their program was puritanical and elitist as well in its advocacy of vegetarianism and teetotalism, and in its call for the excision of "irrational" customs and rituals (animal sacrifices, the worship of godlings, and the like) which were the very stuff of village and popular religion. For the true "Tamil religion" (*tamil1ar matam*), they insisted, was the monotheistic, "rational" worship of Shiva using pure Tamil rituals based on Tamil scriptures performed by Tamil ("non-Brahman") priests through the liturgical medium of divine Tamil (Alarmelmankai 1914; Maraimalai Adigal 1930a, 1974b; K. Subramania Pillai 1940; Swaminatha Upatiyayan 1921).

Neo-Shaivism emerged to counter what was perceived as the disparagement of Dravidian beliefs in colonial narratives, as well as in neo-Hindu formulations produced primarily in northern India. Numerous internal contradictions and changes through time notwithstanding, British colonialism operated on the fundamental assumption that India was primarily Hindu, and that Hinduism, in turn, was made up of at least two principal streams which were historically, philosophically, and racially different from each other. On the one hand, there was the high and morally uplifting religion of the "Aryans" locked away in ancient Brahmanical texts written in Sanskrit, which a whole century of Orientalist research had construed as authentic and pure Hinduism. On the other, there were the "aboriginal," "barbaric," "material demonologies" of the "pre-" or "non-"Aryan tribals, village folk, and uneducated masses, which, by the 1880s, were increasingly identified by many as "Dravidian." Dravidian religion was generally caricatured as "fear ridden," "hideous," and "wholly degrading, intellectually, morally, and spiritually" (e.g., Elmore 1915: 149-52; Whitehead 1921: 152-58). It was deemed "primitive" because of the absence of recognizable scriptural or philosophical traditions such as those possessed by the "civilized" Aryans, and because of its reliance on shamanistic rituals, animal sacrifices, and animistic ceremonies involving petty village deities and bloodthirsty mother-goddesses.

Such colonial speculations also generated an evolutionary theory of Indian religious history (Inden 1990: 117-20). The dark, feminine, materialistic, and sensual religion of the aboriginal Dravidians was conquered by the philosophically and intellectually advanced, virile, white gods of the Aryans. Over the centuries, it was conceded, the two religions did intermesh, the influence of the superior Aryan modifying the "crude animism" of the primitive Dravidian for the better. This had not happened, however, without taking a toll, for latter-day Hinduism reveals the extent to which a pristine Aryan religion had itself come to be eroded by the superstitious and animistic practices of the Dravidian "sub-stratum" (Caldwell 1856: 518-28; Elmore 1915; Whitehead 1921). Nevertheless, "whatever be their present-day union or interminglement, it is difficult to imagine any original connection of the Aryan Brahmans and their subtle philosophies, with the gross demonolatory of the Dravidian peoples who surround them" (Government of India 1912: 51).

Such a theory was extremely useful for a body of thought that we now identify as "neo-Hinduism," which struggled to salvage Hinduism from a colonial scrutiny that savagely denounced some of its aspects, while lavishing praise on others. Like colonialism in whose shadows it was forged, nineteenth-century neo-Hinduism, too, reduced "India" to a Hinduism whose pure and authentic manifestations were limited to the Sanskritic scriptural tradition characterized as "Aryan" (Halbfass 1988: 197-262; K. Jones 1989). In many a neo-Hindu narrative, the progressive admixture of the aboriginal Dravidians had caused the "fall" of Hinduism from its glorious Aryan beginnings, a decline that was only further exacerbated with the invasions of the Muslims. Although not all neo-Hindus or Indian nationalists unanimously participated in the denigration of the Dravidian, they nonetheless shared a lasting conviction that India could be saved by returning to the imagined purity of a pristine Sanskritic Aryanism (Leopold 1970).

By the turn of this century, several neo-Hindu organizations had established themselves in the Madras Presidency; one of the most influential among them was the Theosophical Society, which moved its headquarters to Adayar in 1882-83. The society was heavily patronized by English-educated Tamil Brahmans who found its validation of scriptural and Aryan Hinduism, appropriately scientized and modernized, particularly satisfying (Irschick 1969: 26-54; Suntharalingam 1974: 290-311; Mani 1990). While Brahmans all across India generally prospered under colonial rule, Tamil-speaking Brahmans had especially reaped rich rewards. Barely 3 percent of the population, they disproportionately dominated the bureaucracy and various professions such as education, journalism, law, and medicine, as well as associational politics, into the 1920s, primarily by getting a head start in English and university education (Visswanathan 1982). But even more perniciously, Brahman domination was ensured by a colonial legal culture which institutionalized Brahmanical social theory as the very foundations of the Raj (Derrett 1968: 225-320; Washbrook 1989: 241-44). As a consequence, all those caste Hindus who were not Brahman—almost three fourths of the populace of the Presidency—were unilaterally considered "Shudra," the lowest of the Sanskritic fourfold hierarchy. Such a characterization came to be increasingly resented by the later decades of the nineteenth century by upper-caste "non-Brahman" landholding and merchant elites, growing numbers of whom, especially among Chettis and Vellalas, were also acquiring English education and competing for urban jobs, as well as for political privilege, within a colonial state structure that was undergoing increasing bureaucratization and centralization (Barnett 1976: 22-27; Washbrook 1976: 280-87). So P. Sundaram Pillai, one of the founding fathers of neo-Shaivism, complained thus in 1896 to a fellow Vellala, Nallaswami Pillai:

Vellalas who form the flower of the Dravidian race have now so far forgotten their nationality as to habitually think and speak of themselves as Sudras....In fact to tell them that they are no more Sudras than Frenchmen and that the Aryan polity of castes was the cunningly forged fetters by which their earliest enemies—the Aryans of the North—bound their souls which is worse than binding hands and feet, might sound too revolutionary a theory, though historically but a bare fact.

Many a Brahman intellectual was quick to respond to such charges. M. Srinivasa Aiyangar, amateur historian and litterateur, countered:

Within the last fifteen years, a new school of Tamil scholars have come into being, consisting mainly of admirers and castemen of the late lamented professor...Mr. Sundaram Pillai....Their object has been to disown and to disprove any trace of indebtedness to the Aryans, to exalt the civilization of the ancient Tamils, to distort in the name of historic research current traditions and literature, and to pooh-pooh the views of former scholars, which support the Brahmanization of the Tamil race.

Not least of the consequences of the turn-of-the-century culture wars between these elite products of the "new" education and of the colonial bureaucratic and professional systems was that by the 1920s Brahmans as a community were declared enemies of Tamil and of its speakers. Manickam Nayakar, a devotee of Tamil who also claimed that "his best and tried friends are mostly Brahmans," was compelled to declare in 1917 that "the general disposition of many a Brahmin is to disown his kinship with the rest of his Tamil brethren, to disown his very mother Tamil and to construct an imaginary untainted Aryan pedigree as if the Aryan alone is heaven-born....[T]heir general trend is to assume that they are themselves Aryans and not Tamilians, and to take as an axiom that Tamil and Tamils owe everything to Sanskrit" (Manickam Nayakar 1985: 75). Indeed, as we will see, although individual Brahmans continued to proclaim their *tamil1ppar1r1u* into the 1920s, their devotion was always suspect, tainted as it was by their community's support of Sanskrit, increasingly deemed alien to Tamil and its culture.

In such a charged climate, the ascendancy of the Brahman dominated Indian National Congress in the early 1900s, and the entry of the Theosophical Society into nationalist politics from 1913, only fueled the growing fears of the Vellala and Chetti elite that under the guise of "nationalism," Brahmans would hijack the nation and turn it into a Sanskritic, Aryan, and above all Brahman domain. In such a nation, Tamilians who were not Brahmans would continue to be ritually and socially denigrated as "Shudra," "the sons of concubines" (Maraimalai Adigal 1963, 1974a: 44-45). It is thus not surprising that the earliest efforts to constitute an alternate non-Aryan, non-Sanskritic, and non-Brahmanical religion as the embodiment of all that was truly and originally Tamil were most actively sponsored by these Vellala and Chetti elites. Synecdochically representing the entirety of the "non-Brahman" populace of the region, they vigorously argued that it was only such a "Tamilian religion" that would stem the continuing empowerment of an Aryan-Sanskritic-Brahman-Hinduism which inevitably spelled doom for Tamil and its speakers in the emergent nation. In turn, these "non-Brahman" elites received the support of the colonial state, itself-seeking allies to counter the growing influence of the Congress. The consequence was an informal alliance between them and the colonial administration, which is reflected in the pro-British stance of the Justice Party (founded in 1916-17 to represent "non-Brahman" interests) and in the eulogies of British rule and English that surfaced within neo-Shaivism (Maraimalai Adigal 1967a, 1974a: 45-46).

The Polarization of Tamil and Sanskrit

So, from the turn of this century, neo-Shaivism engaged in a complex set of maneuvers. On the one hand, it had to counter the damaging caricatures of Dravidian religion in colonial narratives. On the other, these very texts also contained much ammunition that could be deployed for its battle against neo-Hinduism and its surrogate, Indian nationalism: the declaration that Dravidian religion far preceded Aryan arrival, not just in the Tamil-speaking country but all over India; the suggestion that Tamil-speaking Brahmans had never participated in this religion; the pronouncement of ancient Tamilian society as egalitarian, untainted by the hierarchical and oppressive caste system of the Aryans; and above all, the possibility that that most important Hindu deity, Shiva, might be Dravidian in origin (Elmore 1915: 13-14; Gover 1871: 1-15). Neo-Shaivism appropriated such colonial propositions, fused them with statements drawn from pre-colonial Shaiva narratives, and proposed the following tenets of the emergent "Tamilian religion," *tamil1ar matam* (also called by some, "Dravidian religion," *tirâvit#a matam*): Shaivism is the true and original religion of all Tamilians who are not Brahman. It is also the most ancient religion of India, predating Sanskritic Hinduism by many centuries. Its principles are enshrined in the devotional and philosophical texts of divine Tamil, and it would be in vain, therefore, to seek it in the demonistic rituals of the populace (as the colonials were wont to). Further, it was not the Dravidians who corrupted a pristine Hinduism (as neo-Hindus were inclined to suggest); on the contrary, it was Brahmanism and Aryanism that had debased the original Tamilian religion and diverted it from its hallowed path of monotheism, rationalism, and egalitarianism into the "gutters" of polytheism, irrational rituals, and unjust social hierarchies (Maraimalai Adigal 1930a: vii-viii; Savariroyan 1900-1901: 269). The removal of such impurities brought in by Sanskritic Brahmanism would lead to the retrieval of pristine Shaivism, the restoration of a pure Tamilian subjectivity, and the growth of self-respect and pride among speakers of Tamil. And it is for this project that Tamil was enlisted by neo-Shaivism, its divinity reemphasized and popularized in the process. Cleansed of its Sanskritic impurities, the divine language would be the beacon that would throw light on all that was originally Tamil/Dravidian. It would sift and separate the pure Tamil Shaiva texts from all those masquerading as such.

The writings and speeches generated by neo-Shaivism show that this was not an easy or consistent project, not least because there was little agreement over what constituted the original Shaivism, and because it was difficult—in certain cases impossible—to dismantle the complex linkages that had developed between Tamil and Sanskrit over the centuries of their coexistence from the early first millennium C.E. In the early decades of neo-Shaiva activity, from around the 1880s to around 1905, there were few explicit statements against Sanskritic Hinduism per se. The focus instead was on countering the negative characterizations of Dravidian religion by asserting its distinctiveness, its uniqueness, its rootedness in high philosophy, and its parity with the Sanskritic tradition. "Moderate" neo-Shaivism, therefore—as exemplified by the writings of J. Nallaswami Pillai, for instance— visioned Tamilian religion as part of a larger Hindu complex, but oriented around divine Tamil and its scriptures rather than around Sanskrit.

Gradually, however, such assertions gave way to overt antagonism towards Sanskritic-Brahmanical-Aryan-Hinduism, and even to calls for a complete break from the latter by the 1920s. This transformation took place in the context of changes in the curriculum of Madras University, which, starting in 1906, became the site of an acrimonious debate over the compulsory study of Sanskrit and the elimination of the "vernaculars" the growing demand for "Home Rule" by the Besant led factions of the Congress, beginning in 1915; the British promise of "self-government" by stages in 1917; the many attempts after that by the colonial state to play off the "non-Brahman" against the Brahman in electoral politics; and finally, the iconoclastic atheism of E. V. Ramasami (1879-1973) and his followers (Irschick 1969; Nambi Arooran 1980: 35-139; Washbrook 1976: 274-87). In the "radical" neo-Shaivism that crystallized in response to these events, and is perhaps best exemplified by the later religious writings of Maraimalai Adigal, a Tamil-speaking Dravidian "non-Brahman" Shaiva community was clearly posited against Sanskritic, Brahmanical, Aryan Hinduism (Maraimalai Adigal 1930b, 1974b; K. Subramania Pillai, 1940: 45-47). Talk of parity between Tamil and Sanskrit gave way to assertions of the superiority of the former. Legends and stories that had accumulated over the centuries about Tamil's divine powers were recycled and embellished, and the very legitimacy of Sanskrit was questioned in this process.

One such story, based on an incident in the life of the nineteenth-century mystic Dandapanisami, is especially popular in neo-Shaiva tellings. When challenged by a Brahman who invoked the superiority of Sanskrit because the *Veda*s were in that language, Dandapanisami declared that unlike them, the Tamil scriptures did not advocate the sacrifice of goats and the consumption of meat. The argument between the two notables continued for a while, and it was finally decided to settle the matter by calling upon the deities. They placed in front of the spear of Lord Murugan three chits with the following messages: "Tamil alone is eminent," "Sanskrit alone is eminent," and "Both are eminent." A virgin maiden was asked to choose among the chits and she picked out the one that declared, unambiguously, "Tamil alone is eminent." Dandapanisami rejoiced, brushed his eyes reverentially with the chit, and then placed it in his mouth. Subsequently, he composed his famous verse on Murugan which praised him as the lord who himself had declared Tamil's superiority over Sanskrit. He then went on to write the *Tamil1alank#âram,* a hundred-verse eulogy of Tamil recounting its various miraculous abilities and supernatural powers (Velayutam Pillai 1971: 124-61).

In the same vein, another of Tamil's admirers, years later, narrated a story his mother had told him about one of his ancestors who had had the power to cure the sick and the dying with the help of Tamil hymns. One day, a cobra, with its hood raised, wandered into the room where he sat, offering his prayers in Tamil. It drank some milk and slithered away, leaving him unharmed. "Is it not clear from this that Tamil has supernatural powers!" he asked rhetorically of his readers. Such stories, of which there are many, reminded Tamil speakers that the Tamil scriptures were infinitely superior in their moral and ethical content, and in their salvific potential, to the Sanskrit *Vedas*. It was a Brahmanical conspiracy that denied the divinity and ritual efficacy of Tamil, designated it as a "Shudra" language, and appropriated all its treasures, including the mighty Shiva himself, for Sanskrit (Maraimalai Adigal 1936a: 105-6; K. Subramania Pillai n.d.: 15-17).

By the time radical neo-Shaivism was under full steam in the 1920s, it was declared unequivocally that Tamil, and not Sanskrit, was the *only* appropriate ritual language for all pious Tamilians. Indeed, Tamil is the world's first divine language, and the religion it expounds the most eminent: "In the whole wide world, there is no greater god than Paramashivam [Shiva]; no religion loftier than Shaivism; no land more superior to the Tamil land; no language more divine than Tamil...and no people more auspiciously pure than Tamilians" (Swaminatha Upatiyayan 1921: 20).

Taking advantage of the technologies and communication possibilities generated in the colonial milieu, neo-Shaiva associations and publications took this message of Tamil's divinity to the public. They urged Tamil speakers to make divine Tamil the center of their renewed religious lives, the core of their (recast) beings. Prior to the neo-Shaiva revival, the cause of divine Tamil and of Shaivism had largely been the purview of religious specialists, temples, and monasteries. Now, lay intellectuals and activists—who were career bureaucrats, lawyers, academics, and even civil engineers—established societies for propagating the message of neo-Shaivism in various cities and towns across the Tamil-speaking parts of the Presidency. They published books and journals, conducted religious and Tamil classes, arranged conferences, and ran local libraries (Nambi Arooran 1980: 20-21; Ramaswamy 1992b: 84-89). Many of these societies as well as their journals were short lived, and suffered throughout their careers for want of support and subscription. Yet there are success stories as well, such as the Tirunelvçli Tenlnlintiya Caivacittânta Nûrlpatippuk Kallakam, founded in 1920. Both this organization and its journal *Centamillc Celvi* (founded in 1923) continue to exist today, albeit not without their share of problems. Although neo-Shaiva organizations eschewed direct participation in associational politics, they threw their influence behind many causes dear to *tamillppar1r1u* such as the demand for education in Tamil, the numerous protests against Hindi, and the movement for renaming Madras state as Tamilnadu, the land of Tamil.

Being Religious, The Tamil Way

Movements for religious reform in colonial India have been extensively studied, and a recent volume clearly shows that spoken, rather than scriptural, languages were the sites of some of the most intense debates and discussion in this regard (K. Jones 1992). Yet, while we have a growing understanding of the recastings of religious doctrines, practices, and conceptions of community, the changes undergone by the languages through which such reconfigurations were attempted have been left largely unexamined. *Tamillppar1r1u*'s divinization of Tamil to authenticate its project(s) reminds us that the medium itself has to be empowered in order to empower the message, to invoke an overused but nevertheless appropriate cliché. Neo-Shaivism declared that Shaivism and divine Tamil are the two "eyes" with which modern Tamil speakers would regain their lost vision and be redeemed. Divine Shiva and his divine Tamil go together, hand in hand, and cannot be separated: each lends power and authority to the other.

Neo-Shaivism emerged to counter what was perceived as the recasting of India as predominantly Aryan, Sanskritic, Brahmanical, and Hindu by both colonialism and neo-Hinduism. Such a countering was necessary because of the fear that "non-Brahman" Tamil speakers would inhabit such an India only in the fissures: ritually denigrated, socially demoted, and symbolically cast out, as "Dravidians" and "Shudras." Yet speakers of Tamil had once been the dominant people of the subcontinent, a preeminence they had lost with the arrival of Sanskritic Aryan Brahmanism. In Maraimalai Adigal's version of this imagined history, "the religion of the land, that is Shaivism, underwent a marked change." Yet, he wrote, this was a change that was limited to the "outer rim," for "in its center, it remained as pure as crystal and as impenetrable as a hard diamond. What is bound and true to its core, what is perfect and complete in itself, requires no change, requires no improvement" (Maraimalai Adigal 1930c: iii).

Neo-Shaivism attempted to recover this imagined pure center and use it as the foundation on which to (re)constitute a true Tamilian religious subjectivity untouched by Brahmanism, Aryanism, Sanskrit, and Hinduism. Cleansed of its Sanskritic impurities, Tamil, the language in which its pure and original scriptures were deemed written, was the means through which this center could be reached. The language had perforce to be (re)divinized for this project, for it had to take on and counter the power of divine Sanskrit. Other religious groups in earlier times had advocated the divinity of Tamil, but not always at the expense of Sanskrit, and not in such a sustained and prolific manner using the modern technologies of print and communication (Ramaswamy 1996). In the changed circumstances of the late colonial period, when a devolving state rewarded communities that could establish their timeless distinctiveness and religious autonomy, there was much to be gained by claiming the existence of a unique Tamilian/Dravidian community, bonded together from time immemorial by its own distinctive religious traditions that were embodied in its own sacred language. Such a claim necessarily called for a delegitimization of Sanskrit and a radical distancing from its scriptures and tradition. Such a project also perforce needed the projection of Tamil as divinity, the ranking favorite of the gods themselves.

Civilizing Tamil: The Language Classical

The search for authentic first principles as the foundation on which to rebuild a modern community did not lead all of *tamil1pparlr1u* towards religion and Shaiva scriptures. Instead, with the help of the secular sciences of comparative philology, archaeology, ethnology, and history, a new source for these was located in ancient Tamil heroic and love poems of the so-called Cank#am age of the early centuries C.E. Hitherto completely outside the horizon of contemporary scholarly awareness, these poems were "discovered" and published between the 1880s and 1920 primarily because of the efforts of C. W. Damodaram Pillai (1832-1901) and U. V. Swaminatha Aiyar (1855-1942). The story of this "discovery" in all its fascinating detail has yet to be told, but it is important to register some of its manifold effects on *tamil1pparlr1u*.

Most immediately, with this "discovery," the antiquity of Tamil literature, dated up until then in colonial histories to the late first millennium, was now pushed back, at the very least, to the early centuries C.E., and in the writings of some devotees to the beginning of time itself. These poems not only deepened the antiquity of Tamil literature, but quite as crucially, within a few years of their being made public, they came to be valorized as the repositories of an ideal and perfect Tamil society, prior to its colonization by either the British or, more enduringly, by the Brahmanical Aryans from the North. They were combed to generate nostalgic portrayals of an ancient Tamil people who were adventurous and heroic; who roamed the high seas in pursuit of gold and glory; who were "hospitable and tolerant in religion," "egalitarian" and "rationalist," fun-loving but contemplative and philosophical as well (Kanakasabhai 1966). Most significantly, these poems were tangible proof that

Tamilians were speakers of the only "living" "classical" language and the proud possessors of a great "civilization," the most ancient in the world. Devotional narratives, regardless of their ideological differences and political commitments, are saturated with the pride that their authors experience in being the modern day inheritors of this ancient literature. In his memoirs, S. Ilakuvan (1910-1973), a Tamil college teacher who was imprisoned in 1965 for his participation in the anti-Hindi protests, has this to say about the effect on his young mind when he learned in college about the antiquity of Tamil and the wealth of its literature:

The glories of the ancient Tamil land and the eminence of Tamilians captured my heart. I became convinced that classical Tamil (*uyartan1ic cemmol1i*) had to have been the mother of all the languages of the world. I was saddened that our great and glorious Tamil country has today lost its name, and languishes away as a small part of Madras [Presidency]. I resolved that my life's mission lay in restoring the rights of the Tamil land, and the preeminence of Tamil. The battle for Tamil is the battle of my life. Similarly, M. P. Sivagnanam (1906-1995), who hailed from an indigent working-class family and could afford only a primary school education, studied these poems on his own when he was in a colonial prison in the early 1940s. He writes of his experience on reading one of the anthologies of the Cank#am corpus, the *Pur1anân1ûr1u:*

I gained consciousness of belonging to a community called Tamilian when I first read the *Pur1anân1ûr1u*. Before that, I knew I was a Tamilian. But it was only on reading the *Pur1anân1ûr1u* that I realized that the Tamil-speaking people had their own unique history, their own unique customs, their own distinctive political traditions, and their own nationality. Tamilians have had their own unique motherland (*tâyakam*) and its name is Tamilnadu, I realized.

Tamilnadu had been ruled for thousands of years by Tamilians. It struck me that no empire from the North had ever subjugated Tamilnadu or Tamilians during the Cank#am period. When I learned that men and women lived as equals in those days, my heart rejoiced. I forgot myself when I read the poems about the heroism of the mothers who sent off their young, innocent sons to the battlefield thronging with spears. I thanked God with all my heart for the good fortune of being born in such a Tamil land.

Again and again, there are similar examples of the wonder and admiration that the poems of this ancient literary corpus elicit from Tamil's devotees. They have been invoked as models for personal belief and behavior, as inspiration for public and political action, and as the founding charter for an ideal society of the future in which Tamil would reign supreme, once again.

The Tyranny of Civilization

An undiluted enchantment with the Cank#am age undoubtedly floods the entire devotional community. But its poems were of special interest to a particular regime of *tamil1ppar1r1u* that I characterize as "counter Orientalist classicism." This regime's fundamental agenda lay in securing acknowledgment—from the world at large, but especially from the colonials and from the Aryan North—of the "civilizational" status of Tamil culture. It went about this task by demanding recognition of an ancient truth that had been grossly overlooked by Orientalism, colonialism, *and* metropolitan nationalism: namely, that Tamil, too, like Sanskrit, was glorious, polished, and perfect. It is *centamil1,* "refined Tamil." Yet Orientalism and the colonial state had classified it as a "vernacular," as a corrupt derivative of Sanskrit, and denied its great texts the status of "literature." Classicism thus sought to rescue Tamil from its current lowly status as a mere "vernacular" (*un#n#ât#t#u mol1i*) and to have it reinstated in all its glory as a "classical" language (*uyartan1ic cemmol1i*) that was, like Sanskrit, Greek, and Latin, the vehicle for a lofty, unique, and refined literature, culture (*pan#pu*), and civilization (*nâkarîkam*) (Suryanarayana Sastri 1903: 132-34). The historian Nambi Arooran (1980: 70-110) has skillfully charted the growing demand among Tamil scholars and politicians from the early decades of this century for recognition of Tamil as a classical language on par with Sanskrit (and Arabic and Persian) in the curriculum of Madras University. I would suggest that there were other gains to be made in securing such a recognition, besides ensuring the victory of "non-Brahman" (Tamil) over "Brahman" (Sanskrit) in the struggle for power in the region.

A less tangible, but nonetheless potent, consequence lay in the possibility that Tamil speakers, too, might now demand membership to that select club of "civilized" cultures of the world whose languages had been deemed "refined" and "classical."

It has been suggested that "the colonies of the European empires were in the nineteenth and early twentieth centuries the context of a new and doomed efflorescence of European discourse about virtue, race, and civilization, even while that discourse was in a process of radical reconsideration in Europe as the alternative ontology of 'political economy' advanced" (Kelly 1991: 11). Tamil devotionalism as conducted in the classicist idiom offers one striking illustration of such an efflorescence, although I will reserve judgment (for now) on whether this was necessarily "doomed." Unlike neo-Shaivism, which retreated into the domain of an (imagined) uncolonized religion to conduct its project of resistance and renewal, classicism took its battle right into enemy territory. For the concept of "civilization" was no innocent classificatory device through which Orientalist and colonial knowledges neatly organized the messy world of culture(s). Instead, it was a fundamental technology of rule in which colonial dominance was secured by institutionalizing a hierarchy of differences, not only between the "West" and the "Orient," but between the various regions, cultures, and communities of the subcontinent as well, on a developmental scale ranging from savage barbarism to civilized perfection. Language was one tangible index by which such differences of cultural and moral worth were measured. The "inflectional" Indo-European, representing the summit of linguistic (and racial) achievement, was the standard by which the "tonal," "isolating," and "agglutinative" languages that were not Indo-European were evaluated: the latter were declared incapable of expressing complex, abstract, refined thought. Correspondingly, their speakers were "primitive," "barbarous," and morally deficient (Curtin 1964; Metcalf 1994; Spadafora 1990).

Such notions were embedded in numerous discourses on language, race, and progress that came to the attention of Tamil's devotees. Consider the following unflattering portrayal of the "Turanians," a linguistic and racial group into which, through much of the late nineteenth century, many colonial narratives placed Tamil speakers:

We may say generally that a large number of them...belong to the lowest Paleozoic strata of humanity[,]...peoples whom no nation acknowledges as its kinsmen, whose languages, rich in words for all that can be eaten or handled, seem absolutely incapable of expressing the reflex conceptions of the intellect or the higher forms of consciousness, whose life seems confined to the glorification of animal wants, with no hope in the future and no pride in the past. They are for the most part peoples without a literature and without a history[,]...peoples whose tongues in some instances have twenty names for murder, but no name for love, no name for gratitude, no name for God.

And consider the response by one of Tamil's devotees, Nallaswami Pillai, to such a characterization:

Did we not all read in our school-days that the Tamilians were aborigines and savages, that they belonged to a dark race, a Turanian one, whom the mighty civilising Aryans conquered and called Dasyus, and that all their religion, language and arts were copied from the noble Aryan. Even a few years ago, a great man from our sister Presidency held forth to a learned Madras audience how every evil in our society, whether moral, social or religious, was all due to the admixture of the civilized Aryan with the barbarous Tamilian. Classicism, like neo-Shaivism, thus set out to contest all such claims—Orientalist as well as metropolitan Indian—that denigrated Tamil speakers as "barbaric" and "primitive," and that unilaterally declared that the "civilized" Aryan was inevitably superior to the "aboriginal" Dravidian.

This battle, however, was fought not on the ground of religion but on the terrains of "literature" and "history," those domains whose very possession spelled the difference between peoples who led moral and civilized lives and those who barely subsisted on immoral "animal wants." In this war, the weapon was the "classicality" (*uyarttan1iccemmai*) of Tamil with which its devotees would demonstrate the originality, autonomy, and antiquity of their culture and history; the distinctiveness of their language from Sanskrit; its crucial role as a parent of many languages; and its status as the fount of an ancient civilization as glorious as, if not more glorious than, the Sanskritic one (Maraimalai Adigal [1948]; Suryanarayana Sastri 1903).

Like neo-Shaivism, classicism, too, was an oppositional discourse that was conducted largely by an educated, urban, and professional middle-class, attracting academics (historians, litterateurs, philologists, and Tamil scholars), schoolteachers, lawyers, and bureaucrats. Unlike neo-Shaivism, however, a number of Brahman admirers of Tamil, among them V. G. Suryanarayana Sastri, T. R. Sesha Iyengar (1887?-1939), and U. V. Swaminatha Aiyar, joined the ranks of devotees who were nominally Christian, such as D. Savariroyan and G. Devaneyan (1902-81), as well as upper-caste "non-Brahmans" like P. Sundaram Pillai, Maraimalai Adigal, and Somasundara Bharati (1879-1959), and those of Sri Lankan origins such as Damodaram Pillai and V. Kanakasabhai (1855-1906). Like neo-Shaivism, classicism primarily conducted its activities through literary and historical societies, the most famous among them (which continue to exist today, although fairly truncated) being the Maturait Tamil1c Cank#am, "Madurai Tamil Academy," founded in 1901 (henceforth Madurai Tamil Sangam); the Karantait Tamil1c Cank#am, "Karanthai Tamil Academy," founded in 1911 (henceforth Karanthai Tamil Sangam); and the Shaiva Siddhanta Kazhagam. Like their neo-Shaiva counterparts, with whom they frequently shared members, their contrary views of Tamil notwithstanding, these associations promoted the cause of Tamil in educational institutions, petitioned for the establishment of a Tamil University, encouraged the battle against Hindi, and so on. But most of all, they focused upon editing and printing ancient manuscripts, publishing periodicals and books, holding literary festivals, running libraries, and conducting classes for the study of classical Tamil. As such, they represent the antiquarian and scholastic aspirations of *tamil1ppar1r1u.*

The Contest with Sanskrit

Classicism, too, was concerned, like neo-Shaivism, with demonstrating the antiquity (*ton1mai*) and primordiality (*mun1mai*) of Tamil, as well as its uniqueness (*tan1imai*) and purity (*tûymai*). These were not established, however, by linking

Tamil to the world of the gods, as in neo-Shaivism. Instead, it was argued that Tamil is the first language of the first humans to flourish on the face of this earth, prior to the emergence of any other language or people (Devaneyan 1966; Maraimalai Adigal 1948). Indeed, classicism drew upon the secular science of comparative philology to dispute ancient religious stories (which neo-Shaivism had revived) about the divine origins of Tamil, insisting instead that the language was not bestowed upon the world by Shiva, but emerged to fulfill the need for human communication (P. T. Srinivasa Aiyangar 1985: 13-15; Suryanarayana Sastri 1903: 51-57).

In all such matters, classicism, too, of course contended with the hegemonic influence of Sanskrit, not so much as a "divine" language but as India's paradigmatic classical tongue. A century of colonial linguistic practice had only reinforced the ancient Sanskritic dogma that all languages (of India) are corruptions of a primordial, eternal Sanskrit. British scholar administrators and their Brahman teacher-assistants based in Calcutta's Asiatic Society and College of Fort William had declared Sanskrit as the fount of Indian "vernaculars," the sole generator of high Hindu civilization, and the only language worthy of comparison with the lofty Greek and Latin. This is a story that has been already told many times (Kejariwal 1988; Kopf 1969).

What has been less noted is the resistance to such formulations that arose almost from the beginning of colonial rule among British administrators and missionaries based in South India. Skeptical about the clubbing together of the languages spoken in "their" part of the subcontinent with the northern tongues, these men were especially critical of the characterizations of Tamil or Telugu as "vulgar derivatives" of Sanskrit. This skepticism was first voiced in Alexander Campbell's *Grammar of the Teloogoo Language* (1816) and in Francis Ellis's introduction to that grammar. Tamil and Telugu, it was argued, form "a distinct family of languages, with which the Sanscrit has, in latter times especially, intermixed, but with which it has no radical connection" (Ellis 1816: 2). In the 1840s and 1850s, other philological analyses reinforced such assertions, frequently referring to Tamil in this process as "copious," "elegant," "refined," and "cultivated" (Asher 1968;

Singh 1969: 78-88). In 1855, Tamil was even declared "a rival of the ancient Sanskrit" (Bower 1855: 158). All such scattered observations were consolidated in 1856 in Robert Caldwell's *Comparative Grammar of the Dravidian or South-Indian Family of Languages,* which used the word "classical" to characterize *centamil1,* "correct Tamil" (Caldwell 1856: 31); authorized the name "Dravidian" to refer to the "family of languages" of South India, distinct from Sanskrit and its Indo-European family of tongues (28-37); insisted that Tamil "can dispense with its Sanscrit altogether if need be, and not only stand alone but flourish without its aid" (31); and suggested that prior to the arrival of Aryan Brahmans, the "elements of civilization" already existed among the Dravidians (77-79).

Tamil's devout found much that was flattering in Caldwell's *Grammar,* which lent the authority of comparative philology (and the West) to the claims of autonomy and distinctiveness of Tamil made in its pre-colonial texts that *tamil1ppar1r1u* resurrected. Yet Caldwell's hallowed status notwithstanding, all his ideas were not wholeheartedly embraced, pace recent scholarly evaluations of the missionary's impact on Tamil cultural politics (Dirks 1995, 1996; Ravindiran 1996). Indeed, many devotees resented his claim that the term *tamil1* had derived from the Sanskrit words *dravid#a* or *drâvid#a* (Chelvakesavaroya Mudaliar 1929: 9; Damodaram Pillai 1971: 3-6, 34-35; R. Raghava Aiyangar 1979: 4-13). Others objected to his attempts to establish affinity between the Dravidian and "Scythian" families of languages, insisting instead that the former was completely distinctive and autonomous (T. Chidambaranar 1938: 5; Devasikhamani 1919: 26). Many also set aside his suggestion that Dravidians had migrated into India, proposing instead an autochthonous origin which placed them in the subcontinent from the beginning of time (T. Chidambaranar 1938: 10). Finally, there were even those who resisted Caldwell's classification of Tamil as a "Dravidian" language, insisting that the word *dravid#a* had been used in the past for Tamil-speaking Brahmans alone (Damodaram Pillai 1971: 34-39; Devasikhamani 1919: 9; Somasundara Bharati 1912:1). Their resistance is not surprising, for in spite of some eulogistic portrayals of Dravidian culture in the writings of some colonials (like C. D. Maclean and Gilbert Slater), which the devotees found useful to invoke, the dominant colonial image of the Dravidian, as created through census records, administrative manuals, and district gazetteers, is captured in this unflattering picture of the 1891 *Census:*

> This was a race black in skin, low in stature, and with matted locks; in war treacherous and cunning; in choice of food, disgusting, and in ceremonial, absolutely deficient. The superior civilisation of the foreigner [the Aryan] soon asserted itself, and the lower race had to give way....The newcomers had to deal with opponents far inferior to themselves in civilisation, and with only a very rudimentary political organisation, so that the opposition to be overcome before the Arya could take possession of the soil was of the feeblest.

In such statements, which were also picked up by many a metropolitan nationalist narrative to pursue the agenda of salvaging Indian pride by taking refuge in Aryanism, the white, virile, civilized, energetic, and superior Aryan is starkly contrasted with the dark, feminine, menial, and aboriginal Dravidian. Correspondingly, the latter's language, too, is "aboriginal," uncivilized, and inferior. So the 1901 *Census of India* observed: "In India, the Indo-Aryan languages—the tongues of civilization...—are continually superseding what may, for shortness, be called the aboriginal languages such as those belonging to the Dravidian, the Munda, or the Tibeto-Burman families....[I]t may be added that nowhere do we see the reverse process of a non-Aryan language superseding an Aryan one" (Government of India 1903: 248-49). This particular statement in the *Census* was authored by George Grierson, who headed the ambitious *Linguistic Survey of India* project for the colonial state (published 1903-28). It is telling that the underlying premise of this authoritative survey was that the "civilized" Aryan languages are inherently superior to the "aboriginal" non-Aryan. So, commenting on the progressive shrinkage in the spread of Dravidian languages, Grierson noted, "Aryan civilization and influence have been too much for [them]" (Government of India 1903: 279). And in the *Linguistic Survey,* although the "importance" of Tamil is recognized, and the antiquity of its literature noted, it is not unambiguously adorned with the mantle of classicality and civilization, as is Sanskrit (Grierson 1906: 298-302).

All the same, slowly but cautiously from the 1920s on, the colonial state began to concede the antiquity and "copiousness" of Tamil, and its status as a "cultivated" language. Dravidian speakers of today, the *Census of 1931* admitted, have "a culture of very great antiquity[;]...speakers of Dravidian languages [were] the ancient inhabitants of Mohenjadaro and perhaps the givers of culture to India" (Government of India 1933: 454-55). The *Census* was here alluding to the recently discovered archaeological remains of the Indus Valley in Mohenjadaro and Harappa, which pointed to a sprawling prehistoric urban civilization rivalling Mesopotamia and Egypt. To the delight of many a Tamil devotee, this prehistoric civilization was declared to have been possibly Dravidian by some colonial archaeologists. Thus Maraimalai Adigal quoted John Marshall in 1941:

> They (the orientalists) pictured the pre-Aryans as little more than untutored savages (whom it could have been grotesque to credit with any reasoned scheme of religion or philosophy). Now that our knowledge of them has been revolutionized and we are constrained to recognize them as no less highly civilized—in some respects, indeed, more highly civilized—than the contemporary Sumerians or Egyptians, it behoves [*sic*] us to re-draw the picture afresh and revise existing misconceptions regarding their religion as well as their material culture....The Indus Civilisation was Pre-Aryan and the Indus language or languages must have been Pre-Aryan also. Possibly, one or other of them...was Dravidic.

Maraimalai then proceeded to overwrite Marshall's tentative conclusion with the following sweeping pronouncement:

> If Sir John Marshall had had a first hand knowledge of the Tholkappiam and some other ancient classics of Tamil, he would have easily shown in corroboration of what he stated as regards the pre-Aryan antiquity of one of the Dravidian languages, that *Tamil, alone, and not any other, as he vaguely affirmed, must have been the language spoken and cultivated by the pre-Aryan inhabitants of the Indus Valley.*

Maraimalai Adigal was not alone in making such a bold assertion. More than a decade earlier, in the late 1920s, soon after Marshall's report on the Indus Valley excavations was first published, fellow devotees T. R. Sesha Iyengar and M. S.

Purnalingam Pillai had already insisted that "future discoveries and dispassionate researches" would confirm Dravidian authorship of the Indus civilization and "the remote antiquity" of Tamil culture (Purnalingam Pillai 1945: 26; Sesha Iyengar 1989: 32-61). They were able to make such assertions confidently, emboldened as they were by the many claims of classicism which challenged the dominant Orientalist wisdom about Tamil's place in India's past, and which proceeded to write an alternate script in which history began not in the North with the Aryans, but in the South with the Dravidians.

Opposing Orientalism

Classicism's status as an oppositional discourse is most apparent in the frequently expressed lament that the achievements of Tamil speakers in India's history had been totally ignored by scholars, especially those based in the North. As Sundaram Pillai dramatically declared in 1897: "The history of Indian Civilization is the old story of the Giant and the Dwarf. The victories in it are the victories of the vaunting Aryan, while the wounds are the wounds of the bleeding pre-Aryan" (quoted by Nallaswami Pillai 1898-99: 113).

The first step lay in overthrowing this "Aryan bigotry and pride" and rewriting the script of India's history so as to show how "Dravidian forebears enriched, strengthened and improved the culture of Aryan India" (Sesha Iyengar 1989: 63). Two basic strategies were adopted for such a rewriting. In the one that I call "compensatory," the aim was to demonstrate that "Hindu" or "Indian" civilization had emerged from a "harmonious commingling of the cultures of the Dravidian and the Indo-Aryan" (Sesha Iyengar 1989: 63). Tamil, it was insisted, "was quite as classical" as Sanskrit, and its literature "is no less ancient, noble, and vast." Tamil and its literature were thus validated by espousing a parity with Sanskrit, whose value was never questioned. Neither is the divide between "Aryan" and "Dravidian," seen as distinctive but complementary halves of "India," nor the legitimacy of the Brahman. As can be expected, compensatory classicism was a strategy that was favored typically, though not always, by devotees who were nominally Brahman, such as R. Raghava Aiyangar (1870-1946), M. Raghava Aiyangar (1878-1960), T. R. Sesha Iyengar, and

Swaminatha Aiyar. Their commitment was to a syncretic Indian civilization jointly produced by the "genius" of Tamil and the "genius" of Sanskrit, both of which are necessary and complementary (P. T. Srinivasa Aiyangar 1985: 85).

From the start, but especially by the 1920s, this strategy was challenged by another that I call contestatory, paradigmatic examples of which may be found in the writings of Suryanarayana Sastri, Savariroyan Pillai, M. S. Purnalingam Pillai, Maraimalai Adigal, G. Devaneyan, K. Appadurai (1907-89), and K. A. P. Viswanatham (1899-1994), among others. Contestatory classicism asserted the superiority of Tamil over Sanskrit, rather than the parity of the two. Sanskrit, after all, was a "dead" language in contrast to the everlasting Tamil (*kan1n1ittamil1*). The "barbarian" Aryans had developed into "civilized beings" on coming into contact with the "highly civilized Dravidians" rather than the other way around. For in the ancient past, Tamilians were settled agriculturists, whereas the Aryans had been mere nomadic pastoralists. Tamilians lived in splendid cities and traded with distant lands, while Aryans were still grazing herds. Tamilians were monotheistic and philosophical, whereas Aryans were polytheistic and ritualistic. Tamil had not evolved from Sanskrit, as the Orientalists maintained; on the contrary, classical Sanskrit itself developed under the influence of Tamil (Maraimalai Adigal 1963, 1966; Purnalingam Pillai 1985: 4-5).

Thus contestatory classicism reversed Orientalism's claim that the true genius of India lay in its Aryan past, asserting instead that it is to Tamil and Tamilian culture that Indian civilization owes all, for, in Sundaram Pillai's words, "what is ignorantly called Aryan philosophy, Aryan civilization, is distinctively Dravidian or Tamilian at bottom" (quoted by Nallaswami Pillai 1898-99: 112). In the logic of contestatory classicism, Aryan Brahmans had not only been responsible for bringing about the end of the Dravidian golden age, but they had also stolen all that was originally and truly Tamil and passed it off as their own (Maraimalai Adigal 1963, 1966; Savariroyan 1900-1901). Misinformed by such crafty Brahmans, Western scholars had got India's history all wrong. So instead of beginning in the North and with "the Aryan Conquest," Sundaram Pillai suggested that the "scientific historian" should begin his study in the South, which was after all, "India proper" (quoted by Nallaswami Pillai 1898-99: 113).

Tamil and the Nostalgia for Civilization

From early in this century, Tamil's classicist devotees went about the task of setting the record straight. The result has been a new—and, from the devotee's perspective, an infinitely more satisfactory—script for the Tamil (and Indian) past. In "the hoary past" (going back millions of years ago, in many accounts), there had been an ancient mega-continent (consisting of present-day Australia, Africa, and southern Asia) where Tamil had flourished. This was the land referred to as "Kumarikkan#t#am" in ancient Tamil texts and attested to as "Lemuria" by Western scientists. Classicism offered brief but nostalgic portrayals of Kumarikkan#t#am, imagined as the home of the first two Tamil academies that produced countless literary masterpieces. This state of prelapsarian bliss came to an end with a series of floods, which destroyed the original Tamil civilization and which compelled Tamil speakers to fan out and civilize different parts of the world, taking their language with them. "Traces of this wide dispersion are found in Palestine, Egypt, Italy, Scandinavia, and far-off Erin in the names of places with the suffix *ur,* in the modes of life pursued, in the resemblances of the Tamilian myths to those of Greece and to the northern sagas" (Purnalingam Pillai 1945: 4). So, the urban remains of the Indus Valley and the great poems of the Cank#am age were only the later remnants of a much more ancient Tamilian civilization, established at the very beginning of time. Orientalism had thus got wrong not only the history of India, but that of the world as well, for it was the Tamil-speaking land which was the "cradle" of the "whole human race" and of "human civilization" (K. Appadurai 1975; Devaneyan 1966; Somasundara Bharati 1912).

The consolidation of industrial modernity in the West has frequently sparked nostalgia for a life in nature, away from city lights and urban sprawls, amid fresh fields and rolling pastures. *Tamil1ppar1r1u,* I have insisted, is a discourse of modernity. But it was conducted in the milieu of a colonial culture whose own ideology of the civilizing mission deemed that the natives lacked "culture" and "civilization." Tamil's modern devotees, therefore, yearn not for nature but for culture and for civilization. The archaeological remains of the Indus Valley and the poems of the Cank#am age, not to mention the antediluvian continent of Lemuria, enabled them to claim that Tamil speakers, too, had "civilization," just "like the Greeks," but even earlier. In 1967, C. N. Annadurai (1909-69), a devotee of Tamil who was also the chief minister of the state of Tamilnadu, gave a speech at Annamalai University in Chidambaram in which he extolled the virtues of the Cank#am poems and the antiquity of "Dravidian civilization." He then called upon the students to carry "the message that our classics contain to the entire world and declare that what was *the most ancient here is what is being introduced today as the most modern*" (quoted in Ryerson 1988: 141-42, emphasis mine). Reversing the logic of Europe's civilizing mission, *tamil1ppar1r1u* thus claimed that Tamil speakers did not need to be granted civilization, for they had possessed it all along, long before any one else, and indeed had bestowed it upon the rest of the world. But such a claim has come with its own costs. For in its anxiety to secure membership in the select club of the civilized, *tamil1ppar1r1u* reinforced Europe's civilizational model of the world. So, ironically, the "uniqueness" of Tamil and its "civilized" state is claimed by demonstrating its similarity with other "civilized" cultures, by insisting Tamil speakers were, after all, "the Greeks of the East" (Purnalingam Pillai 1985: 5-6).

LANGUAGE AND THE NATION: INDIANIZING TAMIL

In the 1890s, around the same time that neo-Shaivism and classicism emerged, a third imaginary also surfaced in the discourses of *tamil1ppar1r1u,* which I call "Indianist." Over the next few decades, it moved from strength to strength, gathering reinforcement from metropolitan Indian nationalism as well as compensatory classicism at home. By the 1930s, however, this regime had to contend with the assertions of both radical neo-Shaivism and contestatory classicism against Hinduism, Brahmanism, and Sanskrit, all of which Indianism deemed necessary to Tamil devotion. More contentiously, it locked swords with the Dravidianist regime of *tamil1ppar1r1u* that was provoked by the Madras government's attempt to institute the compulsory study of Hindi in 1937-38. Dravidianism introduced into Tamil devotion the political and cultural philosophy of E. V. Ramasami, C. N. Annadurai, and their populist Dravidian movement, which the Indianist regime branded as contrary to the spirit of Indian nationalism and hence illegitimate.

In contrast to neo-Shaivism and classicism, however, both Indianism and Dravidianism were overtly political projects concerned with transforming the nature of power relations in the Tamil-speaking region. But here the similarity between the two ends. For Indianism, it was British colonialism and English that had to be replaced by the Indian nation with its family of "national" languages, of which Tamil would be the language of the region, while Hindi would be the "official" language of communication with other Indians. For Dravidianism, on the other hand, "India" itself occupied the space vacated by the colonial, whose legitimacy was only ambivalently questioned. Indeed, the Dravidianist's scathing denunciations of the "imperialism" of India (identified with the North, Aryan Brahmans, Sanskrit, and Hindi) were as passionate as the Indianist's attacks on colonialism. This important distinction notwithstanding, both the Indianist and the Dravidianist are critically concerned with Tamil as the language of politics, and not merely as the language of religion and ritual, or literature and civilization. Their agenda was to ensure that Tamil ruled (again) within *tamil1akam*, "home of Tamil." Therefore, it was not enough to establish learned academies and publish books which proclaimed the glories of divine or classical Tamil. In addition, its devotees had to fight for its institutionalization as the language of government, education, and everyday public communication. As T. V. Kalyanasundaram (1883-1953) demanded in 1924, "What is the condition of our mother tongue, Tamil, today? Where is Tamil1ttây? Does she adorn the seat of government? Does she preside over our associations? Does she flourish in our legislative chambers? Can we at least see her in our schools and colleges? Can we spot her in those political bodies that claim to fight for our rights? At the least, is there a place for her in Tamil newspapers?" (Kalyanasundaranar 1935: 19).

Rather than relying on religious or literary revivalism, as did neo-Shaivism and classicism, these regimes therefore encouraged Tamil enthusiasts to aggressively engage state structures and institutions, and to intervene in political processes, for it was in and through politics that Tamil could be empowered. And in turn, empowered by the claims of Indianism and Dravidianism, many devotees of Tamil went on to become state legislators; members of various government committees on language, education, and cultural policies; even chief ministers by the late 1960s. With Indianism and Dravidianism, *tamil1ppar1r1u* finally enabled its practitioners to secure power, privilege, even profit.

Indianism's prime exponents in the devotional community were V. O. Chidambaram Pillai (1872-1936), especially before the 1920s; T. V. Kalyanasundara Mudaliar prior to the 1940s; V. Ramalinga Pillai (1888-1972), R. P. Sethu Pillai (1896-1961), and M. P. Sivagnanam; and Brahmans like C. Rajagopalachari (1878-1972), V. V. Subramania Aiyar (1881-1925), Subramania Sivam (1884-1925), Suddhananda Bharati (1897-1990), and of course, the most paradigmatic of them all, Subramania Bharati (1882-1921). Generally from upper caste, middle-class, middle-income families—Sivagnanam is a striking exception here—they were professional journalists, lawyers, teachers, litterateurs, poets, and politicians; and in their private lives, they were reformed but devout Hindus. In contrast to Dravidianists, who imagined (away) India in very Tamil terms, these devotees framed their concern with Tamil in terms of India. India, in turn, was sometimes an abstract territorial space; at other times, it was personified, like Tamil, as the goddess and mother, Bhârata Mâtâ, "Mother India." So, the opening lines of one of Subramania Bharati's most popular poems on Tamil incorporates the phrase *vande mâtaram* (homage to [our] mother) from the famous hymn that the Bengali Bankim Chandra Chatterjee had composed in honor of Bhârata Mâtâ:

Long live the glorious Tamil!

Long live the fine Tamil people!

Long live the auspicious Indian nation !

......

Vantç Mâtaram! Vantç Mâtaram!

(Bharati 1987: 50)

It is not accidental that the "mother" whom this verse reverenced is not Tamil1ttây but Bhârata Mâtâ, for Indianism was driven by the terrible anxiety that *tamil1ppar1r1u* would lead Tamil speakers to forget India. Thus Tamilians were chastised in a poem by Ramalinga Pillai first published in 1922:

Intiyattây [Mother India] languishes in sorrow, and you speak of your own community!

That is disgraceful!

O Tamilian, break the chains that enslave that venerable woman....!

Long live the Tamil land!

May our Tamil language flourish, so that our Intiyattây who supports us may find fulfillment.

(Ramalinga Pillai 1988: 29)

Negotiating gingerly between loyalty to Bhârata Mâtâ and devotion to Tamil1ttây, between the shoals of pride in the nation (*tçs#âpimân1am*) and pride in their language (*pâs#âpimân1am*), Indianism reminded Tamil speakers that the liberation of Tamil would have to proceed in tandem with the liberation of India. In his reminiscences, the mystic-poet Suddhananda Bharati recalls how as a young man, his passions were directed as much against the emergent Dravidian movement as against the British, and how he and his young friends countered the cry of "Down with Brahman Rule" with the alternate cry of "Vantç Mâtaram." When we are enslaved to the British, what is the point of saying that we are slaves to Aryanism? he asks. "Relinquishing our home to a foreigner, siblings fight with each other over food. Meanwhile, the foreigner seizes all our food and goes away, leaving us with our squabbles" (Suddhananda Bharati 1950: 143-46). In the Indianist vision, therefore, Tamil speakers had to work together with their Indian "siblings" to throw off the shackles that fettered both Bhârata Mâtâ and Tamil1ttây, instead of fighting with each other. Swayed by the impassioned rhetoric of the Dravidian movement, they ought not to forget that this was their primary goal, Sethu Pillai reminded them on the very eve of Indian independence: "In fifteen more months, we are going to rule over our own nation. India is going to belong to Indians.

Similarly, is there any doubt that Tamilnadu will belong to Tamilians?...Tamilttây in all her former glory and splendor will reign in our hearts" (Sethu Pillai 1968: 1-2).

Not surprisingly, Indianism launched few attacks on Brahmans, Aryanism, or Sanskrit. On the contrary, it produced sympathetic accounts of Brahman contributions to Tamil and its culture, many of whose authors were not Brahmans (Kalyanasundaranar 1935: 37-38; Ramalinga Pillai 1953: 44-48; Sivagnanam 1979: 96-101). Some of its proponents even cast aspersions on (colonial) neologisms such as "non-Brahman" and "Dravidian," whose very legitimacy and historicity they questioned (Bharati 1988: 229, 263; Ramalinga Pillai 1947, 1953: 40-51; Sivagnanam 1979: 63-68). Further, there was always a place for Sanskrit within Indianism's economy of sentiments about Tamil: "In Tamilnadu, Tamil ought to be preeminent. All over India, may Sanskrit flourish, as it always has. To accomplish the unification of our Indian nation, everyone should know Sanskrit. Nonetheless, in Tamilnadu, Tamil should flourish with great eminence" (Bharati 1988: 229).

Given this linguistic division of labor, some even recommended that Sanskrit should be the national language of India (Nuhman 1984: 57-59; Padmanabhan 1982a: 274-76; Rajagopalachari 1962: 51). Correspondingly, Indianist prose was also heavily Sanskritized, especially in the hands of its Brahman practitioners. This lack of hostility towards Sanskrit extended to other Indian languages as well. In the Indianist vision, India is a land where, "along with the glorious Tamil, there flourishes Sanskrit and Urdu and Persian, the unique Telugu, Kannada with its sweet words, lofty Marathi, and fine Malayalam, Gurjaram [Gujarati], Hindi, and eighteen such languages" (Venkatesvara Ayyar 1918: 3). This congenial vision, of course, was severely tested after independence with the struggle over linguistic states and the securing of borders with neighbors, as well as over the Indian state's Hindi policy in the 1950s and 1960s, as we will see.

But in general, Indianism's strategy was to gloss over all internal sources of contention and difference in favor of closing ranks against the real enemy, the English-speaking colonial. Tamilians were reminded, repeatedly, that it was English—rather than Sanskrit or Hindi or any other Indian language—

which was responsible for the current sorry state of their beloved Tamil. Kalyanasundaram thus rebuked the Anglophiles who discarded Tamil1ttây and worshipped Ânk#ilattây (Mother English) instead. "Their birth mother starves; the other mother is well-fed. What a sign of our times!" (Kalyanasundaranar 1935: 21). In his autobiography, Suddhananda Bharati writes that from early in his life, he had to resist pressures brought upon him by his Brahman family to study English. He asked of them, "Why should I study English in order to be a servant to someone else? I am a Tamilian. I will only study Tamil." His resistance to English was fostered partly in response to an environment in which he saw so many young men mortgage their family homes and property to chase after an English education, only to wander around jobless afterwards. What did they acquire, he asks, "by giving up their mother and running after the other woman?" All they can say proudly is " 'I do not know the *Gîtâ,* but I do know Gibbon....' Is Tamil not enough for the Tamilian?" (Suddhananda Bharati 1950: 54-69; see also Bharati 1988: 180-85).

The Indianist dilemma is quite apparent in Suddhananda Bharati's story, however. He tells us that his youthful resistance to English soon gave way to an appreciation for its necessity for Tamilians if they wanted to be citizens of the world (Suddhananda Bharati 1950: 94). Indeed, he soon became "infatuated with English" he often gave public lectures in it, and even taught English to schoolchildren. Even the most anti-English of devotees was aware that English was necessary not just for learning the ways of the West, but also for communicating with other Indians until a suitable national language had been selected. As that latter project ran aground on the reefs of "Hindi imperialism," many devotees who in their early years wrote passionately against English, like Kalyanasundaram and Rajagopalachari, became its advocates, albeit reluctantly, from the 1940s.

In attempting to persuade Tamil speakers that "India" or its languages would not harm Tamil, Indianism came to rely heavily on the emotive metaphor of the mother. Consider the following statement:

The sons of Bhârata Mâtâ speak several languages....Our Indian sons adorn their Intiyattây [Bhârata Mâtâ] with these languages. In adorning her thus, is their unity harmed or affected? Those who say that the existence of so many languages is harmful speak from ignorance. Born from the womb of India, these brothers may speak various languages but are united by the same spirit of love and devotion for their nation.... Therefore, the existence of so many languages in the nation is a sign of excellence.

The Indianist logic was the logic of the family, itself reconstituted as the foundational site of unity, cooperation, and harmony. Could siblings, born from the same mother's womb and reared on her milk, harm each other? So Ramalinga Pillai reminded his fellow speakers that they should not forget: "However many languages there are in the Indian nation, for several thousands of years, the Indian people have been drinking the same mother's milk, and are members of the same culture" (Ramalinga Pillai 1953: 53).

Indianism, of course, presented Tamil speakers with two mothers, Tamil1ttây and Bhârata Mâtâ. It was not a choice between one or the other, as Dravidianism would have it. Instead, in the Indianist imagination, while Tamil1ttây's womb and milk unites all Tamil speakers as *Tamilians,* the womb and milk of Bhârata Mâtâ transfigures them into *Indians,* and ties them with other Indians in webs of sibling solidarity. It is through sharing Bhârata Mâtâ's womb and milk that Tamilians, the children of Tamil1ttây, symbolically become part of the Indian body politic.

It is also the logic of the family and of motherhood that generated that very crucial notion that Indianism (and Dravidianism) popularized among Tamil speakers: namely, that Tamil is their *tâymol1i,* "mother tongue," the language of their home and mother. Part of the challenge that Indianism faced, of course, was to reconcile Tamil's homely status as "mother tongue" with neo-Shaivite attempts to promote its divinity, and classicist efforts to secure its classicality, a task that was not all that easy.

Indianism and Divine Tamil

Like neo-Shaivism, but unlike classicism or Dravidianism, the Indianist regime was willing to accept that Tamil is a divine language (Bharati 1988: 117; Ramalinga Pillai 1953: 13-18).

Unlike neo-Shaivism, however, this did not lead it to question the legitimacy of Sanskrit and of Aryan Brahmanical Hinduism. Consider how Tamilttây introduced herself in one of Bharati's poems published in 1919:

The primordial Shiva gave birth to me;

The Aryan son Agastya saw me and took delight;

That Brahman endowed me with a grammar, complete and perfect. (Bharati 1987: 529)

All the same, even if Indianism thus upheld Tamil's divinity, it did not make this into a fundamental part of its own agenda, as did neo-Shaivism. For there was concern that dwelling on Tamil's divinity would hinder its transformation into a modern language of governance, education, public communication, and politics. As early as 1892, one of its devotees—T. Saravana Mutthu, librarian of the Presidency College, Madras—demanded, "How does it benefit Tamil if we vehemently insist that God created Tamil?" (1892: 3-4). The educationist P. Sivaswami Aiyar similarly suggested in 1917 that "instead of relying on the belief that Tamil was a divine gift and that its vocabulary was copious and its diction rich and self-contained, serious attempts should be made to incorporate into Tamil, from other languages, if necessary, terms that were easy to understand" (Irschick 1969: 304). Recognizing the growing skepticism among many about Tamil's abilities to communicate the modern sciences of the West, Bharati's Tamilttây observed to her "children" in 1919:

"Tamil will die a slow death

The languages of the West will triumph in this world."

So says the simpleton;

Alas! what an accusation!

Go forth in all eight directions!

Bring back here the wealth of all learning!

By the grace of my father, and the penance of our learned scholars, this great taint will be effaced,

With lofty fame I shall last forever in this world!

(Bharati 1987: 531)

It is perhaps not surprising that Bharati saw the task of modernizing and scientizing Tamil as a joint enterprise, made possible through Shiva's grace and human scholarship, for as he insisted elsewhere, Tamil's divine origin was not just fantasy but historically attestable (Bharati 1988: 117). Like Bharati, Indianism was ultimately ambivalent about Tamil's divinity, an ambivalence that is also reflected in its attitude towards religion. As did so many "secular" nationalists in colonial and post-colonial India, devotees of Indianist persuasion upheld the inherent equality of all Indian religions. All the same, Hinduism in particular—in its reformed new "universalist" version which condemned caste hierarchies and irrational rituals, and recommended an action oriented practice of spiritual truths—received special attention. For Bharati, as indeed for others like him, Hinduism was the best religion of the world and Tamil speakers its most eminent practitioners. Correspondingly, a true devotee of Tamil was not exclusively Shaivite (as in neo-Shaivism), nor polemically atheistic (as in Dravidianism), but clearly and proudly a "Hindu." As Bharati insisted in 1917:

A man who has pride in Tamil (*tamil1apimân1am*) is one who embraces Hinduism (*hintu tarmam*). That alone will illuminate the path of the devotee of Tamil. For the man who does not care for the *Tçvâram,* the *Tiruvâcakam,* the *Tiruvâymol1i,* the *Tirukkur1al#,* and the *Kamparâmâyan#am* has no claim to be a devotee of Tamil. One who knows these texts will realize that it is through Hinduism that this world will find salvation.

Thus in contradistinction to radical neo-Shaivism, which adopted an oppositional stance towards Sanskritic Aryan Hinduism in the name of a "Dravidian" Shaivism, Indianism linked the cause of Tamil to an inclusivistic neo-Hinduism (Halbfass 1988: 403-18; Ramalinga Pillai 1953: 39). Indeed, to counter Christian missionary influence in schools (and later, the Dravidian movement's atheism), Indianism advocated a thorough grounding in Tamil and Sanskritic scriptures for Tamil children as part of its "national education" (*tçciya kalvi*) scheme.

All the same, such an embrace of religiosity brought its own share of problems for Tamil's devotees, as it did for others in modern India. Indianism did celebrate the existence of diverse religious beliefs among Tamil speakers, although it employed a distinctly Hindu idiom in such a celebration (Bharati 1937: 35-36; Ramalinga Pillai 1988: 28-29). Nonetheless, there was also considerable anxiety that such a diversity itself could, and did, give rise to sectarian divisiveness and tensions. Not surprisingly, in these circumstances, Indianism placed its hopes in Tamil as the bond which would tie together all Tamil speakers, be they Hindu, Muslim, or Christian. In a public speech that he gave in 1928, Kalyanasundaram pointed out: "If we wish to bind the people born in this [Tamil] nation in the net of unity, there is only one instrument, and that is the Tamil language....We may be attached to different religions, but we cannot forget we are all Tamilians" (Kalyanasundaranar 1935: 25-26).

Kalyanasundaram was able to say this with confidence because he and his fellow devout were simultaneously creators as well as subjects of the founding certitude of *tamil1ppar1r1u:* in contrast to caste and religion, which divided one Tamil speaker from another, their language, especially in its incarnation as "mother tongue" and as Tamil1ttây, bonded them together in the "net of unity," as firmly and surely as the love of their mother(s).

Indianism and Classical Tamil

In the same manner that it affirmed Tamil's divinity, Indianism also confirmed its classicality, especially because the burgeoning classicist scholarship was so convincingly demonstrating to Tamil speakers that while their "mother tongue" might not yet be "scientific," it was certainly more ancient and venerable than English or any other European language being paraded around as a paragon of modernity. So Bharati (1937: 62) declared in 1919 that he had read and appreciated "the exquisite beauties" of Shelley, Victor Hugo, and Goethe, but no "modern vernacular of Europe can boast of works like the *Kural* of Valluvar, the *Ramayana* of Kamban and the *Silappadhikaram* (Anklet Epic) of Ilango."

Like the other regimes of *tamil1ppar1r1u,* the Indianist, too, represented the age of the Cank#ams as free of sectarian strife and caste oppression, when the philosophy of "all towns are our towns, and all men are our kinsmen" had reigned

(Kalyanasundaranar 1935: 28-36; Ramalinga Pillai 1953: 57-59). Its concern with these poems as with other works of Tamil literature, however, was not so much antiquarian as it was utilitarian. The hope was that these would help modern Tamil speakers liberate themselves from their enchantment with English.

If they were exposed to the greatness of their past through the medium of their own language, they would truly appreciate the value of Ilango and Kamban, instead of lauding Shakespeare and Tennyson (Bharati 1937: 62; C. S. Subramaniam 1986: 252-60; Kalyanasundaranar 1919: 122-26). Accordingly, many of Tamil's Indianist devotees, like Subramania Aiyar, Chidambaram Pillai, and Sivagnanam, undertook the publication of accessible (and in many instances Sanskritized) interpretations of ancient Tamil works, which were also popularized through literary conferences, street plays, and movies (Sivagnanam 1970: 97-104, 109-15).

While there was a general consensus that it was important to stress Tamil's classicality so as to bolster the pride and self-respect of its speakers today, there was also concern that an excessive emphasis could detract from the equally urgent task of transforming it into a modern language of rule, education, and everyday communication. And this utilitarian thrust to the Indianist project led it to rebuke, even denigrate, "panditic" and scholarly Tamilians who, it was claimed, resisted efforts to help change Tamil into a useful contemporary language, in their single-minded pursuit of its classicality (Bharati 1987: 527-28; Nuhman 1984: 16-33; C. S. Subramaniam 1986: 264-65). For Indianism, a true Tamil devotee was one who made Tamil suitable for school textbooks, and one who would ensure that it was the language used by its speakers in their assemblies and associations. "The Tamil devotee (*tamil1apimân1i*) is one who produces new knowledges, new literatures, and new life in Tamil," in Bharati's words (Tḥooran 1986: 256-57). The absence of modern, scientific literatures in Indian languages, devotees like Bharati insisted, perpetuated Indian enslavement to English through dependence on the Western mastery of the sciences. The aim therefore was to learn as much as possible from English, in order to displace it from its throne and replace it with Tamil, suitably modernized and scientized.

Their faith in the inherent greatness of Tamil notwithstanding, many of its devotees wondered about its ability to communicate modern, scientific thought. From the turn of this century, these enthusiasts had to face Anglophile critics who claimed that "wallowing in sentimentalism," supporters of Tamil were sacrificing the youth of the country to their "superstitious beliefs in the vernaculars." A contributor to the *Educational Review* in 1916 insisted, "The fact is that our vernaculars are in a most crude state so far as scientific exposition is concerned. It is no answer to say that we have very good poetry and some grandiloquent prose, in the vernaculars. A language that is well-equipped for poetic expression is not necessarily so for a scientific thesis. Kalidasa and Bhavabhuti may well feel handicapped if they were set to translate a modern elementary textbook of science" (quoted in Irschick 1969: 304-5). The challenge therefore lay in scientizing Tamil, in transforming it from a language of great poetry and piety into one of modern science and technology.

A similar challenge was faced by language reformers and modernizers in other parts of the subcontinent, as indeed in other regions of the world (Fishman, Ferguson, and Dasgupta 1968). But in Tamil India, those committed to the creation of scientific vocabularies had to contend not only with all the problems of colonial modernity (such as borrowing from the West without sacrificing pride in the indigenous, embracing the secular without surrendering the religious, and so on), but also with the many languages that rivalled for attention as the reservoir from which to draw for "improving" Tamil—English, Sanskrit, and classical Tamil being the principal contenders. By the 1930s, devotees of Indianist persuasion came to clash with others on this matter because in their logic, Sanskrit was the one language that had the power to displace English, a contention that gave rise to considerable ire, as we can imagine.

This was not the only problem that Indianist devotees faced, for they also sought to ensure that in the process of modernizing and scientizing Tamil, they authorized a language that could easily be used by "the people," its principal consumers. Indianism's clarion call, as captured in Bharati's exhortation "to write as one speaks," meant that the Tamil used in textbooks, newspapers, and political speeches ought to be understood, in the words of V. Ramaswamy (1889-1951), by the rickshaw puller on the street. So Bharati's preface to his famous 1912 poem *Pâòcâli Capatam* (The vow of Panchali), insisted: "Simple words, a clear style, easy rhythms that can be readily comprehended, and simple tunes that the common folk will appreciate—he who composes a poem along these lines today will be breathing new life into our mother tongue" (quoted in Nuhman 1984: 92). Yet the modern Tamil authorized by Indianism in the name of "the common folk" continued to be Sanskritic in its lexicon, betraying both the upper-caste and upper-class prejudices of its practitioners, as we will see.

Indianism and the "Mother Tongue"

In all these struggles—to counter the excessive influence of Tamil's divinity and classicality, to wean Tamil speakers away from their infatuation with English, to create new vocabularies for use in scientific education and modern government, to fashion a language that would be understood by "the common folk"—Indianism relied extensively on Tamil's status as "mother tongue." In the Indianist regime, as indeed in Dravidianism, the speaker's relationship to Tamil is cast in the intimate and familiar terms of a child's interactions with its mother, rather than with some distant abstraction called "the classical tongue" or "the divine language." Early in this century, Bharati (1937: 29) observed that "nations are made of homes." For both these regimes, however, the nation is not merely made of homes; symbolically and discursively, it *is* home, a domain of selfless love and sibling solidarity, a realm of nonpolitics (Chatterjee 1989).

The language of the home acquired potency and validity for Indianism, precisely because it was imagined to be *not* the language of the colonized, Anglicized, public sphere. Untarnished by the West, it was the language of every Tamil speaker's heart, mind, and true self, and hence the means through which anticolonial resistance could be launched. The home, however, was also the abode of the mother, imagined as the true bearer of all that was noble and spiritual about Tamil (and Indian) culture. Just as crucially, the mother was also the vehicle through whom Tamil, the "mother tongue," would continue to be reproduced, even as in the outer, material world, away from the home, Tamil speakers, especially their menfolk, would perforce have to employ English. Not surprisingly, there was much agony among the devout over the alarming escalation in the use of English by women and girls, especially within the intimate and hitherto uncolonized space of the home. Why are we surprised, they asked, that there is no respect for Tamil when "even our women in their kitchens rejoice that they speak English" (Vasudeva Sharma 1928: 18)? An editorial in the nationalist daily *Cutçcamittiran1* (23 August 1917) similarly lamented that if this alarming trend were to continue, "we will be spoiled in every way."

Although the construct of "mother tongue" frequently erupted in neo-Shaiva and classicist discourses, generating paradoxical formations such as "our divine mother tongue" or "our classical mother tongue," it was with Indianism from the turn of the century that the term assumed both popularity and political saliency. English, it was argued, would only turn Tamil speakers (and other Indians) into clerks and accountants; their "mother tongue," however, would transform them into patriots and citizens. As Kalyanasundaram declared in 1924, "The nation in which the mother tongue does not flourish will never achieve freedom....The first step towards freedom is respect for the mother tongue" (Kalyanasundaranar 1935: 21).

Indianism was particularly concerned that such a "respect" for Indian languages was being denied by the colonial state's classification of these as "vernaculars"—"the language of the slaves." Thus S. Satyamurthy, a leading spokesman for the Congress Party, declared to the Madras Legislative Council in November 1928: "Vernacular means the tongue of slaves. I do not think we ought to insult our languages by calling them 'vernaculars' or tongues of slaves. Of course, the answer of the Englishman would be, 'My vernacular is English.' But he never uses the word 'vernacular' in connection with his mother tongue."

Therefore, where classicism protested the categorization of Tamil as a "vernacular" by seeking recognition for its classicality, Indianism did so by insisting on its status as *tâymol1i* (mother tongue)—as the language of the people, of their homes, and of their mothers. Consider the following statement from an essay entitled "Tâymol1i," written by Kalyanasundaram, that appeared in his *Navacakti* in 1924:

Every man reveres the woman who gives birth to him, the nation (*nât#u*) where he was born, and the language he speaks, by referring to these as his "mother." As much as the love he has for the mother who carried him, ought to be his love for the nation that delivers him, and the language that rears him. A man who does not revere his nation and his language is like the sinner who does not reverence his own mother. Indeed, the language that one speaks is the very wellspring of the love for one's mother, and of devotion to one's motherland. A man who is not devoted to the mother tongue he speaks is a man who has reviled his own mother and his own nation.

So endemic does the identification of language with motherhood become with Indianist discourse that even when Tamil1ttây herself was not specifically invoked, Tamil and mothers came to be spoken of in identical terms. In his memoirs Sivagnanam, an autodidact who remembers learning much of his Tamil at his mother's knee in her kitchen, writes, "As far as I am concerned, when I say Tamil is my 'mother tongue,' it is not rhetorical. It is really true. My knowledge of Tamil is my mother's gift. For that reason, Tamil *is* my mother tongue" (Sivagnanam 1974: 868). For its devotees, there was nothing more natural than referring to their language as "mother tongue" because it was literally something they acquired from their mothers. It was, as Sivagnanam reminds us, their mothers' gift.

Indianism and Hindi

From early in the century, in the Madras Presidency as in other parts of the subcontinent, there were many who were concerned with the problem of developing a national language so as to overcome the dependence on English for interregional communication. Hindi was an early favorite candidate among many Tamil speakers, as it was in its own "home" in northern India (Dasgupta 1970). In 1906, in an article he published in *Intiyâ,* Bharati endorsed the view that since Hindi was already spoken by eighty out of India's three hundred million, Tamil speakers, too, should embrace it. Yet, he lamented, no steps had been taken to promote it in the South (C. S. Subramaniam 1986: 443-44). Soon after, in a 1908 letter to the nationalist Tilak, Bharati wrote that he and his friends had started a small

Hindi class in Madras city (Padmanabhan 1982: 48-49; see also Nuhman 1984: 55-61). In subsequent decades, other devotees of the Indianist persuasion backed the cause of Hindi and countered Dravidianism's demonization of the language by reminding their fellow speakers that supporting it did not necessarily amount to the "murder" of their mother, Tamil (Kalyanasundaranar 1935: 21; Sivagnanam 1974: 136-41). Convinced that the regional Congress Party was dedicated to the twin causes of promoting Tamil at the regional level and Hindi at the national level, devotees inclined to Indianism supported that party.

Yet the promotion of Hindi as key to national unity and integration posed many dilemmas for Indianism, caught as it was between devotion to "Tamil" and "India." Over the years and especially in the decade following independence, many an Indianist became increasingly suspicious of the Congress Party's aggressive Hindi policy, which was perceived as endangering Tamil, as Dravidianists had long maintained (Sivagnanam 1974: 138-41, 416-18, 505-7). They came to appreciate the realities of functioning in a multilingual polity in which, contrary to their conviction that all languages are equal "children" of Bhârata Mâtâ, one of them would be the privileged "imperial state language." Ramalinga Pillai captured their conflicting sentiments when he wrote that Tamil speakers were famed the world over for inviting other languages into their home and honoring these. However, he asked, to what extent should they let their own language and culture suffer in this process (Thaninayagam 1963: 12)? What would happen to Tamil and its glorious literature, others demanded, if state funds were redirected towards the support of Hindi? For, as Somasundara Bharati, professor of Tamil and a Congress supporter in his early years, insisted, "clothed with prestige and privileges peculiar to an imperial state language, Hindi is sure to become a dangerous rival to Tamil." Not surprisingly, he wondered if an old "evil," English, was being replaced by a new one, and whether Tamil would continue to suffer in this process (Somasundara Bharati 1937: 17).

Although opposed to compulsory Hindi education, many Indianist devotees like Kalyanasundaram and Sivagnanam continued to extend their allegiance to the Congress's policies into the 1940s, in reaction to the powerful anti-Hindi and anti-India demonology of Dravidianism, and in the face of the Dravidian movement's growing demand for retaining English as the common language. As colonial rule gave way to Congress rule, however, they became convinced that the cause of Tamil would be compromised by the larger cause of the (Hindi-dominated) Indian nation and its needs. Not surprisingly, by the late 1940s, Kalyanasundaram joined forces with the Dravidian movement to oppose Hindi (Kalyanasundaranar 1949). Similarly, in 1946, Sivagnanam formed an interest group called the Tamil1 Aracu Kal1akam, "Association for Tamil Autonomy" (henceforth Tamil Arasu Kazhagam), whose main agenda was to put pressure on the Congress to promote the increased use of Tamil in administration and education, to work towards the creation of an autonomous Tamil state out of a composite Madras Presidency, and to ease up on its pro-Hindi policy. As Sivagnanam wrote in April 1947 on the eve of Indian independence, "The Tamilian is prepared to be Indian. However, he is first and foremost a Tamilian. Only secondarily is he Indian" (Sivagnanam 1981: 105). By 1954, his organization was forced to part ways with the Congress, and in 1967, Sivagnanam even entered into an electoral alliance with the Dravidian movement—the same movement against which through much of the 1950s he had conducted so many campaigns (Sivagnanam 1974: 368-69, 535-55). Most indicative perhaps of Indianism's radical transformation through its dealings with the Hindi question is C. Rajagopalachari's changing stance. The chief promoter of Hindi who made its study mandatory in the late 1930s in the Madras Presidency, he began to insist "English ever, Hindi never" from the late 1950s, and even made electoral deals with his Dravidianist rivals by the 1960s (Rajagopalachari 1962).

The Congress and Indianized Tamil

In 1967, the Congress, the party that prided itself on delivering India from colonialism and that had ruled Madras for the two decades since independence, suffered a stunning defeat at the polls and has never returned to power in the state since. For many a Tamil devotee, the Congress's defeat was its just deserts, for had it not shown, over the years, that it was the enemy of Tamil and Tamil1ttây? Supporters of the Congress have tried to counter such a charge. It was the Congress, more than the non-Brahman elite's Justice Party, that used Tamil from early in this century in party work and popular mobilization. It was under Congress rule that Tamil was extended as medium of instruction in high schools in 1938, and university education in 1960-61. The Congress government also set up, in 1959, the Tamil Development and Research Council entrusted with producing Tamil school and college textbooks in the natural and human sciences, accounting, mathematics, and so on. It also helped finance a series of children's encyclopedias in Tamil, "lucid commentaries" on Cank#am poetry, and an "authentic history of the Tamil people" in 1962-63. And finally, in 1956, it was the Congress that passed the law instituting Tamil as the official language of the state (Karthikeyan 1965-66; C. Subramaniam 1962). Yet, as its critics have been quick to point out, few of these measures seemed to have made any difference to life in the Tamil-speaking land. So, Mohan Kumaramangalam wrote in 1965:

In practice, the ordinary man finds that the Tamil language is nowhere in the picture....In Madras city, English dominates our life to an extraordinary extent....Corporation property tax, electric consumption and water tax bills are only in the English language; all communications of the Collector are in English; in virtually all trade, including the smallest consumer goods, bills, receipts, etc. are made out in the English language. I think it will be no exaggeration to say that a person can live for years in Madras without learning a word of Tamil, except for some servant inconvenience!

As many of its supporters rightly point out, the Congress government's record on *tamil1ppan#i*, "service to Tamil," is not as terrible or as bleak as its critics portray it. Nevertheless, it pursued Tamil policies that were largely Indianist in complexion at a time when the growing Dravidianist discourse was very persuasively pointing to "India" as the source of many of the Tamil speaker's problems, and at a time when even Indianists within the devotional community were turning away from the Congress. Its Indianist predilections meant that the "improvement" of Tamil under Congress rule proceeded side by side with at least tacit support for the Indian state's Hindi policy. The Congress also resisted a number of devotional demands out of fear that these would open the "Pandora's box" of linguistic "balkanization": the renaming of Madras state as "Tamilnadu," the authorization of Tamil as primary liturgical language in temples, the use of pure Tamil instead of Sanskritized Tamil in school textbooks and administrative manuals, and so on. Above all, Congress policies, like orthodox Indianism's, were premised on the fundamental assumption that "Tamil" and "India" were intertwined, an assumption that it felt compelled to uphold if only to counter the separatist agenda of the Dravidian movement. It would be sacrilegious to think exclusively of Tamil as deserving the absolute allegiance of all its speakers. Thus the Congress, and even the Indianist regime, were never animated by the spirit of total and unconditional celebration of Tamil that characterized Dravidianism's attitude towards the language. In the words of one devotee of Tamil whose own sentiments were contestatory classicist and Dravidianist, "None of the Congress Ministers of Tamil Nad was either a Tamil scholar or a Tamil lover. The Congress leaders of Tamil Nad as betrayers of Tamil, cannot represent the State any more. Blind cannot lead the blind, much less the keen sighted" (Devaneyan 1967: 25). In 1967, the Tamil electorate came to the same conclusion.

LANGUAGE OF THE NATION: DRAVIDIANIZING TAMIL

And so, finally, I turn to the Dravidianist regime that crystallized in the 1930s, gained momentum through the 1940s and 1950s, and peaked in the mid-1960s. Its primary terrain of activity was a series of anti-Hindi protests which dramatically drew together diverse elements of the devotional community in opposition to the regional and central governments that sponsored Hindi, itself-caricatured as an evil and demonic force out to destroy pure and sweet Tamil (and its speakers). Contemporaries and participants alike marvelled that the common cause against Hindi threw together religious revivalists like Maraimalai Adigal with such avowed atheists as Ramasami; Gandhians like Kalyanasundaram with men like Annadurai who preached secession from India; university professors and elite antiquarians, such as Somasundara Bharati and Purnalingam Pillai, with populist street poets, pamphleteers, college students, and young men like Chinnasami who immolated themselves. Indeed, the poet Bharatidasan, the paradigmatic Dravidianist, had himself been a self-declared devotee of "India" up until the 1920s, and had published some passionate poems on Bhârata Mâtâ before his conversion to Dravidianism and anti-Hindi politics by the 1930s (Ilango 1982; Ilavarasu 1990). Other events of these decades—the creation of linguistic states out of the erstwhile Madras Presidency, the securing of appropriate borders with neighboring states, the struggle to rename Madras state Tamilnadu—also compelled devotees otherwise inclined, such as Sivagnanam, to turn to Dravidianism. Dravidianism is thus the crisis idiom of *tamil1ppar1r1u,* the regime par excellence for mobilizing—albeit temporarily and sometimes reluctantly—diverse, even opposing, devotees under one umbrella, around events that were deemed to be threatening to the future of Tamil and Tamil1ttây.

The most passionate and radical of all the regimes, Dravidianism routinely elicited from its adherents declarations of willingness to give up their wealth, their lives, and their souls for Tamil. It also produced some antagonistic, even violent, attitudes towards other languages and their speakers, as for instance in the following verse published by Bharatidasan, which is fairly typical: "Our first task is to finish off those who destroy [our] glorious Tamil! / Let flow a river of crimson blood!" Its emphasis on fierce, public displays of devotion meant that images of battlefields, of blood, and of death proliferate in Dravidianist discourse. True Tamilians are those—like Chinnasami—who show their commitment to their mother/tongue by putting their very bodies on the line, and dying for it, if need be. More so than the other devotional regimes, Dravidianism's driving imperative was a vision of the Tamil community as an autonomous racial and political entity (*in1am*), even nation (*nât#u*), whose sacral center is occupied solely by Tamil, from which all its members claim shared descent. So, where neo-Shaivism constituted Tamilian solidarity around the shared worship of Shiva and divine Tamil, and classicism emphasized a common ancient, literary past, Dravidianism focused on descent and kinship. Tropes of motherhood, siblingship, shared blood, the home, and the like mark its discursive style, as they do Indianism's. The significant difference between the two, of course, is that Dravidianism made a commitment to only one entity—namely, Tamil. As Tamil1ttây herself insisted, sometime in the early 1960s: "Do not forget that you are all children who emerged from my womb. I *am* your mother. The learned call me Tamil1ttây. You are called Tamilians (*tamil1ar*). You and I have been inextricably bound together for ever and ever through language. That language is what the good scholars call Tamil....If we look closely, we have a home. That its name is Tamilnadu gives [me] great happiness" (Pancanathan n.d.: 9).

In this statement as elsewhere in Dravidianism, descent is reckoned solely from Tamil, which is not merely one among a "family" of languages *in* a putative Indian nation, as it is in Indianism, but is *the* language *of* the nation, imagined variously as "Tamilian" or "Dravidian." No doubt, by the 1970s Dravidianism became more accommodating on the question of India. But the fundamental imperative of this regime continued to be the establishment of the absolute rule of Tamil through the complete Tamilization of the political apparatus and its accompanying ideology, in a territorial space designated as Tamil or Dravidian, which at least into the early 1960s was seen as independent of, and indeed in opposition to, "India."

The political philosophy of Dravidianism was provided by a broad swathe of ideas associated with "the Dravidian movement" (*tirâvit#a iyakkam*). This movement made its impact on the Dravidianist regime when the elitist "non-Brahman" associational politics of the Vellala dominated Justice Party (1916/17-44) was supplemented by the populist call for radical social reform by E. V. Ramasami and his Self-Respect League (founded in 1926) and the Tirâvit#ar Kal1akam, "Association of Dravidians" (the DK, established in 1944). Although many Self-Respecters were concerned with Tamil (e.g., Velu and Selvaraji 1989), Ramasami himself was extremely critical of *tamil1ppar1r1u*, especially of its valorization of the divinity, antiquity, and motherhood of Tamil. This did not stop Dravidianism from lionizing him and selectively appropriating his ideas of rationalist materialism, iconoclastic atheism, radical anti-Brahmanism, and Dravidian nationalism, for he provided the most polemical and sustained attacks on Indian nationalism, which this regime found useful. Ramasami's obvious dilemma was that Tamil devotion threatened his vision of a Dravidian nation that would incorporate all "Dravidians" of southern India, and not just Tamil speakers. Such a vision had to contend with the resistance of those putative "Dravidians" who were speakers of Telugu, Kannada, and Malayalam. In addition, it was compromised by Tamil speakers who did not necessarily want to participate in a multilingual polity, even if it was "Dravidian." And indeed, as the Dravidian movement itself split, when Annadurai parted company with Ramasami and his DK in 1949 to found his own party, the Tirâvit#a Mun1n1çr1r1ak Kal1akam or "Dravidian Progress Association" (DMK), the inherent tensions between the alternate conceptions of the "Dravidian" and "Tamil" nation came to the fore. By the late 1950s, as the DMK entered the domain of electoral politics, its agenda was primarily formulated in terms of a Tamil nation (albeit one often referred to as "Dravidian"), confined to the territorial space of a Tamilspeaking area, rather than coeval with the more ambitious nation that Ramasami envisaged comprising the speakers of all Dravidian languages.

Like the Dravidian movement, Dravidianism, too, had to contend with the tensions between an exclusive Tamil-speaking nation and a more inclusive Dravidian nation. It adopted various strategies to deal with this, such as suggestions that "Tamil" and "Dravidian" are the same; that since Tamil is the "mother" of all Dravidian languages, the latter are merely extensions of the former; and so on. So, like the other regimes, Dravidianism had its share of contradictions. Notwithstanding these, as a consequence of its discourse, Tamil comes to be firmly "Dravidianized," even as the "Dravidian" category, which had been gaining political and cultural visibility in the region since the 1880s, was unequivocally associated with Tamil. In contrast to neo-Shaivism and classicism, Dravidianism advocated political radicalism and activism as the means to achieve the reign of Tamil: "We have talked enough.... [W]hen are you going to show your sacrifice to [Tamil1ttây]? We are waiting every moment for the honor of being arrested." Under the influence of Dravidianism, *tamil1ppar1r1u* took to the streets, sometimes quite violently. Petition politics gave way to protest politics, increasingly radical and populist. Antiquarian and elite notions about Tamil and Tamilttây, hitherto confined to learned academies and scholastic journals, came to be invoked in street songs, polemical plays, and political speeches at populist anti-Hindi rallies; they were circulated in daily newspapers and street pamphlets, and plastered across billboards and wall posters. Dravidianism typically catered, like the Dravidian movement itself, to the Everyman, generically designated in its texts as *tamillanl,* "Tamilian" (Barnett 1976: 114-15). It attracted its following from devotees who were predominantly from middle and lower castes, and from middle or low-income families with limited or no formal education, like Chinnasami and his fellow self-immolators. At the same time, the DMK's support of literature and language also attracted numerous well-educated Tamil scholars and academics to Dravidianism. In turn, many DMK leaders have been devotees of Tamil. They have assumed titles—*arliòar* (scholar) Annadurai, *kalaiòar* (the artist) Karunanidhi, *nâvalar* (the eloquent) Nedunceliyan—which display both their scholarly aspirations and the close links between populist ideology and high literature in the political culture of the region (Barnett 1976: 56-86). Dravidianism's paradigmatic exponents were undoubtedly well-known poets and politicians like Bharatidasan, Annadurai, "Pulavar" Kulanthai (1906-72), Perunchitran (1920-95), Mudiyarasan (b. 1920), Karunanidhi, and the early Kannadasan (1927-81). But encouraged by the Dravidian movement's populism and by Dravidianism's assertion that Tamil belonged to "the people," the Everyman, who remained anonymous or relatively unknown, took to writing and publishing poems, short stories, and essays on the language and on Tamilttây. Of all the regimes of *tamilppar1r1u,* Dravidianism was thus the one that was truly populist, in spirit as well as constituency.

Dravidianism's fundamental agenda, of course, was to establish the absolute preeminence of Tamil in all spheres of life and being, and to ensure that devotion to the language (and its community) was not diluted by any other passions—for the Indian nation, for the gods of the Hindu pantheon, or even for the families and mothers of individual devotees. For Tamil is everything; it is the life (*uyir*), breath (*âvi*), and consciousness (*un#arvu*) of every true Tamilian. In its purest form, there were no divided commitments in Dravidianism, no subordination of

Tamil to Shiva, to literature and learning, or to India. Tamil was not a means through which to construct something else, be it an alternate religious or civilizational formation, or allegiance to India. In and of itself, it ought to be the very center of everything in the devoted Tamil speaker's life. Without it, there is nothing. So Bharatidasan wrote in a poem suggestively entitled "Living for Tamil Is the Only Life":

O Tamil! Homage to you!

......

Your well-being is ours as well.

Your victories are ours as well.

We may as well be dead if we live for ourselves.

Living for Tamil is the only life!

For the Dravidianist devotee, Tamil was so much a part of the Tamilian's very essence that it would be impossible to separate the language from its speaker. So Bharatidasan insisted:

We can turn mountains into pits;

We can dry up the ocean bed;

We can fly speedily through the skies.

......

We can even bring the dying back to life.

The Tamilian cannot be separated from Tamil

Even for a moment, by anyone.

This conviction, that Tamil and its speaker devotee had so blended into each other that it would be impossible to separate them, is echoed in other poems as well. Consider this verse by Kannadasan addressed to Tamil1ttây:

Would I ever forget you? Would I cease to sing about you?

Even if they set me on fire,

In the burning flames of the fire,

The world will see only you, O dear mother of mine!

(Kannadasan 1968: 89)

Elsewhere, in 1954, in lines that eerily anticipate Chinnasami's immolation a decade later, the poet wrote, "even in death, Tamil should be on our lips. Our ashes should burn with the fragrance of Tamil. This is our undying desire" (Kannappan 1995: 22).

Given such sentiments, Dravidianism was particularly concerned with all alternate objects of passion that might draw its speakers away from Tamil, such as "India," their gods, and their families. It therefore focused as much energy to convince Tamil speakers of the illegitimacy of these other entities as to emphasize that it is Tamil that sustains their life and consciousness.

Dravidianism and India

While Indianism emphatically asserted that the liberation of Bhârata Mâtâ and Tamil1ttây would have to proceed in tandem, Dravidianism, particularly in its early years, and most especially as expressed by its more radical exponents, saw in the very establishment of the Indian nation the downfall of Tamil. A poem that was published in the *Tirâvit#an1* on 31 August 1947, a fortnight after India was officially liberated from colonial rule, declared: "The foreign Bhârata Mâtâ (*an1n1iyap pâratattây*) has attained glory. / Our own dear Tamil1ttây has been greatly disgraced."

Dravidianism, at its peak, portrayed the newly emergent Indian nation as an imperialist formation, as a tool in the hands of Brahmans and Banias (North Indian merchants), and as an instrument with which the material interests of Dravidians would continue to be subordinated to Aryan Indians (Annadurai 1974: 39-48, 1985: 22-23; Pancanathan n.d.; M. S. Ramasami 1947: 5-6, 19-20). Consider the following verse from a 1947 pamphlet revealingly entitled *Songs of Separation for the Dravidian Nation:*

The Brahmans and Banias have united;

We are all children of Bhârata Mâtâ, they lie to us[.]

......

Our own Tirâvit#attây [Mother Dravida] is our mother;

Bhârata Mâtâ who belongs to the duplicitous, is a deceitful mother;

If the Dravidians realize this, they will have no trouble.

If we let down our guard, the Northerners will loot and plunder.

(M. S. Ramasami 1947: 14)

Indianism, we have seen, offered Bhârata Mâtâ to Tamil speakers as a mother who would reproduce them as "Indians." In the logic of Dravidianism, however, she was clearly a false mother who sought to lure gullible Tamilians away from their true mother with promises of milk, nourishment, and even jobs. So, in 1958, Bharatidasan, who in his early years had waxed passionately on Bhârata Mâtâ and even declared her his true mother, published a poem in which he ridiculed the Tamilian who is confused about his "real" mother. The poem is addressed to Tamil1ttây:

"O glorious Tamilian! What is the name of your nation?"

When I ask thus, he sheepishly says "India," O mother!

How will this child ever improve if he confuses the evergreen

Tamil nation with India, O mother!

Will he ever change, the one who does not recognize his mother as mother, and declares the evil that destroys his motherland as mother, O mother!

Sitting in [his] mother's lap and nursing on the breast milk of Tamil, how can this child not know [his] mother's name, O mother!

Tamil *is* [his] mother tongue, and Tamilnadu is his motherland.

Does not the Tamilian realize this?

So, while Indianism sought to naturalize "India" by presenting it in the familiar terms of the home and the mother, the Dravidianist logic lay in demonizing it as a "deceitful" or "evil" mother, and substituting Tamil1ttây in its stead as the authentic, *sole* mother of all true Tamil speakers.

Dravidianism's antagonism towards India came to the fore in the numerous protests against Hindi, presented in its discourses as a blood-sucking demoness, lowly maid, seductive temptress, and false mother out to destroy the noble, righteous, but endangered Tamilttây. Such Manichean images were deployed to create fear and hatred of Hindi, and to generate sentiments of love, loyalty, and filial piety for Tamil, which its loyal speakers were obliged to protect with life and limb. Just as crucially, the regional state government (in the control of the Congress) and the Indian nation were also rendered into objects that deserved the Tamilians' deepest opprobrium and the withdrawal of their support, emotional *and* electoral. Dravidianism thus seized upon the linguistic fact that Hindi was related to Sanskrit, and translated the assertions of radical neo-Shaivism and contestatory classicism against Aryan Brahmanism into political action against the Indian nation. For Dravidianism, the battle against Hindi was not only inevitable and natural, but necessary and morally legitimate; it was a "holy war" (*arlappôr*) fought against evil and on behalf of the good and righteous (Ramaswamy, forthcoming). Although Hindi was in effect legislated out of Tamilnadu government schools in 1968 by the DMK, and although all kinds of accommodations with the North have been made since the 1960s, to this day the threat of Hindi has continued to be effectively used to reiterate the autonomy and uniqueness of a Tamil space within a larger Indian whole, to summon up the specter of non-Tamil elements entering the pure Tamil body politic, and to remind Tamil speakers of the dangers that await them if they cease supporting the Dravidian movement and its Tamil cause.

Dravidianism and Hinduism

In the years between the late 1920s and 1950s, when the influence of the iconoclastic and atheistic Ramasami was at its peak and before the DMK actively entered the fray of electoral politics, Dravidianism also sought energetically to dissociate Tamil from all religious affiliations. Like radical neo-Shaivism, it castigated Hinduism as a Brahmanical, Sanskritic, and Aryan conspiracy hatched to destroy Tamil and Dravidian society. So, for Dravidianism, a true Tamilian/Dravidian is one who is emphatically *not* a Hindu. "A Hindu in the present concept may be a Dravidian, but the Dravidian in the real sense of the term cannot and shall not be a Hindu" (quoted in Harrison 1960: 127). Tamil speakers were therefore repeatedly called upon to destroy all (Hindu) irrationalisms and foolish beliefs, and to rescue themselves from *ârya mâyai*, "Aryan illusion" (Annadurai 1969). Thus Bharatidasan, who in the 1920s had written passionate poems on Hindu deities and continued occasionally to publish religious verse into the 1930s, insisted in the 1950s that "there is no god" and told the Tamilian that his duty lay in weaning away his hapless fellow speakers from their false belief in divinities.

And here is where Dravidianism parted company with neo-Shaivism: for in its attacks on religion, it did not spare either Shiva or the reformed "rational" version of Shaivism that Maraimalai Adigal and others were attempting to popularize (Sivathamby 1978: 30-31; Venkatachalapathy 1990). Neo-Shaivism may have insisted that Shaivism is the authentic Tamilian religion, radically different from Aryan Brahmanical Hinduism, but Dravidianism was not convinced about this. Nor was it ready to brook neo-Shaivite resistance to reforming and rationalizing the Tamil script, believed by many devout Shaivites to be Shiva's own handiwork (Sivathamby 1979: 71). Dravidianism was also not willing to define the Tamil/Dravidian community as Shaiva, for what would then happen to Tamilians/ Dravidians who were nominally Vaishnavas, Christians, and Muslims?

So Tamil is the life, the consciousness, and the soul of the Tamilian. It is indeed everything, but it certainly is not "divine Tamil," for to imagine it as such would entangle it with the irrationalisms, inequalities, and idiocies of Hinduism. Tamil speakers, too, consequently would be subordinated and demeaned in an inherently Brahmanical order of things, and they would lose all their "self-respect." In a revealing speech of 1944, Ramasami offered the following advice to his fellow Dravidians: "You may well ask, 'If we give up Hinduism, what religion can we profess to have?' Have courage and claim that religion which will not demean you as untouchable and lowly in society. If there is objection to this, you may always say you are Dravidian and that your religion is Dravidianism. If you have problems even with that, say that your religion is humanity" (Anaimuthu 1974: 446).

Contrary to Marguerite Barnett (1976: 274), who has suggested that "within the Dravidian ideology there was no coherent alternative to religion or Hinduism," I would argue that especially within the Dravidianist regime of *tamil1ppar1r1u,* various efforts were made to create alternatives to both religion and Hinduism. Given the complex entanglements between Tamil devotion and Hinduism, however, such efforts were not entirely successful, nor were they as autonomous as Dravidianism would have desired. Minimally, those devotees of Tamil who turned to active electoral politics as members of the DMK distanced themselves from Ramasami's iconoclastic irreverence for Hindu scriptures, gods, and images. By the 1950s, both the DMK and Dravidianism generated a curious combination of agnosticism ("we do not ask whether there is god or not"), monism ("there is only one god and one community"), populism ("god lives in the smile of the poor"), and humanism ("we must develop that kind of outlook which treats all humanity as one"). This medley of diverse beliefs that Anita Diehl (1977: 29) has shrewdly characterized as "pragmatic, agnostic humanism" opened up a space for the steady incorporation of all kinds of elements from popular as well as the devotional religious practices of the region into the ideology of Dravidianism, such as the celebration of the harvest festival, Pongal; the worship of Murugan; and the apotheosis of Valluvar and his *Tirukkur1al#* (Ramanujam 1971: 168, 175; Ryerson 1988: 108-93).

One other important strategy is followed by Dravidianism in filling up the space vacated by Hindu gods. Consider this 1959 poem by Bharatidasan, addressed to a *tampirân1,* "Shaiva monk preceptor," in response to the opposition of the orthodox to the growing demand for use of Tamil as ritual language in temples:

Is it religion (camayam) that is important, O *tampirân1*[?]

It is fine Tamil that is indeed eminent, O foolish *tampirân1*[.]

Why do you hate Tamil, O *tampirân1*[.]

Why do you hate your mother, O *tampirân1*[?]

Even if religion is destroyed, Tamilians will flourish[.]

If good Tamil is destroyed, can there be a Tamil community[?]

Do service to Tamil! O *tampirân1*[.]

Tamil is the life of the Tamilian! O foolish *tampirân1*[.]

Is it God who is great[?] O *tampirân1*[!]

It is glorious Tamil that is indeed great[!] O foolish *tampirân1*[.]

Even if God disappears, the Tamil community will flourish[.]

If Tamil dies, its community, too, will die, O *tampirân1*[.]

Do you intend to destroy the Tamil creed (*tamil1ner1i*) by invoking Shaivism (*caivaner1i*), O foolish *tampirân1?*

Service to Shaivism is not great, O *tampirân1*[.]

It is auspicious service to Tamil that is eminent, O *tampirân1*[.]

......

Only one thing is greater than [our] mother(s)! O *tampirân1!*

Is that not Tamil, O foolish *tampirân1?*

There are few clearer statements than this of Dravidianism's attempt to displace conventional gods and the religious beliefs associated with them, and to substitute Tamil in their stead. Indeed, Dravidianism sacralized Tamil, even while refusing to participate, at least overtly and consciously, in its divinization. Dravidianism's ambivalence towards religiosity and Hinduism notwithstanding, Tamil was offered to its speakers as an iconic object that deserves all the adulation, adherence, and service they had hitherto reserved for their gods. In this process, even within Dravidianism, Tamil was imagined as desired by the gods, and was every now and then deified. So, in his controversial 1945 poem, *Tamil1iyakkam* (The resurgence of Tamil),Bharatidasan asked whether Tamil, "which is life itself," is not dear to the gods (Bharatidasan 1969: 27). On a more personal note, in his autobiography the poet Mudiyarasan, who identifies himself as an ardent follower of Ramasami and Annadurai, asks, "I consider Tamil as god (*kat#avul#*). How can I be an atheist (*nâttikan1*)?" (Mudiyarasan n.d.: 86-87). A similar sentiment undergirds the DMK government's institution of the homage to Tamil1ttây as the state song in 1970. The government may have announced that it was doing this because the song had no "religious or sectarian associations," an assertion it was able to make because it carefully edited out Sundaram Pillai's original title, *Tamil1t teyva van#akkam,* "Homage to *Goddess* Tamil." Nonetheless, in its official statement (in English), Tamil1ttây herself is referred to as "goddess of Tamil," and the hymn is characterized as "prayer song."

Dravidianism and the Tamil Family

Dravidianism did not just have to delegitimize the "other mother," Bhârata Mâtâ it also had to ensure that flesh-and-blood Tamil-speaking mothers themselves did not pose a threat to the absolute devotion and loyalty owed to the sacralized language. This was a very complicated task, for motherhood was the ground on which both Indianism and Dravidianism constituted *tamil1ppar1r1u.* Indeed, Dravidianism was not content with merely establishing similitude between language and one's mother; more strikingly, it insisted that language *is* that mother:

When I was a child, you snuggled me and placed me on your lap;

You placed flowers in my hair, and adorned me, and admired my beauty;

You are the sweet mother who protected me, in the shade and in the heat;

O my ancient Tamil! May you live long!

(Ulakanathan 1969: 4)

Similarly, the well-known DMK rhetorician R. Nedunceliyan, who later became a key member of the government, insisted in 1960 that there was no difference between one's mother and Tamil:

There is *no distinction at all* between our mother who bore us for ten months, gave birth to us, watched over us, sang lullabies to us, and fed us milk and guarded us, and our Tamil language which taught us about good conduct and tradition, and granted us good values and knowledge, and which is the very reason that we live well and in prosperity. We have the same attachment to our language as we have for our mother; we have the same devotion to our language as we have for our mother; we have the same love for our language as we have for our mother. He who disregards his language...is like he who disregards his mother and forsakes her. Dravidianism may have invited speakers of Tamil to imagine it as their mother. At its most dramatic, however, it elevated Tamil to a position of absolute preeminence, even transcending the status and authority of one's birth mother. For instance, the poet Pulavar Kulanthai declared passionately:

I will never refuse to obey my [own] mother's words;
But if harm befalls my precious Tamilttây,
I will not fear to set aside my own mother's words.
I will chop off the head of [Tamilttây's] enemy,
Even if [my] mother prevents me.
(Pulavar Kulanthai 1972: 21)

By extension, this kind of loyalty extended to fellow Tamil speakers as well, as is apparent from Bharatidasan's much-cited declaration: "I will not leave alone the man who scorns the greatness of Tamilians / *Even if [my] mother prevents me*" (Bharatidasan 1958: 5, emphasis mine). Indeed, Dravidianism even insisted that service to Tamil and to Tamilttây should take priority over the Tamilian's family—over spouses, children, and parents. So Perunchitran demanded as late as 1975: "Are the troubles of your own mother more important than the terrible suffering of our glorious Tamilttây? /.../ Are the words of your own mother sweeter than our Tamil language, which is like ambrosia?" (Perunchitranar 1979: 109).

Yet in thus subordinating the family to Tamil, Dravidianism only overtly and consciously articulated a sentiment that was widespread in the devotional community as a whole. As we will see later, in the life stories of individual devotees as these are narrated in memoirs and biographies, their families are typically superseded in favor of devotion to the Tamil cause. The family, which is a primary site for cultivating devotion to the language, is ultimately transcended within the regimes of *tamilpparru*. Such a transcendence is deemed necessary, for not even the family can—or can be allowed to—intervene between the devotee and his language.

The DMK and Dravidianized Tamil

Deriving considerable political capital from its self-appointed role as the guardian of Tamil and from demonizing the Congress as an agent of "evil" North Indian interests during the prolonged anti-Hindi protests of the 1950s and 1960s which it spearheaded, the DMK swept the state polls in 1967. Two days after the party's victory was assured, its leading newspaper, *Nam Nât#u*, carried the headline, "Tamil1ttây's Desire of Many Years Fulfilled." The *Muracoli's* front-page cartoon showed Tamil1ttây, a smile on her face, placing a crown on Annadurai, her "chief son." And it was declared that Tamil1ttây's victory was the fruit of penances undergone by her followers for Tamil's sake: "In order that Tamil1ttây be enthroned, in order that Tamil1ttây should abide with honor, so that Tamil1ttây may be crowned...so many became prey to gunfire, so many drowned in an ocean of red blood, so many martyrs set themselves on fire, so many great ones passed away. This we know. Today, we see Tamil blooming everywhere. You must all go to the Legislative Assembly. You will hear good Tamil there." The DMK takes great pride that so many of its leaders—Annadurai, Nedunceliyan, and Karunanidhi, among others—have been hailed as great scholars of Tamil and of literature in their own right. So, for many Dravidianists, the DMK's victory finally fulfilled Bharatidasan's dream, voiced years earlier in 1945, that "only the Tamilian who knows Tamil should rule as the chief minister of Tamilnadu" (Bharatidasan 1969: 19).

Regardless of what its opponents may say or statistics may reveal, the DMK has promoted itself as selflessly dedicated to the Tamil cause. Party literature as well as government publications provided details of the measures that it undertook to promote the language: the increasing use of "chaste" and "good" Tamil in administrative and public facilities; the publication of Tamil encyclopedias, scientific manuals, and textbooks; the increasing support of Tamil scholars and Tamil studies both within and outside Tamilnadu; and so on—programs pursued by the Congress government as well to varying degrees. In addition, under the DMK, Hindi was in effect legislated out of state schools in 1968; steps were taken, although not successfully, to introduce Tamil as the exclusive language of higher education and as medium of worship in high Hindu temples; and the state itself was renamed Tamilnadu, "land of Tamil." DMK cultural policy also focused on creating a new literary and historical canon, by drawing upon the findings of *tamil lppar lr lu,* especially upon contestatory classicism and Dravidianism. Not surprisingly, the poems of the Cank#am corpus occupy a hallowed place in this canon, Karunanidhi himself offering a new interpretation in 1987 (Karunanidhi 1987a). Similarly, the *Tirukkur lal#,* the new "scripture" of Dravidianism, is valorized, as is the *Cilappatikâram,* as exemplars of the "secular," "egalitarian," and "chaste" essence of true and pure Tamil culture, free from the influences of Sanskritic Aryan Brahmans with their priestly ways.

Correspondingly, a new pantheon of secular icons surrounding the presiding deity, Tamil lttây, has sprung up. It includes Tiruvalluvar, the author of the *Tirukkur lal#* Kattabomman, who died a martyr's death during the late-eighteenth-century British expansion into South India, and who is considered a paradigmatic symbol of Tamil heroism (Ramaswamy 1994); and Kannagi, the heroine of the *Cilappatikâram,* who is imagined as the ideal Tamil woman, renowned for her chastity and wifely fidelity (J. Pandian 1982). Similarly, Ramasami and Annadurai were lionized for giving Tamil speakers their "self-respect," and many DMK narratives contain laudatory poems on their achievements. And it was under DMK rule that Chinnasami and his fellow devotees who burned themselves alive were immortalized. New mythologies and praise poems on all these figures were written and circulated. Their life stories were narrated and offered as paradigms for Tamil speakers to emulate. Commemorative memorials were set up, and festivals conducted in their honor. In 1968, the government used an academic gathering in Madras, the Second International Conference of Tamil Studies, to treat the populace to a spectacular celebration of Tamil, featuring giant floats of Tamil lttây, Tiruvalluvar, and other Tamil icons. The party's leaders must believe that such acts carry symbolic as well as political capital, for as recently as 1984, its election manifesto chose to present its achievements to the electorate in the following terms:

In order that Tamil lttây's jeweled crown should shine,

We built the historic temple to Valluvar whose fame reaches the very skies;

And the world-famous new town of Poompukar with its *Cilappatikâram* museum, seven stories high!

And a fort in the memory of Virapandya Kattabomman at Panjalamkurichi.

We enabled all these, not just one, not just two, but plenty! plenty!

And yet, as critics as well as supporters of the DMK are quick to ask, have such gestures really helped the cause of Tamil? I quote Sivagnanam, who, despite his recent rapprochement with the DMK, lamented thus:

A museum commemorating the *Cilappatikâram* and a memorial celebrating Kattabomman have been built. The names of ministers and homes have been changed. Street names have been changed, and so have the names of towns. But Tamil's fortunes have not changed. Formerly, Tamilttây was worshipped three times a day. Today, she is worshipped six times a day. She is worshipped with great pomp and splendor. But the chains that fetter her arms and legs have not been destroyed....Tamil will not grow by changing the names of streets, towns, and gardens.

Dravidianism and its Discontents

And this is a lament that we continue to hear to this day, even after about a century of Tamil devotional activity. Sivagnanam's statement points to a fundamental problem with which the Tamilnadu state has had to contend, especially in the past three decades or so, when it has been under the rule of political parties which are ostensibly dedicated to the Tamil cause. In addition to confronting the crucial issue of which Tamil to promote—"classical" Tamil, "pure" Tamil, the "people's" Tamil, and so on—there has been growing awareness that the socioeconomic and political realities of Tamil's status as a regional language within the linguistic economy of a multilingual nation-state, itself embedded within a larger global environment in which English dominates as the world language, preclude the active implementation of public policies that will ensure the supremacy of Tamil in all spheres at all times, the ideal of Dravidianism (on this, see Tamilkudimagan 1990). Strapped by financial and political constraints, it has been easier for the state to indulge in symbolic activities, such as changing street names and instituting official anthems, rather than to ensure high quality education in Tamil studies, or to create job opportunities that would convince Tamil speakers that the study of Tamil is a viable end in itself. Tamil's devotees undoubtedly recognize the value of the symbolic act, but Sivagnanam's lament also reminds us that Tamil devotionalism demands much more, especially from a party that claims to be ruling on behalf of Tamilttây. From the start, Dravidianism, like Indianism, placed its hopes in the political process. The establishment of a Tamil state and the Tamilization of the political apparatus, it was proclaimed, would ensure the triumph of Tamil, everywhere and in everything. And yet, this has not happened. This is a tragedy that casts its long shadow not just on Dravidianism, but on the rest of the Tamil devotional community as well.

This has not been the only cross that Dravidianism has had to bear. The Congress's policies caused the increasing disenchantment of devotees of Indianist sentiment and compelled several to embrace Dravidianism. Similarly, the empowerment of the DMK has accompanied the progressive Indianization of the message of Dravidianism, as its radical separatist vision and its credo that Tamil is everything have been progressively diluted in favor of the Tamil community's coexistence with India. Numerous compromises made by the DMK government on linguistic and cultural policies may be cited to support this claim, but perhaps the most illuminating here is the sanitized version of Sundaram Pillai's 1891 hymn that was instituted as the state "prayer song" in 1970.

Of course, the state song is still loyal to Dravidianism's "secular" recasting of Tamiltteyvam, "Goddess Tamil," as Tamilttây, "Mother Tamil." The lines from the 1891 hymn that likened Tamilttây to the primordial lord Shiva—which neo-Shaivism kept alive through the next century—are excised, on the grounds that an appropriate prayer song for a modern Tamil community should have no religious or sectarian associations. This significant erasure is not surprising given radical Dravidianism's antagonism to the divinization of Tamil and to Hinduism. And yet, the government order explicitly refers to Tamilttây as the "goddess of Tamil," a slippage that is not accidental. For it indexes the progressive accommodation with religiosity that characterizes DMK cultural policy through the 1950s and 1960s. It also reminds us that within Dravidianism itself, Tamil increasingly took on the mantle of conventional Hindu deities, even as it displaced them.

Next, the recast anthem comes close to compensatory, rather than contestatory, classicism's stance on Tamil, for the government also deliberately excised the much-quoted lines of the original hymn that had referred to Sanskrit as a "dead" language and had declared the superiority of the ever-enduring Tamil (*kan1n1ittamil1*). In his reminiscences, Chief Minister Karunanidhi maintains that these lines were not incorporated into the state prayer song because "it is not appropriate to disparage or ridicule other languages, and to use inauspicious words such as 'ruined' or 'dead' in a hymn in praise of Tamil1ttây to be recited at government functions" (Karunanidhi 1987: 233). Yet, as we have seen, both contestatory classicism and Dravidianism built their arguments on the assumption that Sanskrit was a "dead" language whose very presence had sucked the life out of Tamil.

Finally, Sundaram Pillai's hymn was selected over numerous others precisely because it simultaneously acknowledges the legitimacy of both *tirâvit#a nât#u* (Dravidian nation) and *paratak kan#t#am* (Indian nation). Indeed, the government insisted that the state's prayer song would in no way supplant the Indian national anthem: while the former would be sung at the commencement of official functions, the latter—and no other—would be recited at their conclusion. Thus the modern Tamil community—as envisioned by the DMK government in this hymn—has been symbolically framed in terms of its dual "Dravidian" and "Indian" heritages, a position that clearly conforms more closely to the Indianist, rather than to the radical Dravidianist, imagining of Tamil. In what ought to have been Dravidianism's paradigmatic moment of triumph—the institution of a daily celebration of Tamil and Tamil1ttây by the DMK—it appears as if it is Indianism, and its vision of Tamil as part of the Indian whole, that wins out.

THE MANY FACES OF TAMIL

This chapter has taken its cue from a number of recent studies which claim allegiance to a new area of scholarly inquiry called "language ideology." As the anthropologists Kathryn Woolard and Bambi Schieffelin note, language ideology provides a "much-needed bridge between linguistic and social theory, because it relates the micro-culture of communicative action to political economic considerations of power and social inequality" (Woolard and Schieffelin 1994: 72). My own analysis here has allied itself with one subset of concerns in this burgeoning field in its focus on "ideologies of language," those networks of representations and significations about language which emerge within particular literary, social, political, and religious formations. However natural and timeless they might appear, conceptions about a language among its interested speakers are rarely neutral or innocent; they are produced at specific historical moments, they are generally linked to efforts to create or retain power and control, and they change through time. Such conceptions are "partial, contestable, and contested, and interest laden": disguising their historicity, they present themselves as eternally true; hiding their cultural specificity, they masquerade as universally valid and commonsensical (Woolard and Schieffelin 1994: 58; see also Joseph and Talbot 1990).

I have suggested that the endowing of Tamil with various extraordinary attributes—divinity (*teyvattan1mai*), classicality (*uyarttan1icemmai*), purity (*tûymai*), antiquity (*ton1mai*), motherhood (*tâymai*), and so on—has to be located within larger social and political projects conducted by its numerous devotees. Other languages in other places—Afrikaans, Arabic, English, Hebrew, to name a random few—have been similarly empowered. But few have been studied in any historical depth to reveal the extent of ideological work necessary to transfer them into sites of privilege, potency, and power (for examples of this, see Alter 1994; Ferguson 1968; R. Jones 1953; Roberge 1992). My analysis of such work done on Tamil suggests that although consensus eventually emerges around such certain key contentions, this is a process that is riddled with contradiction and contrariety. The very importance of Tamil for its adherents has meant that there is much at stake in the manner in which it is constituted, and hence its imaginings are subject to many negotiations within the community united in devotion to it. *Tamil1ppar1r1u* is neither a wholly homogenous nor an entirely consensual activity, because the principal entity at its center is itself not conceived in a singular manner. Instead,

Tamil's devotees bring their own varying visions and shifting agendas to bear on their imaginings about their language and its role in their lives. As a consequence, Tamil devotion flourishes as a multifaceted enterprise, fissured by countervailing purposes and contrary passions, as we have seen.

But important questions remain. If the language has been subjected to all these alternate imaginings, as I have suggested, how are its devotees able to mobilize so many of their fellow speakers to rally around it? What is it that led many of them to claim as they did that they lived for its sake, and would die for it? Indeed, what is it that compelled them to speak and write with so much passion and fervor about its state of being—its past glory, its present ignominy, and its future fate? To answer such questions, I turn to the figure of Tamil1ttây.

3. FEMINIZING LANGUAGE

Tamil as Goddess, Mother, Maiden

Tamil's devotees do not merely relate to it as their language. They are able to breathe so much life and inject so much passion into practicing *tamil1ppar1r1u* because Tamil to them is more than an intangible abstraction. Instead, embodied in the figure of Tamil1ttây, it is a near and dear being—their personal goddess, their devoted mother, even their beloved lover—who commands their veneration and adulation, and deserves their love and loyalty. Yet, like the language she embodies, Tamil1ttây appears differently to different devotees at different moments in their lives, and is thus variously represented as *teyvam,* "goddess" *tây,* "mother" and *kan1n1i,* "virgin maiden." Consequently, she does not have a singular persona. Indeed, this is how Tamil devotion, fundamentally a network of patriarchal discourses conducted largely by men, solves the "problem" of having a female figure enshrined at the very heart of its enterprise. She is first isolated and abstracted from the "real" world in which Tamil-speaking women of all shades have been disempowered through much of this century; she is then endowed with a plenitude of powers and possibilities which transform her into a strikingly exceptional Woman, not readily confused with the flesh-and-blood women on whom she is also obviously modelled. Though she may be thus empowered, her potential to exceed the control of her (male) creators is contained through her fragmentation. The plethora of multiple personae that she is endowed with works to prevent her consolidation as a threatening, all-powerful being, even as it simultaneously opens up the possibility that her various selves may be deployed in contradictory ways for the different projects of her devotees. Tamil1ttây thus is yet another classic example of the objectification of woman as a thing "to be appropriated, possessed, and exchanged in the social relations of cooperation and competition among men" (Uberoi 1990: 41). Although we will see later that some Tamil-speaking women have their own way with her, Tamil1ttây, like other exemplary female icons, is far from cutting a feminist figure in her guise as tame goddess, benevolent mother, and pure virgin. Visible and valorized she may be, but she is very much a figment of the patriarchal imaginations of modernity in colonial and post-colonial India.

THE POETICS AND POLITICS OF PRAISE

The founding narrative which popularized the habit of imagining Tamil as goddess, mother, and maiden is P. Sundaram Pillai's 1891 hymn, "Tamil1t teyva van#akkam," "Homage to Goddess Tamil." Sundaram Pillai, of course, occupies a hallowed niche in the pantheon of *tamil1ppar1r1u* as a truly loyal son of Tamil1ttây. As his fellow devotees exclaim, was it not remarkable that although he lived all his life in Kerala, a non-Tamil-speaking region, he confessed to Tamil1ttây, "I may reside in [the land of] Malayalam, but I think of [only] you às my mother" (Sundaram Pillai 1922: 23)?

Born in 1855 in Allepey into a middle-income Vellala family of traders, Sundaram Pillai had a master's degree in philosophy. Aside from a brief bureaucratic stint as commissioner of separate revenues for Travancore (1882-85), he taught history and philosophy at the Maharaja's College in Trivandrum until his death in 1897. His historical researches on Tamil literature secured for him membership in the Royal Asiatic Society and the coveted title of Rao Bahadur from the colonial state (Pillai et al. 1957).

In writing his hymn on Tamil1ttây, Sundaram Pillai took great care in locating it within a prior Shaiva tradition of deifying Tamil (Sundaram Pillai 1922: 9; Kailasapathy 1970: 102-9). Like his seventeenth-century predecessor, Karunaiprakasar, he refers to Tamil as deity and even boldly establishes a parity between the mighty Shiva and his Tamil1tteyvam, both of whom are deemed "primordial," "everlasting," and "boundless." Nonetheless, Sundaram Pillai was indeed inaugurating a new sensibility when he explicitly feminized Tamil as goddess, mother, and maiden. Aside from a few verses, the feminization of the language was quite underdeveloped prior to his hymn, but since then it has gained an immense following. Furthermore, large numbers of subsequent poets, especially those influenced by the Dravidian movement, have abandoned the conventional practice of beginning their works by calling upon the traditional Hindu deities to shower their benedictions on them. Instead, they more typically appeal to Tamil1ttây as their sole muse and guardian deity (Kailasapathy 1970). In doing so, they broadcast their allegiance to the Tamil cause and secure membership for themselves in the Tamil devotional community, even as they elevate the language to a status commensurate with that of the gods.

Equally striking, since Sundaram Pillai's time many devotees have not just been content with short invocatory verses on Tamil1ttây; instead they have also produced long and elaborate praise poems on her, many of which have been—and continue to be—published in literary journals and popular newspapers, or printed in anthologies (e.g., Nagarajan 1980; Somasundara Pulavar n.d.; Velayutam Pillai 1971). Indeed, praise poetry is one of the principal technologies through which devotion to Tamil1ttây is produced and circulated. For while there are a number of devout prose writings in which Tamil1ttây figures, it is praise poetry written in Tamil that is her favored niche.

Praise poetry has a long history in the literary cultures of the region, and it may be traced back through the devotional verses of the second millennium to the royal panegyrics of the ancient Cank#am corpus. Most such praise poems focused on deities, sovereigns, and spiritual notables, although occasionally other subjects of praise, like Tamil itself, materialized (Krishnan 1984; Ramaswamy 1996). As literary practice, praise poems enabled poets to articulate sentiments of love and adulation for their chosen subjects, to recount the salvific powers and glorious actions of the deity or the sovereign, to dwell lovingly upon his or her beautiful form and appearance, and the like. Many conventional genres of praise—such as the *tirupal#l#iyel1ucci,* the *tirutacânk#am,* the *pil#l#aittamil1,* the *tûtu,* and so on—have been extremely productive over the centuries, offering standardized templates that a poet could readily deploy in the praise of a chosen subject or patron (Zvelebil 1974: 193-219).

Remarkably, such genres, which were predominantly reserved for deities or sovereigns in the premodern praise literature, are used from the early decades of this century to laud Tamil. Thus, there are many examples of *Tamil1ttây pal#l#iyel1ucci,* "the awakening of Tamil1ttây from sleep" *Tamil1ttây tirutacânk#am,* "the ten constituents of [the kingdom of] Tamil1ttây" and of *Tamil1ttâyppil#l#aitamil1,* "Tamil1ttây as extraordinary child." There are innumerable versions of *Tamil1ttâymâlai,* "garland of Tamil1ttây" at least two poems written in the ancient *âr1r1uppat#ai,* "guide," genre in which poets direct their fellow speakers to the presence of a glorious and bountiful Tamil1ttây whom they had forgotten; and two poems featuring Tamil as messenger, *tûtu* (Amirtham Pillai 1906; Arangasami [1977]; Parantama Mudaliar 1926; Somasundara Pulavar n.d.: 8-10, 35-43; Sundara Shanmugan 1951; Velayutam Pillai 1971: 56-61, 83-84; Pekan 1986). Additionally, popular and folk genres such as the *kur1lavaòci* and the *villuppât#t#u* have also been appropriated in narratives such as the *Tamil1aracikkur1lavaòci* (The fortuneteller song on Queen Tamil) and *Tamil1 Val#arnta Katai* (The story of Tamil's growth) (Navanitakrishnan 1952; Varadananjaiya Pillai [1938]). At the very least, all this suggests the energy with which modern devotees of Tamil have colonized high as well as popular forms, so that a space may be cleared for their chosen one among the more conventional objects of adulation in the Tamil life-world. Through the deployment of such poetic genres and praise strategies, they have endowed their language with the powers and charisma that have gathered around gods, sovereigns, and notables over the centuries—the right to command allegiance, demand loyalty, and mobilize followers. In turn, her devotees are encouraged to relate to Tamil1ttây as they have interacted with these figures—with a mixture of adulation, reverence, and deep love.

Praise, Arjun Appadurai suggests, is a "regulated, improvisatory practice" that creates a "community of sentiment involving the emotional participation of the praiser, the one who is praised, and the audience of that act of praise" (A. Appadurai 1990: 94). The praise poem on Tamil1ttây personalizes the language, presenting it to its devotee as a tangible being who is familiar, even intimate—a personal god, patron sovereign, guardian muse, object of desire, and increasingly, mother figure. The praise poem also knits together the language and its devotees into a community of adulation and worship, each act of praise allowing them an opportunity to dwell lovingly upon the wonders and powers of their beloved Tamil. Finally, the praise poem allows its authors to renew their faith in themselves and in each other as devotees of Tamil1ttây. The praise of Tamil1ttây through poetry thus is more than just a literary or political gesture, signifying one's adherence to Tamil; it is, also, crucially, a *ritual* act through which *tamil1ppar1r1u* is continually renewed and reaffirmed. It is therefore not surprising that many such praise poems, particularly by hallowed devotees such as Sundaram Pillai, Subramania Bharati, or Bharatidasan, are recited over and over again in devotional circles, especially at times that call for a heightened demonstration of piety and loyalty.

All this is not to say that poetry is the only form of expression in Tamil devotion. Certainly, its devotees wrote a great deal about Tamil in prose, especially on matters relating to language and cultural policy, on the promotion of Tamil in education, government, and public activities, and so on. In such prose narratives, however, especially when they were written in English, it is comparatively rare to find Tamil1ttây. Instead, Tamil generally appears in prose as a nonpersonified language—not as an animate being, as it frequently does in its poetry. This in itself is perhaps not surprising, for prose narratives on Tamil were often produced for the consumption of the state, in the process of petitioning the government for various favors. In contrast, poetry on Tamil1ttây is typically generated for the consumption of its speakers. Indeed, especially in the colonial period, the state appears to have been remarkably disinterested in this whole sphere of activity that was so prolific and widespread among Tamil's devout. So the striking dependence on poetic discourse in Tamil devotional circles was more than just a literary habit, dictated by the norms of a culture in which poetry, rather than prose, was until fairly recently the privileged mode of literary expression. Rather, the recourse to Tamil poetry was also a strategic practice through which its devotees expressed and constituted their devotion to their language through a medium (Tamil) that is considered their very "own," through a form (poetry) that is deemed authentically and deeply "Tamil," and through forums (such as community based literary and revivalist activities) that were outside the interests of the state. Poetry made possible intimate, even veiled, discourse about the language, allowing participation only to those who were familiar with its imagery, meters, rhetorical nuances, and so on. Thus poetry enabled Tamil's devout to practice what I would characterize as "intimate politics" in which affect and passion were deployed to establish the boundaries of a community united in devotion to the language.

And yet, although poetry had been the preferred mode of pre-colonial literary work, with the onset of modernity and its privileging of prose as rational, objective, and scientific, poets were increasingly pushed to the margins of social prestige and economic well-being in many parts of colonial India, and certainly in the Tamil-speaking region. Paradoxically, this itself may account for poetry's popularity as a discursive form among Tamil's devotees. Because prose, especially prose in English, was so closely associated with the existing power structures, poetry, I suggest, emerged as the favored form for the disenfranchised and the disempowered. Concomitantly, poetry also presents itself as a form of expression for those who want to oppose the existing system and the dominant ideology. In her marvellous ethnography on the ideology of poetry in Bedouin society, Lila Abu-Lughod suggests as much and notes that among the Bedouins, "poetry is, in so many ways, the discourse of opposition to the system[,]...[a] symbol of defiance" (1986: 233-59). I appropriate her suggestion, applying it as well to the production of poetry by *tamil1ppar1r1u,* which has clearly been a discourse of opposition conducted around sentiments of decline, loss, and disempowerment. On the one hand, poetry is widely believed to encapsulate the best of Tamil's literary tradition; it is associated with the Tamil past, especially the past of the ancient Cank#am age when poets, we are repeatedly told, commanded even kings. Poetry, it is nostalgically believed, is a deeply and authentically Tamil form. On the other hand, at least in the past century or so, its very subordination to prose within the regimes of colonial modernity meant that it emerged not just as a means but as a site of resistance to dominant ideologies, as well as to the new literary and linguistic forms that threatened what was perceived as authentically Tamil. For all these reasons, when Tamil's devotees want to write most passionately, intimately, and fiercely about their language, they turn to poetry.

In the praise poetry on Tamil and Tamil1ttây since the time of Sundaram Pillai, there is no singular conception of *par1r1u,* "devotion," that reigns. Instead, like the language and like Tamil1ttây, devotion, too, is multifaceted, and here I examine three of its modalities. In what I wish to call its "pietistic" mode, it is Tamil1ttây's persona as *teyvam,* "goddess," that is foregrounded, and the devotee casts himself as a pious worshipper. The predominant sentiment of this modality is reverence for a divine being, the relationship between the language and its *pious* devotee modelled on the ritual relationship between an omniscient goddess and her subordinate worshipper. I characterize the second of the modalities as the "somatics of devotion." Here, the emphasis is on Tamil1ttây's persona as *tây,* the "mother" of her devotees, who correspondingly cast themselves as her "children." In this modality, the relationship between the language and its *filial* devotee is biological and corporeal, modelled on the genealogical and familial bonds that tie a mother to her child. Here, devotion takes on a distinctly filial flavor, predominantly expressed in the domestic idiom of the family and the home. And then, there is a third modality that I characterize as the "erotics of devotion." Here, it is Tamil1ttây's persona as woman that is highlighted, the devotee casting himself as a desiring man. In this modality, the relationship between the language and its *desiring* devotee is charged with eroticism, although Tamil1ttây's status as *kan1n1i,* "virgin maiden," obviously complicates an already ambivalent situation.

3

Buddhism in Myanmar

There are four dominant ethnic groups in the recorded history of Myanmar: the Mon, the Pyu, the Myanmar, and the Shan. Uncertainty surrounds the origins of the Mon; but it is clear that, at least linguistically, they are related to the Khmer. What is known is that they settled in the south of Myanmar and Thailand while the Khmer made northern Thailand, Laos, and Cambodia their home. These two peoples were probably the first migrants to the region, apart from Indian merchants who established trading colonies along the coast. The Mon with their distinct language and culture competed for centuries with the Myanmar. However, today their influence and language is limited to remote areas of the south.

The Pyu, like the Myanmar, are a people of Tibeto-Burman origin with a distinct culture and language. They lived in the area around Prome long before the Myanmar pushed into the plains of Myanmar from the north. Their language was closely related to the language of the Myanmar and was later absorbed by it. Their script was in use until about the fourteenth century, but was then lost.

The Myanmar people began to colonise the plains of Myanmar only towards the middle of the first millennium AD. They came from the mountainous northern regions and may well have originated in the Central Asian plains.

After the Myanmar, the Shan flooded in from the North, finally conquering the entire region of Myanmar and Thailand. The Thai people are descended from Shan tribes. The northeast region of modern Myanmar is still inhabited predominantly by Shan tribes.

The Region

In the sixth century BC, most of what we now know as Myanmar, Thailand, Laos, and Cambodia was sparsely populated. While migrants from the east coast of India had formed trading colonies along the coast of the Gulf of Martaban, these coastal areas of Myanmar and Thailand were also home to the Mon. By this time, the Khmer probably controlled Laos, Cambodia, and northern Thailand, while Upper Myanmar may already have been occupied to some extent by Myanmar tribes.

As these early settlers did not use lasting materials for construction, our knowledge of their civilization remains scant. We do know, however, that their way of life was very simple — as it remains today in rural areas — probably requiring only wooden huts with palm-leaf roofs for habitation. We can assume that they were not organised into units larger than village communities and that they did not possess a written language. Their religion must have been some form of nature worship or animism, still found today among the more remote tribes of the region.

There were also more highly developed communities of Indian origin, in the form of trading settlements located along the entire coast from Bengal to Borneo. In Myanmar, they were located in Thaton (Suddhammapura), Pegu (Ussa), Yangon (Ukkala, then still on the coast), and Mrauk-U (Dhannavati) in Arakan; also probably along the Tenasserim and Arakan coasts. These settlers had mainly migrated from Orissa on the northeastern coast of the Indian subcontinent, and also from the Deccan in the southeast. In migrating to these areas, they had also brought their own culture and religion with them. Initially, the contact between the Hindu traders and the Mon peasants must have been limited. However, the Indian settlements, their culture and traditions, were eventually absorbed into the Mon culture.

G.E. Harvey, in his *History of Burma,* relates a Mon legend which refers to the Mon fighting Hindu strangers who had come back to re-conquer the country that had formerly belonged to them. This Mon tale confirms the theory that Indian people had formed the first communities in the region but that these were eventually replaced by the Mon with the development of their own civilization. As well as the Indian trading settlements, there were also some Pyu settlements, particularly in the area of Prome where a flourishing civilization later developed.

Also, it is assumed that some degree of migration from India to the region of Tagaung and Mogok in Upper Myanmar had taken place through Assam and later through Manipur, but the "hinterland" was of course much less attractive to traders than the coastal regions with their easy access by sea. A tradition of Myanmar says that Tagaung was founded by Abhiraja, a prince of the Sakyans (the tribe of the Buddha), who had migrated to Upper Myanmar from Nepal in the ninth century BC. The city was subsequently conquered by the Chinese in approximately 600 BC, and Pagan and Prome were founded by refugees fleeing southward. In fact, some historians believe that, like the Myanmar, the Sakyans were a Mongolian rather than an Indo-Aryan race, and that the Buddha's clansmen were derived from Mongolian stock.

First Contacts with the Buddha's Teachings

The source of information for many of the events related forthwith is the *Sasanavamsa*. The *Sasanavamsa* is a chronicle written in Pali by a bhikkhu, Pannasami, for the Fifth Buddhist Council held in Mandalay in 1867. As the *Sasanavamsa* is a recent compilation, many events mentioned therein may be doubted. However, as it draws on both written records, some of which are no longer available, and on the oral tradition of Myanmar, information can be included in this account with the understanding that it is open to verification.

There are many instances in the history of Southeast Asian tribes in which a conquering people incorporates into its own traditions not only the civilization of the conquered, but also their clan gods, royal lineage, and thereby their history. This fact would explain the visits of the Buddha to Thaton and Shwesettaw in the Mon and Myanmar oral tradition, and the belief of the Arakanese that the Buddha visited their king and left behind an image of himself for them to worship. Modern historiography will, of course, dismiss these stories as fabrications made out of national pride, as the Myanmar had not even arrived in the region at the time of the Buddha. However, it is possible that the Myanmar and Arakanese integrated into their own lore the oral historical tradition of their Indian predecessors. This does not prove that the visits really took place, but it seems a more palatable explanation of the existence of these accounts than simply putting them down to historical afterthought of a Buddhist people eager to connect itself with the origins of their religion. The *Sasanavamsa* mentions several visits of the Buddha to Myanmar and one other important event: the arrival of the hair relics in Ukkala (Yangon) soon after the Buddha's enlightenment.

The Arrival of the Hair Relics

Tapussa and Bhallika, two merchants from Ukkala, were traveling through the region of Uruvela and were directed to the Buddha by their family god. The Buddha had just come out of seven weeks of meditation after his awakening and was sitting under a tree feeling the need for food. Tapussa and Bhallika made an offering of rice cake and honey to the Buddha and took the two refuges, the refuge in the Buddha and the refuge in the Dhamma (the Sangha, the third refuge, did not exist yet). As they were about to depart, they asked the Buddha for an object to worship in his stead and he gave them eight hairs from his head. After the two returned from their journey, they enshrined the three hairs in a stupa which is now the great Shwedagon Pagoda in Yangon.

It is believed in Myanmar that the hill upon which the Shwedagon Pagoda stands was not haphazardly chosen by Tapussa and Bhallika but was, in fact, the site where the three Buddhas preceding the Buddha Gotama in this world cycle themselves deposited relics. Buddha Kakusandha is said to have left his staff on the Theinguttara Hill, the Buddha Konagamana his water filter, and Buddha Kassapa a part of his robe. Because of this, the Buddha requested Tapussa and Bhallika to enshrine his relics in this location. Tapussa and Bhallika traveled far and wide in order to find the hill on which they could balance a tree without its touching the ground either with the roots or with the crown. Eventually, they found the exact spot not far from their home in Lower Myanmar where they enshrined the holy relics in a traditional mound or stupa. The original stupa is said to have been 27 feet high. Today the Shwedagon pagoda has grown to over 370 feet.

The Buddha's Visits to the Region

The Myanmar oral tradition speaks of four visits of the Buddha to the region. While these visits were of utmost significance in their own right, they are also important in having established places of pilgrimage up to the present day.

The Visit to Central Myanmar

According to the *Sasanavamsa,* the city of Aparanta is situated on the western shore of the Irrawaddy river at the latitude of Magwe. The *Sasanavamsa* gives only a very brief summary of the events surrounding the Buddha's visit to Aparanta, presumably because these were well known and could be read in the Tipitaka and the commentaries.

Punna, a merchant from Sunaparanta, went to Savatthi on business and there heard a discourse of the Buddha. Having won faith in the Buddha and the Teachings, he took ordination as a bhikkhu. After sometime, he asked the Buddha to teach him a short lesson so that he could return to Sunaparanta and strive for arahatship. The Buddha warned him that the people of Sunaparanta were fierce and violent, but Punna replied that he would not allow anger to arise, even if they should kill him. In the Punnovada Sutta, the Buddha instructed him not to be enticed by that which is pleasant, and Punna returned and attained arahatship in his country. He won over many disciples and built a monastery of red sandalwood for the Buddha (according to some chronicles of Myanmar, the Buddha made the prediction that at the location where the red sandalwood monastery was, the great king Alaungsithu of Pagan would build a shrine). He then sent flowers as an invitation to the Buddha and the Buddha came accompanied by five hundred arahats, spent the night in the monastery, and left again before dawn.

Sakka, the king of the thirty-three devas living in the Tavatimsa plane, provided five hundred palanquins for the bhikkhus accompanying the Buddha on the journey to Sunaparanta. But only 499 of the palanquins were occupied. One of them remained empty until the ascetic Saccabandha, who lived on the Saccabandha mountain in central Myanmar, joined the Buddha and the 499 bhikkhus accompanying him. On the way to Sunaparanta, the Buddha stopped in order to teach the ascetic Saccabandha. When Saccabanda attained arahatship, he then joined the Buddha and completed the total of 500 bhikkhus who usually traveled with the Master.

On the return journey, the Buddha stopped at the river Nammada close to the Saccabandha mountain. Here, the Blessed One was invited by the Naga king, Nammada, to visit and preach to the Nagas, later accepting food from them. The tradition of Myanmar relates that he left behind a footprint for veneration near this river, which would last as long as the Sasana (i.e. 5000 years). Another footprint was left in the rock of the Saccabandha mountain. These footprints, still visible today, were worshipped by the Mon, Pyu, and Myanmar kings alike and have remained among the holiest places of pilgrimage in Myanmar. In the fifteenth century, after the decimation of the population through the Siamese campaigns, knowledge of the footprints was lost. Then, in the year 1638, King Thalun sent learned bhikkhus to the region; fortuitously, they were able to relocate the Buddha's footprints. Since then Shwesettaw, the place where the footprints are found, has once again become an important place of pilgrimage in Myanmar. And in the dry season thousands of devout Buddhists travel there to pay respects.

The Visit to Arakan

In Dhannavati, whose walls are still partially visible today, the Mahamuni temple is located on the Sirigutta hill. In this temple, for over two millennia, the Mahamuni image was enshrined and worshipped. The story of the Mahamuni image, at one time one of the most revered shrines of Buddhism, is told in the *Sappadanapakarana,* a work of a local historian.

Candrasuriya, the king of Dhannavati, on hearing that a Buddha had arisen in India, desired to go there to learn the Dhamma. The Buddha, aware of his intention, said to Ananda: "The king will have to pass through forests dangerous to travelers; wide rivers will impede his journey; he must cross a sea full of monsters. It will be an act of charity if we go to his dominion, so that he may pay homage without risking his life."

So the Buddha went there and was received with great pomp by King Candrasuriya and his people. The Buddha then taught the five and eight precepts and instructed the king in the ten kingly duties, namely, (1) universal beneficence, (2) daily paying homage, (3) the showing of mercy, (4) taxes of not more than a tenth part of the produce, (5) justice, (6) punishment without anger, (7) the support of his subjects as the earth supports them, (8) the employment of prudent commanders, (9) the taking of good counsel, and (10) the avoidance of pride. The Buddha remained for a week and on preparing for his departure the king requested that he leave an image of himself, so that they could worship him even in his absence. The Buddha consented to this and Sakka the king of the gods himself formed the image with the metals collected by the king and his people. It was completed in one week and when the Buddha breathed onto it the people exclaimed that now there were indeed two Buddhas, so alike was the image to the great sage. Then the Buddha made a prophesy addressing the image: "I shall pass into Nibbana in my eightieth year, but you will live for five thousand years which I have foreseen as the duration of my Teaching."

The Mahamuni image remained in its original location until 1784 when King Bodawpaya conquered Arakan and had the image transported to Mandalay where a special shrine, the Arakan pagoda, was built to enshrine the three-meter image. To have this image in his capital greatly added to his prestige as a Buddhist king, as it was one of the most sacred objects in the region. The king himself went out of his city to meet the approaching image with great devotion and "through the long colonnades leading to the pagoda, there used to come daily from the Myanmar palace, so long as a king reigned there, sumptuous offerings borne in stately procession, marshalled by a minister and shaded by the white umbrella."

The Missionaries of the Third Buddhist Council

The Third Buddhist Council was held in the reign of Emperor Asoka in the year 232 BC in order to purify the Sangha, to reassert orthodox teaching and to refute heresy. But the work of the Council did not stop there. With the support of Emperor Asoka, experienced teachers were sent to border regions in order to spread the teachings of the Buddha. This dispersal of missionaries is recorded in the *Mahavamsa*, a Sinhalese chronicle on the history of Buddhism: When the thera Moggaliputta, the illuminator of the religion of the Conqueror, had brought the (third) council to an end and when, looking into the future, he had beheld the founding of the religion in adjacent countries, then in the month of Katthika he sent forth theras, one here and one there. The thera Majjhantika he sent to Kasmira and Gandhara, the thera Mahadeva he sent to Mahisamandala. To Vanavasa he sent the thera named Rakkhita, and to Aparantaka the Yona named Dhammarakkhita; to Maharattha he sent the thera named Mahadhammarakkhita, but the thera Maharakkhita he sent into the country of the Yona. He sent the thera Majjhima to the Himalaya country and together with the thera Uttara, the thera Sona of wondrous might went to Suvannabhumi...

According to the *Sasanavamsa,* the above mentioned regions are the following: Kasmira and Gandhara is the right bank of the Indus river south of Kabul; Mahisamandala is Andhra; Vanavasa is the region around Prome; Aparantaka is west of the upper Irrawaddy; Maharattha is Thailand; Yona, the country of the Shan tribes; and Suvannabhumi is Thaton. The *Sasanavamsa* mentions five places in Southeast Asia where Asoka's missionaries taught the Buddha's doctrine, and through their teaching many gained insight and took refuge in the Triple Gem. There are two interesting features mentioned in the text. First, in order to ordain nuns, bhikkhunis, other bhikkhunis had to be present, and secondly, the Brahmajala Sutta was preached in Thaton.

The *Sasanavamsa* goes on to describe sixty thousand women ordaining in Aparanta. It states that women could not have been ordained without the presence of bhikkhunis, as in Sri Lanka where women could only be ordained after Mahinda's sister Sanghamitta had followed her brother there. In this case, the author surmises that bhikkhunis must have followed Dhammarakkhita to Aparanta at a later stage.

The Brahmajala Sutta, which the arahats Sona and Uttara preached in Thaton, deals in detail with the different schools of philosophical and religious thought prevalent in India at the time of the Buddha. The fact that Sona and Uttara chose this Sutta to convert the inhabitants of Suvannabhumi indicates that they were facing a well-informed public, familiar with the views of Brahmanism that were refuted by the Buddha in this discourse. There can be no doubt that only Indian colonisers, not the Mon, would have been able to follow an analysis of Indian philosophy as profound as the Brahmajala Sutta.

BUDDHISM IN THE MON AND PYU KINGDOMS

While there is no conclusive archaeological proof that Buddhism continued to be practiced in southern Myanmar after the missions of the Third Council, the *Sasanavamsa* refers to an unbroken lineage of teachers passing on the Dhamma to their disciples.

The Mon

In a third century AD inscription by a South Indian king in Nagarjunakonda, the land of the Cilatas is mentioned in a list of countries visited by a group of bhikkhus. Historians believe the Cilatas or Kiratas (also mentioned by Ptolemy and in Sanskrit literature) to be identical to the Mon populations of Lower Myanmar.

The inscription states that the bhikkhus sent to the Cilata country converted the population there to Buddhism. In the same inscription, missions to other countries such as Sri Lanka are mentioned. It is generally believed that most of these countries had received earlier Buddhist missionaries sent by Buddhist kings, but as civilization in these lands was relatively undeveloped, teachings as profound as the Buddha's had probably become distorted by local religions or possibly been completely lost. It is possible that these missions did not so much re-establish Buddhism, but rather purify the type of Buddhism practiced there. Southern India was then the guardian of the Theravada faith and obviously remained in contact with countries that had been converted in earlier times but were unable to preserve the purity of the religion.

As has been already mentioned, the first datable archaeological finds of the Mon civilization stem from the Mon kingdom of Dvaravati in the South of Thailand. They consist of a Roman oil lamp and a bronze statue of the Buddha which are believed to be no later than the first or second century AD. In discussing the Mon Theravada Buddhist civilization, we cannot remain in Myanmar only. For only by studying the entire sphere of influence of the Mon in this period, can a comprehensive picture be constructed. This sphere includes large parts of present day Thailand. In fact, the Chinese Buddhist pilgrim, Yuan Chwang, who traveled to India in about 630 AD, describes a single Mon country stretching from Prome to Chenla in the east and including the Irrawaddy and Sittang deltas. He calls the country Dvaravati, but the annals of the court of China of the same period mention Dvaravati as a vassal of Thaton. We can, therefore, safely conclude that the Mon of the region formed a fairly homogenous group in which the distribution of power was obviously not always evident to the outsider.

The Pyu

Lower Myanmar was also inhabited by another ethnic group, the Pyu, who were probably closely related to the modern Myanmar. They had their capital at Sri Ksetra (near modern day Prome) and were also followers of the Theravada Buddhist faith. Chinese travelers' reports of the mid-third century AD refer to the kingdom of Lin-Yang where Buddha was venerated by all and where several thousand monks or bhikkhus lived. As Lin-Yang was to the west of Kamboja and could not be reached by sea, we can infer that the Chinese travelers must have been referring to the ancient kingdom of Prome. This is all the more likely as archaeological finds prove that only about one century later Pali Buddhist texts, including Abhidhamma texts, were studied by the Pyu.

The earliest highly developed urban settlement of the Pyu was Beikthano, near Prome. However, its importance dwindled towards the sixth century, when Sri Ksetra became the center of Pyu civilization. A major monastery built in the fourth century has been unearthed at Beikthano. The building, constructed in brick, with a stupa and shrine located nearby, is identical to the Buddhist monasteries of Nagarjunakonda, the great Buddhist center of southern India. It is situated near a stupa and a shrine, a design which is identical to the one used in South India. Bricks had been used by the Pyus since the second century AD for the construction of pillared halls, which formed the temples of their original religion. Interestingly, the Pyu bricks have always been of the exact dimensions as those used at the time of Emperor Asoka in India. But the brick laying techniques used in the monastery in Beikthano were far inferior to the ones used in their southern Indian counterparts.

For such a major edifice as the monastery at Beikthano to have been constructed, the religion must have been well established at least among the ruling class. How long it took for Buddhism to become influential in Pyu society is difficult to determine, but some historians assume that the first contacts with Asokan religious centers in India took place in the second century AD. This would allow for a period of development of two hundred years until the first important shrine was built. Despite the Indian architectural influence, the inferior brick laying techniques found in Beikthano indicate that indigenous architects and artisans, rather than imported craftsmen or Indian colonisers, were employed in the construction of monasteries and other important buildings.

It should, of course, not be forgotten that the Pyu possessed an architecture of their own and a highly developed urban culture that had evolved quite independently of Indian influences. Theravada Buddhism found a fertile ground in this highly developed civilization. It is probable that the Pyu civilization was more advanced than that of the Mon. The Pyu sites found around Prome are the earliest urban sites in Southeast Asia found to date. The urban developments and datable monuments in Thailand and Cambodia are only from the seventh century. Older artifacts may have been found in Thailand, but they were not products of indigenous people and do not prove the existence of a developed civilization.

The information we have of the state of the religion in the Mon and Pyu societies during the first four centuries AD is very limited. However, by the fifth century, with the development of religious activity in the region, information becomes more substantive. The historical tradition of Myanmar gives the credit for this religious resurgence to a well-known Buddhist scholar, Acariya Buddhaghosa.

Buddhaghosa and Myanmar

Acariya Buddhaghosa was the greatest commentator on the Pali Buddhist texts, whose *Visuddhimagga* and commentaries to the canon are regarded as authoritative by

Theravada scholars. The chronicles of Myanmar firmly maintain that Buddhaghosa was of Mon origin and a native of Thaton. They state that his return from Sri Lanka, with the Pali scriptures, the commentaries, and grammatical works, gave a fresh impetus to the religion.

However, modern historians do not accept that Buddhaghosa was from Myanmar while some even doubt his existence. Despite this contention, Eliot, in his *Hinduism and Buddhism,* gives more weight to circumstantial evidence and writes:

The Burmese tradition that Buddhaghosa was a native of Thaton and returned thither from Sri Lanka merits more attention than it has received. It can easily be explained away as patriotic fancy. On the other hand, if Buddhaghosa's object was to invigorate Hinayanism in India the result of his really stupendous labors was singularly small, for in India his name is connected with no religious movement. But if we suppose that he went to Sri Lanka by way of the holy places in Magadha [now Bihar] and returned from the Coromandal coast [Madras] to Burma where Hinayanism afterwards flourished, we have at least a coherent narrative.

The Sinhalese chronicles, especially the *Mahavamsa,* place Buddhaghosa in the first half of the fifth century. Although he spent most of his active working life in Sri Lanka, he is also credited with imbuing new life into Theravada Buddhism in South India, and developing such important centers as Kancipura and Uragapuram that were closely connected with Prome and Thaton. Proof of this connection can be found in archeological finds in the environs of Prome which include Pali literature inscribed in the Kadambe script on gold and stone plates. This script was used in the fifth and sixth century in southern India. All in all, Myanmar has a valid case for claiming some connection with Buddhaghosa. It is, of course, impossible to prove that he was born there or even visited there, but his influence undoubtedly led to great religious activity in the kingdoms of Lower Myanmar.

Buddhism in Lower Myanmar: 5th to 11th Centuries

From the fifth century until the conquest of Lower Myanmar by Pagan, there is a continuous record of Buddhism flourishing in the Mon and Pyu kingdoms. The Mon kingdoms are mentioned in travel reports of several Chinese Buddhist pilgrims and also in the annals of the Chinese court. In the fifth century, Thaton and Pegu (Pago) are mentioned in the Buddhist commentarial literature for the first time. They were now firmly established on the map as Buddhist centers of learning. Despite this, Buddhism was not without rivals in the region. This is shown, by the following event some chronicles of Myanmar mention.

A king of Pago, Tissa by name, had abandoned the worship of the Buddha and instead practiced Brahmanical worship. He persecuted the Buddhists and destroyed Buddha images or cast them into ditches. A pious Buddhist girl, the daughter of a merchant, restored the images, then washed and worshipped them. The king could not tolerate such defiance, of course, and had the girl dragged before him. He tried to have her executed in several ways, but she seemed impossible to kill. Elephants would not trample her,while the fire of her pyre would not burn her. Eventually the king, intrigued by these events, asked the girl to perform a miracle. He stated that, if she was able to make a Buddha image produce seven new images and then make all eight statues fly into heaven, she would be set free. The girl spoke an act of truth, and the eight Buddha statues flew up into the sky. The king was then converted to Buddhism and elevated the girl to the position of chief queen.

Until now, archaeological finds of Mon ruins in Myanmar are meager, but at P'ong Tuk, in southern Thailand, a Mon city, dating from the second half of the first millennium AD, has been unearthed. Here, excavations have revealed the foundations of several buildings. One contained the remains of a platform and fragments of columns similar to the Buddhist vihara at Anuradhapura in Sri Lanka; another, with a square foundation of round stones, seems to have been a stupa. Statues of Indian origin from the Gupta period (320-600 AD) were also found at the site. The Theravada Buddhist culture of the Mon flourished in both Dvaravati and Thaton. However, the Mon civilization in Thailand did not survive the onslaught of the Khmer in the eleventh century who were worshipping Hindu gods. In Myanmar, the Mon kingdom was conquered by Pagan. The Myanmar were eager to accept the Mon culture and especially their religion, while the Khmer, as Hindus, at best tolerated it.

The Pyu culture of this period is well documented because of archaeological finds at Muanggan, a small village close to the ancient ruins of Hmawza. There two perfectly preserved inscribed gold plates were found. These inscriptions reveal three texts: the verses spoken by Assaji to Sariputta *(ye dhamma hetuppabhava...),* a list of categories of the Abhidhamma *(cattaro iddhipada, cattaro samappadhana...),* and the formula of worship of Buddha, Dhamma, and Sangha *(iti pi so bhagava...).* At the same site, a book with twenty leaves of gold protected with golden covers, was discovered. It contained texts such as the *paticca-samuppada* (dependent origination), the *vipassana-nanas* (stages of insight knowledge), and various other excerpts from the Abhidhamma and the other two baskets of the Buddhist scriptures. The scripts in all these documents are identical to scripts used in parts of southern India, and can be dated from the third to the sixth century AD.

In addition to these golden plates, a number of sculptures and reliefs were found in Hmawza. They depict either the Buddha or scenes from his life, for example, the birth of the Buddha and the taming of the wild elephant Nalagiri. The sculpture is similar in style to that of Amaravati, a center of Buddhist learning in South India. There were also unearthed remains of Brahman temples and sites of Mahayana worship of east Indian origin; hence it would appear that several faiths, of which the Theravada was the strongest, co-existed in Sri Ksetra, the then capital of the Pyu. The script used by the Pyu is indicative of major links with Buddhist kingdoms in South India rather than with Sri Lanka. And it can be surmised that the bhikkhus of the Deccan and other regions of southern India were the teachers of both the Mon and the Pyu in religious matters as well as in the arts and sciences.

The inscriptions show how highly developed scholarship of the Pali Buddhist texts must have been in Lower Myanmar even in these early days. Learning had gone well beyond the basics into the world of Abhidhamma studies. Pali was obviously well known as a language of learning, but unfortunately no original texts composed in Sri Ksetra or Thaton have come down to us. Interestingly, some of the texts inscribed on these gold plates are not identical to the same canonical texts as they are known today. Therefore, the Tipitaka known to the Pyu must have been replaced by a version preserved in a country that had no close contact with the Pyu. This could well have been Sri Lanka, as this country came to play an important role in the history of Buddhism in Myanmar through the friendship between the conqueror of Lower Myanmar, Anawratha, and the king who drove the Hindus from Sri Lanka, Vijayabahu.

The finds on the site of the ancient Pyu capital confirm the reports of the Chinese pilgrims and also the Tang imperial chronicles of China which state: "They (the Pyu) dislike taking life. They know how to make astronomical calculations. They are Buddhists and have a hundred monasteries, with brick of glass embellished with gold and silver vermilion, gay colours and red kino... At seven years of age the people cut their hair and enter a monastery; if at the age of twenty they have not grasped the doctrine they return to the lay state."

Both Buddhist cultures in the south of Myanmar, the Mon and the Pyu, were swept away in the eleventh century by armies of the Myanmar who had found a unifying force in their leader, the founder of Pagan and champion of Buddhism, Anawratha.

THERAVADA BUDDHISM COMES TO PAGAN

The Beginnings of Pagan

Pagan is believed to have been founded in the years 849-850 AD, by the Myanmar, who had already established themselves as rice growers in the region around Kyauksai near Mandalay. Anawratha began to unite the region by subjugating one chieftain after another and was successful in giving the Myanmar a sense of belonging to a larger community, a nation. The crucial event in the history of Myanmar is not so much the founding of the city of Pagan and the building of its walls and moat, but more Pagan's acceptance of Theravada Buddhism in the eleventh century. The religion was brought to the Myanmar by a Mon bhikkhu named Shin Arahan.

The religion prevailing among the Myanmar before and during the early reign of Anawratha was some form of Mahayana Buddhism, which had probably found its way into the region from the Pala kingdom in Bengal. This is apparent from bronze statues depicting Bodhisattas and especially the "Lokanatha," a Bodhisatta believed, in Bengal, to reign in the period between the demise of the Buddha Gotama and the advent of the Buddha Metteyya. Anawratha continued to cast terracotta votive tablets with the image of Lokanatha even after he embraced the Theravada doctrine.

In India, Buddhism had split into numerous schools, some of which differed fundamentally from the teachings of Pali Buddhism, which is also called Theravada Buddhism (the doctrine of the Theras). The Ari, the monks or priests of this Mahayana Buddhist form of worship, are described, in later chronicles of Myanmar, as the most shameless bogus ascetics imaginable. They are said to have sold absolution from sin and to have oppressed the people in various ways with their tyranny. Their tantric Buddhism included, as an important element, the worship of Nagas (dragons), which was probably an ancient indigenous tradition.

At this time, the beginning of the eleventh century, the Buddhist religion among the Mon in Suvannabhumi was on the decline as people were disturbed by robbers and raiders, by plagues, and by adversaries of the religion. These most probably came from the Hindu Khmer kingdom in Cambodia and the north of Thailand. The Khmer were endeavoring to add Thaton and the other Mon kingdoms of the south to their expanding empire. Shin Arahan must have feared that bhikkhus would not be able to continue to maintain their religious practice and the study of the scriptures under these circumstances. He went, therefore, upcountry where a new, strong people were developing, prosperous and secure from enemies.

It is interesting to note that in this same period, Buddhism was under attack in other places as well. The Colas, a Hindu dynasty strongly opposed to Buddhism, arose in southern India, one of the last strongholds of Theravada Buddhism. They were able to expand their rule to include most of Sri Lanka between 1017 and 1070. The great Mon city, Dvaravati, a Theravada center in southern Thailand, fell to the Khmer, the masters of the whole of Thailand, who were Shaivaite Hindus. In the north of India, Muslim armies were trying to destroy what little was left of Buddhism there. "In this perilous period," writes Professor Luce, "Buddhism was saved only by such valiant fighters as Vijayabahu in Sri Lanka and Anawratha."

Shin Arahan Converts the King

Shin Arahan arrived in the vicinity of Pagan and was discovered in his forest dwelling by a hunter. The hunter, who had never before seen such a strange creature with a shaven head and a yellow robe, thought he was some kind of spirit and took him to the king, Anawratha. Shin Arahan naturally sat down on the throne, as it was the highest seat, and the king thought: "This man is peaceful, in this man there is the essential thing. He is sitting down on the best seat, surely he must be the best being."

The king asked the visitor to tell him where he came from and was told that he came from the place where the Order lived and that the Buddha was his teacher. Then Shin Arahan gave the king the teaching on mindfulness *(appamada),* teaching him the same doctrine Nigrodha had given Emperor Asoka when he was converted. Shin Arahan then told the monarch that the Buddha had passed into Parinibbana, but that his teaching, the Dhamma, enshrined in the Tipitaka, and the twofold Sangha consisting of those who possessed absolute knowledge and those who possessed conventional knowledge, remained.

The king must have felt that he had found what had been missing in his life and a genuine alternative to the superficial teachings of the Ari monks. He built a monastery for Shin Arahan, and according to some sources, stopped all worship of the Ari monks. Tradition has it that he had them dressed in white and even forced them to serve as soldiers in his army. The Ari tradition continued for a long time, however, and its condemnation is a feature of much later times, and not, as far as contemporary evidence shows, of the Pagan era.

The *Sasanavamsa* gives an alternate version of Anawratha's conversion according to which Shin Arahan had originally come from Sri Lanka to study the Dhamma in Dvaravati and Thaton and was on his way to Sri Ksetra in search of a text when he was taken to Anawratha by a hunter. The king asked him, "Who are you?" — "O King, I am a disciple of Gotama." — "Of what kind are the Three Jewels?" — "O King, the Buddha should be regarded as Mahosadha the wise, his doctrine as Ummagga, his order as the Videhan army."

This version is interesting in that Anawratha is portrayed as being a Buddhist with knowledge of Jataka stories, such as the Mahosadha Jataka referred to above, even before meeting Shin Arahan. This assumption that he was no stranger to Buddhism is supported by the fact that earlier kings had been followers of Buddhism in varying degrees. Caw Rahan, who died about 94 years before Anawratha's accession, is said to have built a Sima and five Pagodas, and Kyaung Pyu Min built the white monastery outside Pagan. Kyaung Pyu Min is believed to have been Anawratha's father.

Anawratha Acquires the Scriptures

Through Shin Arahan, Anawratha had now found the religion he had been yearning for and he decided to set out and procure the scriptures and holy relics of this religion. For he wished his kingdom to be secured on the original teachings of the Buddha. He tried to find the scriptures and relics of his new religion in different quarters. In his enthusiasm he did not limit his quest to Thaton, but also searched among the Khmer in Angkor, and in Tali, the capital of the Nanchao, a kingdom in modern day Yunnan, in China, where a tooth of the Buddha was enshrined. But everywhere he was refused. He then went to Thaton, where his teacher Shin Arahan had come from, to request a copy of the scriptures. According to the tradition of Myanmar, Anawratha's request was refused, and unable to endure another refusal he set out with his army in the year 1057 to conquer Thaton and acquire the Tipitaka by force. Before conquering Thaton, however, he had to subjugate Sri Ksetra, the Pyu capital. From there, he took the relics enshrined in King Dwattabaung's Bawbaw-gyi Pagoda to Pagan.

Some think that the aim of his campaign was mainly to add the prosperous Indian colonies of Lower Myanmar to his possessions, while others think he may have actually been called to Thaton to defend it against the marauding Khmer. Whatever the immediate cause of his campaign in the lower country, we know for certain that he returned with the king of Thaton and his court, with Mon artists and scholars and, above all, with Thaton's bhikkhus and their holy books, the Tipitaka. Suvannabhumi and its Mon population were now in the hands of the Myanmar and the Mon culture and religion were accepted and assimilated in the emergent Pagan with fervor.

Initially the fervor must have been restricted to the king and possibly his immediate entourage, yet even they continued to propitiate their traditional gods for worldly gain as the new religion was considered a higher practice. Theravada Buddhism does not provide much in the way of rites and rituals, but a royal court cannot do without them. So the traditional propitiation of the Nagas continued to be used for court ceremonials and remained part of the popular religion, while the bhikkhus were accorded the greatest respect and their master, the Buddha Gotama, was honored with the erection of pagodas and shrines.

There were contacts between the new kings of Myanmar and Sri Lanka that are recorded not only in the chronicles of the two countries but also in stone inscriptions in South India. As the Hindu Colas had ruled Sri Lanka for more than half a century, Buddhism had been weakened and King Vijayabahu, who had driven out the Vaishnavite Colas, wanted to re-establish his religion. So in 1070, he requested King Anawratha of Myanmar, who had assisted him financially in his war against the Colas, to send bhikkhus to re-introduce the pure ordination into his country. It is interesting to note that the *Culavamsa* refers to Anawratha as the king of Ramanna, which was Lower Myanmar, also called Suvannabhumi. He was approached as the conqueror and master of Thaton, a respected Theravada center, rather than as the king of Pagan, a new and unknown country. The bhikkhus who traveled to Sri Lanka brought the Sinhalese Tipitaka back with them and established a link between the two countries which was to last for centuries.

Anawratha is mentioned in the Myanmar, Mon, Khmer, Thai, and Sinhalese chronicles as a great champion of Buddhism because he developed Pagan into a major regional power and laid the foundation for its glory. He did not, however, build many of the temples for which Pagan is now so famous as the great age of temple building started only after his reign. It is important to realize that his interest was not restricted only to Pagan. He built pagodas wherever his campaigns took him and adorned them with illustrations from the Jatakas and the life of the Buddha. Some maintain that he used only Jatakas as themes for the adornment of his religious buildings because that was all he possessed of the Tipitaka. Such a conclusion is negative and quite superficial. After all, during Asoka's time Jatakas and scenes from the life of the Buddha were used for illustrations in Bharut and Sanchi, the great stupas near Bombay. We cannot therefore deduce that the builders of Bharut and Sanchi were acquainted only with the Jatakas. These edifying stories which teach the fundamentals of Buddhism so skillfully are singularly suited to educate an illiterate people beset by superstitions through the vivid visual means of the stone reliefs depicting these stories. It is almost unthinkable that the Mon Sangha, who taught Anawratha, had no knowledge of at least all of the Vinaya. Otherwise, they would not have been able to re-establish a valid ordination of bhikkhus in Sri Lanka.

Anawratha left behind innumerable clay tablets adorned with images of the Buddha, the king's name, and some Pali and Sanskrit verses. A typical aspiration on these tablets was: "By me, King Anawratha, this mould of Sugata (Buddha) has been made. Through this may I obtain the path to Nibbana when Metteyya is awakened." Anawratha aspired to become a disciple of the Buddha Metteyya, unlike many later kings of Myanmar who aspired to Buddhahood. Is this an indication that this warrior had remained a modest man in spite of his empire building?

PAGAN: FLOWERING AND DECLINE

Anawratha was succeeded by a number of kings of varying significance to Buddhism in Myanmar. His successors inherited a relatively stable and prosperous kingdom and consequently were able to embark on the huge temple building projects for which their reigns are still remembered.

This is the time when kings such as Kyanzitta and others built pagodas, libraries, monasteries, and ordination halls. These kings must have possessed coffers full of riches collected from their extensive kingdom which they lavished on the religion of the Buddha. Their palaces were probably built of wood as was the last palace of the Myanmar dynasty. Though the palaces must have reflected the wealth and power of the rulers, the more durable brick was not deemed necessary for such worldly buildings. This is similar to views still found in rural areas of Myanmar today. The only structure adorned to any extent in a village is the monastery and the buildings attached to it, such as the rest house. The villagers are very modest with regard to their private houses and even consider it improper to decorate them. Their monastery, however, is given every decoration affordable.

Kyanzitta Strengthens Theravada Buddhism

Kyanzitta (1084-1113), who had been Anawratha's commander-in-chief and had succeeded Anawratha's son to the throne, consolidated Theravada Buddhism's predominance in Pagan. In his reign, such important shrines as the Shwezigon Pagoda, the Nanda, Nagayon, and Myinkaba Kubyauk-gyi temples were built.

With the three latter temples, Kyanzitta introduced a new style of religious building. The traditional stupa or dagoba found in India and Sri Lanka is a solid mound in which relics or other holy objects are enshrined. The area of worship is situated around them and is usually marked by ornate stone railings. In the new style of building, however, the solid mound had been hollowed out and could be entered. The central shrine was surrounded by halls which housed stone reliefs depicting scenes from the Buddha's life and Jataka stories. Kyanzitta's aim was the conversion of his people to the new faith. Whereas Anawratha had been busy expanding his empire and bringing relics and the holy scriptures to Pagan, Kyanzitta's mission was to consolidate this enterprise. Enormous religious structures such as the Nanda Temple attracted the populace and the interiors of the temples allowed the bhikkhus to instruct the inquisitive in the king's faith.

Professor Luce writes:

> *The Nanda (temple)... he built with four broad halls. Each hall had the same 16 scenes in stone relief all identically arranged. The bhikkhus could cope with four audiences simultaneously. The scenes cover the whole life of the Buddha. When well grounded in these, the audience would pass to the outer wall of the corridor. Here, running around the whole corridor are the 80 scenes of Gotama's life up to the Enlightenment. The*

later life of the Buddha is shown in hundreds of other stone reliefs on the inner walls and shrines.

Kyanzitta's efforts for the advancement of Buddhism were not limited to his own country. For in one of his many inscriptions, he also mentions that he sent craftsmen to Bodhgaya to repair the Mahabodhi temple, which had been destroyed by a foreign king. The upkeep of the Mahabodhi temple became a tradition with the kings of Myanmar, who continued to send missions to Bodhgaya to repair the temple and also to donate temple slaves and land to the holiest shrine of Buddhism.

Kyanzitta also initiated an extensive review and purification of the Tipitaka by the bhikkhus. This was the first occasion in Myanmar's history when the task of a Buddhist Sangayana or Synod, comparing the Sinhalese and Suvannabhumi's Tipitaka, was undertaken. It is possible and even probable that this huge editing work was carried out along with visiting Sinhalese bhikkhus.

By nature of Myanmar's geographical position, external influences swept in predominantly from northern India, and therefore tantric Buddhism, dominant especially in Bengal, remained strong. However, Kyanzitta succeeded in firmly establishing the Pali Tipitaka by asking the bhikkhus to compare the ancient Mon Tipitaka with the texts obtained from the Mahavihara in Sri Lanka. In this way, he also made it clear that confirmation of orthodoxy was to be sought in Sri Lanka and not in any other Buddhist country. Though Mahayana practices were tolerated in his reign (his chief queen was a tantric Buddhist), they were not officially regarded as the pure religion. It is characteristic of Pagan that these two branches of Buddhism co-existed — the religion of the Theras, which was accepted as the highest religion — and the tantric practices, which included the worship of spirits or *nats* and gave more immediate satisfaction. Pagodas are often adorned with figures of all types of deities, but the deities are normally shown in an attitude of reverence towards the pagoda, a symbol of the Buddha. The ancient gods were not banished, but had to submit to the peerless Buddha. Tradition attributes to King Anawratha the observation: "Men will not come for the sake of the new faith. Let them come for their old gods, and gradually they will be won over."

An approach such as this, whether it was Anawratha's or Kyanzitta's, would suggest that the practice of the old religion of the Ari monks was allowed to continue and that the conversion of the country was gentle and peaceful as befits the religion of the Buddha. Although later Myanmar chronicles refer to the Ari monks as a debased group of charlatans who were totally rooted out by Anawratha, this is far from the truth.

A powerful movement of "priests" who incorporated magic practices in their teachings continued to exist throughout the Pagan period, and though they may have respected the basic rules of the Vinaya and donned the yellow robe, their support was rooted in the old animistic beliefs of the Myanmar. It should not be forgotten that the Myanmar first started to settle in the area of Kyauksai in the sixth century AD and that the "man in the field" was in no way ready for such highly developed a religion as Theravada Buddhism. The transition had to be gradual, and the process that started remains still incomplete in the minds of many people, especially in the more remote areas of the hill country.

The example of Kyanzitta's son Rajakumar, however, shows how even in those early days the teachings of the Buddha were understood and practiced not only by the bhikkhus, but also by lay people and members of the royal court. Rajakumar's conduct is proof of his father's ability to establish men in the Dhamma and survives as a monument just as the Ananda temple does.

Rajakumar was Kyanzitta's only son and his rightful heir. Due to political misadventures Kyanzitta was separated from his wife and therefore not aware of the birth of his son for seven years. When his daughter gave birth to his grandson he anointed him as future king immediately after his birth. Rajakumar grew up in the shadow of his nephew, the crown prince, but neither during his father's reign nor after his death did he ever try to usurp the throne through intrigue or by force. He was a minister zealous in the affairs of state, prudent and wise. He was also a scholar of the Tipitaka and instrumental in its review, vigorously supporting his father in his objective to establish Buddhism. But he is best known for his devotion to his father in his last years when his health was failing. In order to restore the king's health he built five pagodas which to this day are called Min-o-Chanda, "The Welfare of the Old King." When the king was on his deathbed:

Rajakumar, remembering the many and great favors with which the king had nourished him, made a beautiful golden image of the Buddha and entering with ceremony presented it to the king, saying: "This golden Buddha I have made to help my lord. The three villages of slaves you gave me, I give to this Buddha." And the king rejoiced and said "Sadhu, sadhu, sadhu." Then in the presence of the compassionate Mahathera and other leading bhikkhus, the king poured on the ground the water of dedication, calling the earth to witness. Then Rajakumar enshrined the golden image, and built around it a cave temple with a golden pinnacle.

Later Kings

Rajakumar's nephew was King Alaungsithu (c.1113-67), who continued the tradition of his dynasty of glorifying the Buddha's religion by building a vast temple, the Sabbannu Temple, probably the largest monument in Pagan. During his many travels and campaigns, he built pagodas and temples throughout Myanmar. The faith that Shin Arahan had inspired in Anawratha and his successors continued to inspire Alaungsithu. Shin Arahan, who had seen kings come and go and the flowering of the religion he brought to Pagan, is believed to have died during the reign of King Alaungsithu, in about 1115.

After the death of Alaungsithu, Pagan was thrown into turmoil by violent struggles for the throne. Several kings reigned for short periods and spent most of their time and resources in power struggles. One even succeeded in alienating the great king of Sri Lanka, Parakramabahu, by mistreating his emissaries and breaking the agreements between the two countries. Eventually Parakramabahu invaded Myanmar, devastating towns and villages and killing the king. The new king, Narapati (1174-1210), blessed the country with a period of peace and prosperity. This conducive atmosphere was to allow outstanding scholarship and learning to arise in Pagan.

Kyawswa (1234-50) was a king under whom scholarship was encouraged even more, undoubtedly because the king himself spent most of his time in scholarly pursuits including memorizing passages of the Tipitaka. He had relinquished most of his worldly duties to his son in order to dedicate more time to the study of the scriptures. Two grammatical works, the *Saddabindu* and the *Paramatthabindu*, are ascribed to him. It would appear that his palace was a place of great culture and learning as his ministers and his daughter are credited with scholarly works as well.

During the twelfth century, a sect of forest dwellers also thrived. They were called *arannaka* in Pali and were identical with the previously mentioned Ari of the later chroniclers of Myanmar. This was a monastic movement that only used the yellow robes and the respect due to them in order to follow their own ideas. They indulged in business transactions and owned vast stretches of land. They gave feasts and indulged in the consumption of liquor, and, though they pretended to be practicing the teachings of the Buddha, their practices were probably of a tantric nature. It would appear that they had a considerable amount of influence at the royal court and one of the main exponents of the movement was even given the title of royal teacher. Superstition and magic were gaining dominance once again and Anawratha's and Kyanzitta's empire was slowly sliding into decadence.

The last king of Pagan, Narathihapate, whom the Myanmar know by the name Tayoupyemin (the king who fled the Chinese), repeatedly refused to pay symbolic tribute to the Mongol emperors in Peking who in 1271 had conquered neighbouring Yunnan. He even went so far as to execute ambassadors of the Chinese emperor and their retinue for their lack of deference to the king. He became so bold and blinded by ignorance that he attacked a vassal state of the Mongols. The emperor in Peking was finally forced to send a punitive expedition which defeated the Pagan army north of Pagan. The news of this defeat caused the king and his court to flee to Pathein (Bassein). As the imperial court in Peking was not interested in adding Pagan to its possessions, the Yunnan expedition did not remain in the environs. When the king was later murdered and the whole empire fell into disarray, the Yunnani generals returned, looting Pagan. The territories were divided amongst Shan chiefs who paid tribute to the Mongols.

G.E. Harvey honors the kings of Pagan with the following words:

> *To them the world owes to a great measure the preservation of Theravada Buddhism, one of the purest faiths mankind has ever known. Brahmanism had strangled it in its land of birth; in Sri Lanka its existence was threatened again and again; east of Burma it was not yet free from priestly corruptions; but the kings of Burma never wavered, and at Pagan the stricken faith found a city of refuge.*

Contacts with Sri Lanka and the First Controversies

The contact with Sri Lanka was very important for the growth of the religion in Pagan. As was shown previously, it started with the friendship of Anawratha and Vijayabahu, both of whom fought for Buddhism: Anawratha to establish a new kingdom, Vijayabahu to wrench an old one from the clutches of the Hindu invaders. They supported each other in their struggles and then together re-established the Theravada doctrine in their respective countries, Anawratha sending bhikkhus to Sri Lanka to revive the Sangha, while Vijayabahu reciprocated by sending the sacred texts. The continued contact between the two countries was beneficial to both: many a reform movement, purifying the religion in one country spread to the other as well. Bhikkhus visiting from one country were led to look at their own traditions critically and to reappraise their practice of the Dhamma as preserved in the Pali texts. After the fall of the main Buddhist centers in southern India, centers which had been the main allies of the Mon Theravadins in the south, Sri Lanka was the only ally in the struggle for the survival of the Theravada tradition.

Leading bhikkhus of Pagan undertook the long and difficult journey to Sri Lanka in order to visit the holy temples and study the scriptures as they had been preserved by the Sinhalese Sangha. Shin Arahan's successor as the king's teacher left the royal court for Sri Lanka, returning to Pagan only to die. He was succeeded by a Mon bhikkhu, Uttarajiva, who led a pilgrimage to Sri Lanka in 1171. This was to cause the first upheaval in the Sangha of Pagan. Uttarajiva traveled to Sri Lanka accompanied by Chapada, a novice who remained behind on the island in order to study the scriptures in the Mahavihara, the orthodox monastery of Sri Lanka and the guardian of the Theravada tradition. After ten years, he returned to Pagan accompanied by four elders who had studied with him. The Kalyani inscription, written about three hundred years later, relates that Chapada considered the tradition of the Myanmar bhikkhus impure. He had consequently taken four bhikkhus with him because he needed a chapter of at least five theras in order to ordain new bhikkhus.

It is possible that the Myanmar bhikkhus, who seemed to have formed a group separate from the Mon bhikkhus, had paid more attention to their traditional worship than was beneficial for their practice of the Dhamma. It is also possible that there was an element of nationalist rivalry between the Mon bhikkhus and the Myanmar bhikkhus. As he showed a penchant for the reform movement, the Myanmar king Narapati seems to have accepted the superiority of the Mon bhikkhus, though he did not neglect the other bhikkhus. Chapada and his companions refused to accept the ordination of the Myanmar bhikkhus as legitimate in accordance with Vinaya. They established their own ordination, following which the Myanmar bhikkhus sent a delegation to Sri Lanka to receive the Mahavihara ordination for themselves.

After Chapada's death, the reform movement soon split into two factions, and eventually each of the four remaining bhikkhus went his own way, one of them leaving the order altogether. "Thus in the town of Arimaddana (Pagan) there were four schools... Because the first of these to come was the school of the Elder Arahan from Sudhamma (Thaton) it was called the first school; while the others, because they came later, were called the later schools."

Scholarship in Pagan

It is surprising how quickly a relatively simple people absorbed the great civilization that arrived in their midst so suddenly. Even before the conquest of Thaton, Pagan possessed some ornate religious buildings, which is indicative of the presence of artists and craftsmen. It is quite likely, however, that these were Indians from Bengal and the neighbouring states.

The type of Buddhism that had come to Pagan from India was an esoteric religion, as some old legends indicate. It was the jealously guarded domain of a group of priests, who made no attempt to instruct the people but were happy if their superiority remained unquestioned by a superstitious populace.

The advent of Theravada Buddhism with its openness and its aim to spread understanding must have been quite revolutionary in Pagan and obviously the people were eager to acquire the knowledge offered to them by the bhikkhus. Mabel Bode says in her *Pali Literature of Burma:*

Though the Burmese began their literary history by borrowing from their conquered neighbours, the Talaings (Mon)— and not before the eleventh century — the growth of Pali scholarship among them was so rapid that the epoch following close on this tardy beginning is considered one of the best that Burma has seen.

The principal works of the Pagan period still extant are Pali grammars. The most famous of these is the *Saddaniti,* which Aggavamsa completed in 1154. Uttarajiva gave a copy of this work to the bhikkhus of the Mahavihara in Sri Lanka and it "was received with enthusiastic admiration, and declared superior to any work of the kind written by Sinhalese scholars."

The *Saddaniti* is still used to teach grammar in the monasteries in Myanmar and has been printed many times. B.C. Law regards it as one of the three principal Pali grammars along with the grammars by Kaccayana and Moggallana. K.R. Norman says: "The greatest of extant Pali grammars is the *Saddaniti,* written by Aggavamsa from Arimaddana [Pagan] in Burma..." Aggavamsa was also known as the teacher of King Narapatisithu (1167-1202) and was given the title Aggapandita. Unfortunately, no other works by this author are known today.

The second famous author of Pagan was Saddhammajotipala who has been previously mentioned under his clan name of Chapada. He was a disciple of Uttarajiva and is credited with a great number of works, but in the case of some it is doubtful whether he actually composed them himself or merely introduced them from Sri Lanka. His works deal not only with grammar, but also with questions of monastic discipline (Vinaya) and the Abhidhamma, which in later centuries was to become a favorite subject of Myanmar scholars.

His work on Kaccayana's grammar, the *Suttaniddesa,* formed the foundation of his fame. However, his specialty would appear to have been the study of Abhidhamma, as no less than four noted works of his on the subject attained fame: *Samkhepavannana, Namacaradipani, Matikatthadipani,* and *Patthanagananaya.* According to the Pitaka-thamain, a history of Buddhism in Myanmar, he also devoted a commentary to the *Visuddhimagga* by Buddhaghosa called the *Visuddhimagga-ganthi.* There are no written records that refer to meditation being practiced in Myanmar before this century. However, his interest in the *Visuddhimagga* is indicative of an interest in meditation, if only in the theory rather than in the practice. Another scholar of Pagan, Vimalabuddhi, also wrote a commentary concerning Abhidhamma, the *Abhidhammatthasangahatika,* in addition to another important grammatical work, the *Nyasa,* a commentary on Kaccayana's grammar.

Other grammatical works of some importance were written, but none acquired the standing of Aggavamsa's *Saddaniti.* However, a rather peculiar work worth mentioning is the *Ekakkharakosa* by Saddhammakitti. It is a work on Pali lexicography enumerating words of one letter.

SHAN RULE

Upper Myanmar

After Narathihapate had fled Pagan in fear of the Mongol army, he was never able to re-establish his authority, even though the Mongols supported the Pagan dynasty. The Mongol court in Peking preferred a united neighbouring country under a single ruler, but in spite of its efforts Myanmar was divided into several principalities mainly under Shan tribal leaders. These self-styled princelings paid tribute to the Chinese Mongol court and were nominally its subjects. The Shan, at this time still nomadic tribes in the north, broke into an already destabilized Myanmar like a tidal wave. They penetrated the entire region as far as the Mon country and established themselves as rulers in many towns and cities. The intrigues, fratricidal wars, and murders that make up the history of their courts are innumerable.

A division of the country into Upper and Lower Myanmar is somewhat arbitrary, as, after the fall of Pagan, the two regions were composed of many competing principalities. However, there were the two principle kingdoms of Ava in Upper Myanmar and Pago (Pegu) in Lower Myanmar. Hostilities between these two prevailed, as well as with the neighbouring smaller states including the Shan fiefs of Chiang Mai and Ayutthaya in Thailand. Intrigues within and between courts were rife. Sometimes these claimed victims only within the circle of the powerful and mighty, and sometimes whole towns were looted and destroyed, and their population massacred or carried off into slavery.

But, in spite of politically unsettled conditions, the Sangha survived, because the new rulers, initially somewhat barbaric, soon accepted the religion of their subjects. Just as the Myanmar had adopted the religion and culture of the more refined Mon, so the Shan submitted to the sophisticated civilization of the peoples they subjugated. The Shan initially established their capital at Pinya in Upper Myanmar to the north of Pagan and transferred it to Ava in 1312. Ava was to remain the capital of Upper Myanmar until the eighteenth century.

The *Sasanavamsa* praises Thihathu, the youngest of three Shan brothers who wrested power from the Pagan dynasty in Upper Myanmar, as a Buddhist king who built monasteries and pagodas. He had a bhikkhu as his teacher and supported thousands of bhikkhus in his capital Pinya and later Ava. However, Pagan remained the cultural and religious capital of the region for the whole of the fourteenth century. Scholarly works were composed in its monasteries throughout this period whereas no such works are known to have been written in the new centers of power. The works of this period of scholarship were mostly concerned with Pali grammar.

Two generations later, a descendant of Thihathu secured himself a place in religious history as a great patron of scholarship. As in the courts of some previous kings, his court was also devoted to scholarly learning; and not only bhikkhus, but also the palace officials, produced treatises on religious subjects and the Pali language.

Although the political situation remained unsettled in Upper Myanmar throughout the fifteenth century, in the main, this affected only those in power and their usurpers. Consequently the Sangha appears to have flourished, while the traditional devotion to the support of the Sangha through gifts of the four requisites remained unchanged. The royal court, followed by the leading families, made great donations of monasteries, land, and revenue to the bhikkhus.

In approximately 1440, two Mahatheras from Sri Lanka settled in Ava. Here they joined a group of famous scholars, of whom Ariyavamsa was the most outstanding. The *Sasanavamsa* tells us of his great wisdom and humility in an anecdote.

The elder Ariyavamsa had studied the books of the Abhidhamma Pitaka, but felt he had not gained real understanding. Eventually he came to a bhikkhu in Sagaing who kept his mouth always filled with water in order not to have to engage in meaningless chatter. Ariyavamsa did not talk to "the Elder Water-bearer," as this bhikkhu was known in the Myanmar language, but simply performed the duties of a disciple to his teacher for two days. On the third day, the Venerable Water-bearer spat out the water and asked Ariyavamsa why he was serving him. When Ariyavamsa told him that he wanted to learn from him, the Venerable Water-bearer taught him the *Abhidhammattha-vibhavani-tika,* a subcommentary on the *Abhidhammattha-sangaha.* After two days, Ariyavamsa grasped the meaning and his teacher asked him to write a commentary on this book in order to help others to gain understanding.

During the composition of his first work, Ariyavamsa submitted his writings to the assembled bhikkhus on every Uposatha day, reading out what he had composed and asking his brethren to correct any mistakes they found. On one occasion, a visiting bhikkhu twice made a sound of disapproval during the reading. Ariyavamsa carefully noted the passages where the sound of disapproval had occurred. On reflecting on them in the evening, he found one error of grammar where he had used the wrong gender and also a repetition, an error of style. He approached the bhikkhu who had made the sounds during the reading and out of gratitude for the correction gave him his own outer robe.

Ariyavamsa composed several works in Pali: works on the Abhidhamma, on grammatical subjects, and a study of the Jatakas. But his very important contribution to Buddhism in Myanmar was the fact that all his writing was in the Myanmar vernacular. He was probably the first bhikkhu to write treatises on religious subjects in the local idiom, thus making the religion accessible to a greater number of people. The work by Ariyavamsa still known today is a commentary on the anutika (sub-commentary) of the Abhidhamma.

Towards the end of the fifteenth century, a bhikkhu by the name of Silavamsa composed several epic poems in Pali. They were, of course, of a religious nature dealing with subjects such as the life of the Buddha, or Jataka stories. This genre was later very popular in the Myanmar language and there are many poems relating Jataka stories which were sung by bards throughout the country until recently. In the *Sasanavamsa,* however, Pannasami disapproves of bhikkhus writing or reciting poetry as he considers it to be in breach of the Vinaya rules. He says that because of this, Silavamsa's name was excluded from the Theraparampara, a listing of eminent bhikkhus of Myanmar by ancient chroniclers.

Lower Myanmar

The Mon civilization in Lower Myanmar flourished after Pagan's importance waned, once again reliving the era of glory that it had experienced prior to Anawratha's conquest.

Wareru, the Shan ruler who had established himself in Martaban in 1287, was soon converted to Buddhism. He was a Shan peddler who had astutely wrested power from a son of the last king of Pagan, a son who had revolted against his father and founded an independent kingdom. Under Wareru's rule, scholarship in the Mon monasteries flourished and a code of law was compiled which still forms the foundation of the legal literature of Myanmar. The Mon bhikkhus based this code on ancient Hindu codes of law which had found their way into Mon tradition through Indian colonisers and merchants.

At the beginning of the fourteenth century two respected Mon theras named Buddhavamsa and Mahanaga revived the tradition of their countryman Chapada in making a pilgrimage to Sri Lanka. There, they accepted new ordination in the Mahavihara monastery, the guardian of Sinhalese orthodoxy. The bhikkhus of the Mahavihara asked those ordained in other countries to revert to the lay-state before being re-ordained as novices and full bhikkhus, as it was considered of the utmost importance that the ordination be handed down in an unbroken tradition from the time of the Buddha. This was especially significant in Myanmar where there were some reservations about the continuity of the tradition. By disrobing, a bhikkhu forgoes the seniority he has acquired through the years spent in robes and, in this case, he also states that he considers his former ordination invalid. One can imagine that such a step is not taken lightly but only after careful consideration.

The Great Reformation of the Sangha

King Dhammazedi (1472-92) takes a special place in the history of the religion in Myanmar. He unified the Sangha in the Mon country and purified the order of the bhikkhus. He recorded his great service to the country in the Kalyani inscription, which will be quoted below.

Dhammazedi was a bhikkhu of Mon origin who taught one of the queens at the royal palace in Ava. This lady, Shin Sawbu, was the daughter of the king of Pago. She had been queen to several unfortunate kings of Upper Mynamar and had beeen conveyed into the hands of the subsequent kings along with the throne. She had become disenchanted with the life of a queen and desired to return to her native land. Dhammazedi and a fellow Mon bhikkhu helped her to escape and brought her back to Pago. Eventually she became queen of Pago, but after reigning only a few years she wished to retire and do works of merit. She found that the only people worthy of the throne of Pago were her teachers, the two bhikkhus. She let fate decide which would be the future king by concealing miniature imitations of the regalia in one of the two bowls in which she offered them their daily alms food.

She handed the throne over to Dhammazedi who had received the fateful bowl and spent the rest of her life at Dagon

(Yangon) building the terrace around the Shwedagon Pagoda and gilding the sacred mound. The Shwedagon became what it is today chiefly thanks to Shin Sawbu's munificence.

Dhammazedi assumed government in Pago after leaving the Order of the bhikkhus. He moved the capital closer to the Swemawdaw Pagoda and built several pagodas and shrines. His name is also connected with a collection of wise judgments and the translation of Wareru's Code of Law into the vernacular. In 1472, Dhammazedi sent a mission to Bodhgaya to repair the temple and make plans and drawings of it.

Dhammazedi had received his education in monasteries of Ava which adhered to the Sihala Sangha. The Sihala Sangha was the faction of the Sangha of Myanmar that accepted only the Mahavihara of Sri Lanka as the ultimate authority in religious questions. King Dhammazedi knew from direct experience the state of the Sangha in Lower Myanmar and was determined to improve it. Having lived as a bhikkhu for so many years, he was also singularly qualified to change the Sangha for the better.

He chose twenty-two senior bhikkhus to lead the reform movement and informed them:

Reverend Sirs, the *upasampada* ordination of the bhikkhus of the Mon country now appears to us to be invalid. Therefore, how can the religion, which is based on such invalid ordination, last to the end of 5000 years? Reverend Sirs, from the establishment of the religion in the island of Sri Lanka up to this present day, there has been existing in this island an exceedingly pure sect of bhikkhus... Receive at their hands the *upasampada* ordination... and if you make this form of the *upasampada* ordination the seed of the religion, as it were, plant it, and cause it to sprout forth by conferring such ordination on men of good family in this Mon country... Reverend Sirs, by your going to the island of Sri Lanka, much merit and great advantage will accrue to you.

At the beginning of 1476 the chosen bhikkhus with their twenty-two disciples embarked on the journey to Sri Lanka. They sailed in two ships, one taking about two months while the other needed six full months to arrive on the shore of the Buddhist island. They received the *upasampada* ordination at the Mahavihara from 17th to 20th July 1476. The return journey of the forty-four Mon bhikkhus was not so smooth, however. One group arrived home in August 1476, while the other group took three years to return to Pago and ten of the bhikkhus died en route. Following their return, Dhammazedi had a pure ordination hall*(sima)* consecrated and made the following proclamation:

May all those who possess faith and desire to receive the bhikkhu's ordination at the hands of the bhikkhus ordained in Sri Lanka come to the Kalyani sima and receive ordination. Let those who have not faith and do not desire to receive the bhikkhus ordination of the Sinhalese, remain as they are.

In order to confer the bhikkhu ordination outside the middle country (i.e. northern India), a chapter of five bhikkhus is needed, one of whom must be qualified to serve as preceptor *(upajjhaya)* and another as teacher *(acariya).* The latter two must have spent at least ten years in robes as fully ordained bhikkhus. So if Dhammazedi wanted to have local bhikkhus ordained in the new ordination, it was necessary to find two senior bhikkhus. Since those returning from Sri Lanka had been ordained for a period of only three years, they could not act as preceptor or teacher. Local bhikkhus who had not received the ordination of the Mahavihara in Sri Lanka were unacceptable, as otherwise the ordination would again have been invalidated by one who was not of pure descent. Fortunately, the two theras who had undertaken a pilgrimage to Sri Lanka at the beginning of the century and had received the Sinhalese ordination at that time, were still alive. As a result, one was able to act as preceptor and the other as teacher of the newly ordained bhikkhus. The stage was now set for the reformation and unification of the Mon Order of bhikkhus and soon the re-ordination of almost the entire Order of bhikkhus began. The Kalyani inscription records the number of 15,666 ordinations in hundreds of ordination halls newly constructed for the purpose.

It is interesting to note how forcefully the king reformed the Order through royal decrees that would hardly be tolerated today. He declared that all bhikkhus who were, for example, practicing medicine or other arts and crafts or who even slightly infringed on the Vinaya rules would be expelled. The king as a layman, however, did not have the power to defrock a bhikkhu who had not broken one of the four Parajika rules. Dhammazedi circumvented this by threatening to punish with royal penalties the mother, father, relatives, and lay supporters of bhikkhus whose behavior was not in accordance with the rules of the Vinaya.

It goes without saying that a king who could allow himself to take such drastic measures in regard to the Sangha must have had the support of a broad section of the Order and also the people. After years spent in robes, he was keenly aware of the problems of monastic life and because of this even senior bhikkhus respected and accepted his council. We can assume that all his actions to reform the Order were firstly discussed with his bhikkhu teachers and then implemented with their blessings. There being no such thing as a Buddhist Church with a central authority, the Sangha has little possibility to regulate itself. Only the committed support of a worldly power can protect the Order of bhikkhus from those who take advantage of the respect that is given to the yellow robe.

Dhammazedi's support for the religion was so great that his fame spread well beyond the borders of Myanmar and bhikkhus from neighbouring countries such as Thailand came to his realm to receive ordination there. Though the reform movement did not spread to Upper Myanmar and cause the same mass ordinations there, it did not remain without influence in the kingdom of Ava and other principalities, and many bhikkhus came to the Mon bhikkhus to receive the Kalyani ordination.

THE MYANMAR BUILD AN EMPIRE

Shan versus Myanmar

The beginning of the sixteenth century was one of the most difficult periods for Buddhism in Upper Myanmar. While the religious fervor of Dhammazedi still lived on in the kingdom of Pago in Ava, Shan rulers were endeavoring to bring about the destruction of the Sangha. A Shan king named Thohanbwa (?1527-1543) was particularly well-known for his barbarity. He destroyed pagodas and monasteries and robbed their treasures. Although he was a king, he was uneducated and ignorant.

Hence fearing the influence of the bhikkhus and suspicious of their moves, he brought about the massacre of thousands. Under these terror regimes of the Shan rulers the Myanmar did not feel safe. Many, including learned bhikkhus, fled to Toungoo, the stronghold of the Myanmar race in the south. Despite the anarchy prevailing, some respected treatises on Pali grammar were written in Upper Myanmar in these years.

Better times, however, lay ahead for Buddhism in the Golden Land. Two successive kings of Myanmar origin from Toungoo would unite the country and fulfill the duties of Buddhist kings. The wars fought by these two kings, King Tabinshwehti (1531-50) and King Bayinnaung (1551-81), were long in duration and exceedingly cruel. They succeeded in gaining control of the Mon kingdom in Lower Myanmar and the kingdom of Ava. They conquered all of what is today Myanmar including the Shan states as far east as Chiang Mai, and made incursions into lower Thailand and Yunnan where some kings paid tribute to the Myanmar court.

Bayinnaung deferred to the Mon as far as culture and religion were concerned and dressed in Mon style. Under his royal patronage, the Mon Sangha produced scholarly works on grammar and the Abhidhamma and also helped with the collection and standardisation of a code of law based on the old Mon code compiled during Wareru's reign.

Bayinnaung not only unified the country politically, but also made Buddhist principles the standard for his entire dominion. He forbade the sacrificial slaughter of animals, a custom still practiced by the Shan chiefs, the worshippers of certain spirits, and the followers of some other religions. He built pagodas and monasteries in all the newly conquered lands and installed learned bhikkhus in order to convert the often uncivilized inhabitants to gentler ways. The main religious building of his reign is the Mahazedi Pagoda, a majestic monument to the Buddha in the capital, Pago. He also crowned the main pagodas in Myanmar with the jewels of his own crown, a custom practiced by many rulers of the country. He continued in the tradition of Dhammazedi, in supporting the Sihala Sangha and in sponsoring the ordination of many bhikkhus in the Kalyani Ordination Hall near Pago. It is said that he built as many monasteries as there were years in his life.

It remains a mystery how a king who had such deep devotion to the religion of the Buddha and who was so generous towards it could spend his life fighting campaign after campaign to expand his realm. He caused bloodshed and suffering in the conquered regions and at home people starved because farmers were drafted into the army. However this may be, Bayinnaung seems to have been able to reconcile fighting expansionist wars with being a pious Buddhist.

After King Bayinnaung, Pago rapidly lost its significance. Bayinnaung's son persecuted the Mon and consequently reignited racial tensions that would plague Myanmar for centuries. Later, Pago was to fall into the hands of a Portuguese adventurer who pillaged the pagodas and monasteries. Eventually the whole of Lower Myanmar, already depopulated by the incessant campaigns of Bayinnaung and his successors, was pillaged by all the surrounding kings and princelings. The country was devastated and people starved.

The *Sasanavamsa* records one major problem of the Vinaya during the sixteenth century. At the beginning of the century, the bhikkhus of Toungoo were divided over whether or not bhikkhus could partake of the juice of the toddy palm which was generally used to prepare fermented drink. The dispute was settled by a respected thera who decided that toddy juice was permissible only if it was freshly harvested.

Political Influence of the Sangha in Early Myanmar

What motivated the royal court probably remained largely a mystery to the ordinary citizens, except when they were pressed into service in the king's army. There was little sense of collective responsibility as it is cultivated in today's democracies. Everyone looked after himself and his immediate circle and governments were sometimes more of a scourge than a protection. Kings did not always provide a visible administration beyond appointing governors at whose mercy local people were. These governors often endeavored to establish independence as soon as they perceived inherent weaknesses in their masters. Many accumulated great wealth for themselves.

There was, however, one element in the policy of rulers which, with a few exceptions, remained fairly stable throughout Myanmar history. Most kings supported Buddhism and the Sangha provided a framework of continuity as no other entity could. Ray writes:

They (the kings) were good Buddhists and never did they waver from their kingly duty of acting as the patron-guardian of the faith of the country. Moreover, whatever their numerical strength, the bhikkhus were real spokesmen of the people and the monasteries were the popular assemblies as it were; and each king that came to the throne sought to win the bhikkhus over to his side. The best insurance of a peaceful life in Myanmar was to become a bhikkhu, as they were not drafted into armies or enslaved by conquerors and as long as the lay people had food to eat they were also fed. The bhikkhus not only provided a link between the people and those in power, they often played a role in the affairs of state. This is illustrated by an event which occurred in the middle of the seventeenth century and is related by the *Sasanavamsa.*

The king, Ukkamsika, popularly known as King Thalun, was a devoted Buddhist and thanks to him, learning flourished in Myanmar. The king's son, however, tried to dethrone his father, and Thalun, taken by surprise, had to flee accompanied only by two companions. Coming upon a river, the only vessel in sight was the boat of a samanera. The samanera agreed to take them onboard as passengers, and they ended up in the samanera's monastery where they revealed their true identities and asked for protection from their persecutors. They were referred to another monastery where lived a bhikkhu wise in worldly affairs. Following his advice, the bhikkhus formed a living wall around the monastery and, as no Buddhist will attack a man in robes, the rebels who had come to kill the king had to withdraw. Another example of the beneficial influence of the Sangha is their appeal for clemency to King Bayinnaung. Bhikkhus often tried to stay executions in accordance with the principles of *metta* (loving kindness) and *karuna* (compassion) and sometimes their efforts achieved success.

During one of Bayinnaung's Thai campaigns, the peasantry around Pago revolted and razed the royal city to the ground. Bayinnaung, after hurrying back from Ayutthaya, captured several thousand rebels and was ready to burn them alive. It was the custom then to burn deserters from the army alive and obviously rebellion was considered to be a crime of similar gravity. The bhikkhus of all races intervened on behalf of the poor wretches and were able to save all from the pyre, except for seventy ring leaders, the most serious offenders.

There are several instances in Myanmar history when bhikkhus also mediated between contending kings or princes and helped to avoid bloodshed. This was often the case when cities were besieged and both parties realised that they could not win. The king who was besieged would normally take the initiative and send his bhikkhus to the king in attack. Often the bhikkhus were authorized to negotiate on behalf of the monarch. An armistice agreed by or in the presence of bhikkhus was more likely to be honored than a promise given without their blessings. Therefore, if the two parties were sincere in their offers to negotiate, they usually requested bhikkhus to be mediators and judges.

The Spread of Abhidhamma

The seventeenth century was a period of dynamic growth in the history of Buddhism in Myanmar. Many outstanding developments took place, and principal among these were the numerous translations of texts into the Myanmar language and the great increase in the study of the Abhidhamma. It is quite possible that the two developments were inter-connected.

In the first half of the century, Manirathana Thera translated the following texts into the Myanmar language: *Atthasalini, Sammohavinodani, Kankhavitarani, Abhidhammatthavibhavini, Sankhepavannana.* Of these five, only the *Kankhavitarani,* Buddhaghosa's commentary on the Patimokkha, is not concerned with Abhidhamma. In the second half of the century Aggadhammalankara translated Kaccayana's Pali grammar, the *Abhidhammatthasangaha, Matika, Dhatukatha, Yamaka,* and the *Patthana* into the Myanmar tongue. Later, the *Nettippakarana* was also translated.

It cannot be a coincidence that nine out of twelve translated works were texts of the Abhidhamma or its commentaries. The reason for these translations must have been a developing interest in the psychology of Buddhism among the Buddhist followers who could not themselves read Pali. Whether these were only bhikkhus or whether lay people were also interested in exploring the scriptures for themselves is difficult to determine now. However, what is known is that almost every boy and many of the girls attended monastic schools, whose curriculum was probably established by this period, if not earlier. Included in the curriculum were studies of the Mangala Sutta, Metta Sutta, Ratana Sutta, and the other parittas, as well as basic literacy which included some Pali. In addition a number of the Abhidhamma texts had to be committed to memory.

The intention behind these translations and commentaries in the Myanmar language was obviously to make the words of the Buddha accessible to a wider audience who would, then, not be solely dependent on the authority of the Pali scholars.

In the later half of the century, the bhikkhu Devacakkhobhasa designed a system for the study and teaching of the *Patthana,* the last book of the Abhidhamma, which in Myanmar is believed to be the highest teaching of the Buddha. The king at the time of Devacakkhobhasa was so impressed by the bhikkhu's proficiency in these higher teachings and by his system of instruction, that he ordered the *Patthana* to be studied in all the monasteries of Myanmar. It is not unreasonable to assume that the king himself studied these teachings. Otherwise he would hardly have been in a position to appreciate them and make them compulsory reading for the Myanmar bhikkhus.

This emphasis on Abhidhamma in general and the *Patthana* in particular has survived in Myanmar to the present day. The movement, therefore, that began in the seventeenth century is still of great significance for Buddhism there. The *Patthana,* for instance, is ubiquitous in Myanmar.

The twenty-four conditions of the *Patthana* can be found printed on the fans of the bhikkhus, on calendars, and on posters. In some monasteries, the bhikkhus are woken every morning by twenty-four strokes on a hollow tree trunk, while the bhikkhu striking the tree trunk has to recite the twenty-four conditions as he does so. Even little children learn to recite the twenty-four conditions along with the suttas of protection. As the *Patthana* is the highest and most difficult teaching of the Buddha, it is believed that it will be the first to be lost. In order to slow the decline of the Sasana, many people of Myanmar, bhikkhus and lay people alike, memorize the *Patthana* and recite it daily.

In Pagan, the Jataka stories and the history of the Buddha's life were the main subjects of religious study. In later centuries, Pali grammar and the study of the Vinaya were foremost on the agenda. Dhammazedi's reform movement drew the attention back to the foundations of all monastic life, the code of conduct for the bhikkhus as laid down by the Buddha himself.

Though stricter observation of the Vinaya would have to be re-emphasised in the future, its foundation was firm enough to insure that progressive reform movements would be instigated within the Sangha and not be dependent on external impetus. How far a bhikkhu was allowed to stray from the ideal had been defined in strictures that had become integral to the Sangha. Based on this foundation of *sila* (right conduct, morality), the Sangha was now free to give increased attention to higher teachings.

The age of the Abhidhamma had dawned. The Abhidhamma remained no longer the domain of a chosen few, but began to be studied by many. The wealth of translations from the Abhidhamma would suggest that in the seventeenth century it had become so popular that it may have been taught even to lay people. The Myanmar language had developed and had been enriched with Pali terms so that it could convey the difficult concepts of Abhidhamma. civilization had matured to an extent never seen before. Myanmar was ready to study the analysis of mind and matter as taught by the Buddha. The stage was being set for the widespread practice of insight meditation *(vipassana bhavana)* in later times.

THE EIGHTEENTH AND NINETEENTH CENTURIES

In the succession of rulers of the eighteenth century some were strong and despotic, while others were ineffective and withdrawn. Some tried to expand their power and fought wars, while others appeared satisfied with existing conditions. There were several wars with Thailand and the population of Myanmar had to bear the deprivations that war invariably brings not only to the conquered, but also to the country where the conquering armies are levied. After a war between the Mon and the Myanmar in which the Mon initially attacked and then conquered Ava itself, the Myanmar king Alaungpaya (1752-60), who believed himself a Bodhisatta, crushed Mon resistance once and for all. After Pago had fallen into his hands in 1756, Lower Myanmar was devastated and many of the Mon survivors fled to Thailand or were deported as slaves.

Like Bayinnaung, Alaungpaya established a Myanmar empire, at the same time decimating the population of the country by drafting the peasantry into the army for campaigns against Ayutthaya (Thailand) and other countries. The *Sasanavamsa* does not comment on the atrocity of war. War is perceived as it is, cruel and pitiless — but it is the affair of rulers, not of bhikkhus. The manner in which rulers conduct their affairs is entirely their responsibility. Pannasami probably took very seriously the Buddha's injunction that a member of the Sangha should not talk about rulers and royal affairs.

The *Sasanavamsa* pays much attention to a controversy which raged in monastic circles throughout the eighteenth century. At the beginning of the century, some bhikkhus began to wear their robes outside the monasteries as they were worn within them, that is, covering only one shoulder. Even when going on their daily alms round, they failed to drape the robe in the traditional way. When challenged as to the orthodoxy of this practice, they produced various interpretations and opinions, but could not validate their practice through the authority of the scriptures. Different kings endorsed one or other of the two opinions and bhikkhus of the orthodox school even died for their conviction when a king had outlawed the covering of both shoulders.

The most interesting aspect of this historical period of the religion is not so much the actual controversy as the power the king had in religious affairs. The kings of Myanmar were not normally expert in the Vinaya and yet they took the final decision in matters of monastic discipline after due consultation with the leaders of the Sangha. In the more than one hundred years that this controversy prevailed, different kings supported the orthodcxy of either view. This shows that this system is not entirely satisfactory. However, the right view which was in accordance with the Vinaya did eventually triumph due to the persistence of the majority of the Sangha. Only the worldly power was in a position to regulate the Sangha into which undesirable elements entered repeatedly. To keep the Order pure, it had to be always under careful scrutiny and bogus ascetics had to be removed. The kings of Myanmar in co-operation with the Sangharajas and the other senior bhikkhus had established a system of supervision of the bhikkhus by royal officials. In every township, the king's representatives were responsible for ensuring that the bhikkhus adhered scrupulously to the rules of the Vinaya. Bhikkhus who transgressed were taken before religious courts and punished according to the code of discipline.

The controversy concerning the correct manner of wearing the robes came up for arbitration for the last time under Bodawpaya (1782-1819), the fifth son of Alaungpaya. He decided in favor of orthodoxy and thenceforth all bhikkhus had to cover both shoulders on the daily alms round. This ruling created one unified sect throughout Myanmar under the leadership of a council of senior bhikkhus appointed by the king. These were called the Thudhamma Sayadaws and the Thudhamma sect has survived in Myanmar down to the present day.

Bodawpaya appointed a chapter of eight eminent bhikkhus as Sangharajas, leaders of the Sangha, and charged them with the duty to safeguard the purity of the Order of bhikkhus. As a direct result of the discipline and stability created by the work of these senior bhikkhus, the Sangha prospered, and consequently scholarship flourished under Bodawpaya's reign.

The name of the Mahasangharaja Nanabhivamsa is especially noteworthy in this respect. Nanabhivamsa was an eminently learned bhikkhu who had proven his wisdom even as a young man. Only five years after his ordination as a bhikkhu, he had completed a commentary *(tika)* on the *Nettippakarana*. Eight years after full ordination, at the age of twenty-eight, he became Sangharaja, and then Mahasangharaja, the title conferred by the king on the highest bhikkhu in his realm. Soon after this, he wrote his well respected "new sub-commentary" on the Digha Nikaya, the *Sadhujjanavilasini*. At the request of the king, he wrote a commentary on Buddhaghosa's *Jatakatthakatha* and several other treatises.

The king was so devoted to the head of the Sangha that he dedicated a "very magnificent five storied monastery" to him and later many other monasteries as well. According to the *Sasanavamsa,* Nanabhivamsa was not only a scholar, but also practiced the ascetic practices *(dhutanga)* sitting always alone. He divided his time between the various monasteries under his tutelage and was an indefatigable teacher of the scriptures.

Scholarship flourished in the reign of King Bodawpaya and Myanmar was able, for the first time, to return thanks to Sri Lanka for nurturing the religion in the Golden Land. The bhikkhu ordination *(upasampada)* preserved in Myanmar was re-introduced to Sri Lanka where the Sasana had been interferred with by an unwise king.

The Amarapura Nikaya in Sri Lanka

In the later half of the eighteenth century, the *upasampada* ordination in Sri Lanka was barred to all except the members of the landed aristocracy. This was a result of royal decree probably issued with the support of at least a section of the Sangha. However, this was a flagrant defilement of the letter and the spirit of the Buddha's instructions. The conferring of the *upasampada* ordination is dependent only upon such conditions as the candidate being a man, free from government service, free of debt, free of contagious diseases, and upon his having his parents' consent, etc. Members of the lower castes had now only the possibility of becoming novices (samanera), a condition that created dissatisfaction. A sizeable section of ordained bhikkhus also disapproved of the royal order, but were in no position to defy it within the country. The only recourse for those of the lower castes desiring the higher ordination was therefore to travel to other Buddhist countries to ordain. At first, missions were sent to Thailand where Dhammazedi's reforms lived on through the ordination conferred to Thai bhikkhus in Pago and through the scores of Mon bhikkhus who had found refuge in Thailand from the Myanmar armies.

At the beginning of the nineteenth century, however, Sinhalese bhikkhus began traveling to Myanmar to find the pure ordination there. The fame of the then Mahasangharaja of Myanmar, Nanabhivamsa, influenced their choice.

Scholarship had developed in all fields: Pali grammar, the Vinaya, the Suttanta, and the Abhidhamma. Myanmar had, after a long period of development, become the custodian of Buddhism.

The first delegation from Sri Lanka arrived in 1800 and was welcomed with a magnificent reception by King Bodawpaya himself. Nanabhivamsa, the wise Sangharaja, ordained the samaneras as bhikkhus and instructed them for some time in the scriptures. On returning to Sri Lanka, they were accompanied by five Myanmar bhikkhus and a letter from Nanabhivamsa to the Sinhalese Sangharaja. Five bhikkhus form a full chapter and apparently the Myanmar bhikkhus were permitted to ordain bhikkhus without class distinction. Even today, Sri Lanka possesses three schools, the Amarapura Nikaya, the Siyama Nikaya (Thai school), and the Ramanna Nikaya.

The Amarapura Nikaya was so called because King Bodawpaya had established his capital in Amarapura (between Mandalay and Ava) and the bhikkhus had received their ordination there. The Ramanna Nikaya was presumably founded by bhikkhus who had received ordination from Mon bhikkhus in the tradition of the Dhammazedi reforms and who had fled to southern Thailand from the wrath of the Myanmar kings. Both these schools were allowed to ordain bhikkhus without discriminating against the lower classes. Only the Siyama Sangha (the Thai ordination) continued to follow the royal command, and ordained only novices of the higher castes as bhikkhus. Missions from Sri Lanka continued to travel to Amarapura to consult with its senior theras and they were all given royal patronage and sent back with gifts of the Pali scriptures and commentarial texts.

Bodawpaya's Relationship with the Sangha

Although King Bodawpaya would appear to have been a pious and devout king, his relationship with the Sangha was somewhat problematic. He supported it at times and even used it to extend his own glory, but at times he seemed almost jealous of the respect the bhikkhus received from the people. He realised that the bhikkhus were not respected out of fear, but were held in genuine esteem and affection by his subjects.

His jealousy became apparent on different occasions. At one time, he declared that from then on the bhikkhus were no longer to be addressed by the traditional title "Hpoungyi" meaning "The One of Great Merit." This form of address was to be reserved for the king. Then again he tried to confiscate land and other goods given to the Sangha and to pagodas by previous generations. When the Sangharajas could not answer his questions to his satisfaction, he invited the Muslim clergy for a meal to test their faith. He had heard that they were so strict in the observance of their discipline that they would rather die than eat pork. Unfortunately for them, they did not display great heroism as they all ate the pork offered to them by the king. Bodawpaya is also reputed to have been beset by a form of megalomania. He wanted to force the Sangha to confirm officially that he was the Bodhisatta of the next Buddha to come in this world cycle, the Buddha Metteyya. On this issue, however, the Sangha was not to be bent even in the face of royal wrath. The bhikkhus refused, and the king was finally forced to accept defeat. Another expression of his inflated self-esteem was the Mingun Pagoda near Sagaing. It was to be by far the biggest temple ever built. Scores of slaves and laborers worked on its construction until funds were depleted. However, it was never completed and remains today as a huge shapeless square of millions of bricks.

To his credit, King Bodawpaya imposed the morality of the Five Precepts in his whole realm and had offenders executed immediately. Capital punishment was prescribed for selling and drinking alcohol, killing larger animals such as buffaloes, spreading heretical views, and the smoking of opium. Bodawpaya ruled the country with an iron fist and brought offending lay people as well as bhikkhus to heel. His successors were benevolent, but possibly they could be so only because of the fear his rule had instilled in the populace.

The Fate of Buddhism in Upper and Lower Myanmar

Bodawpaya's successor, Bagyidaw (1819-1837), was the first of the Myanmar kings to lose territory to the white invaders coming from the West. The Myanmar court was so out of touch with the modern world that it still believed Myanmar to be the center of the world and her army virtually invincible. Hence the king was not unduly disturbed when the British raj, governing the Indian sub-continent, declared war on the Kingdom of Ava in 1824 (Bagyidaw had moved the capital back to Ava). It came to a battle near the coast in which the Myanmar general Mahabandhula achieved little or nothing against modern British arms. The Indian colonial government occupied all of the Myanmar coast as far south as Tenasserim in 1826 and forced the treaty of Yandabo on King Bagyidaw. In the treaty, he was forced to accept the new borders established by the Indian government and pay compensation to the invaders for the annexation of the coast of Lower Myanmar.

However, Bagyidaw made a very important contribution to the development of the Sangha and to the literature of Myanmar in general. His predecessor, Bodawpaya, had united the Sangha by resolving the dispute relating to the draping of the robe over one or two shoulders. Bagyidaw saw the necessity of creating stability for the Sangha. He felt that this could be achieved to some extent by bestowing on it a sense of its own history. He commissioned a work on the history of the religion starting from the time of the Buddha, which was to show an unbroken succession of the pure tradition from teacher to pupil. Its purpose was to praise the diligent theras and expose the shameless ones.

This work, the *Thathana-lin-ga-ya-kyan,* was composed at the king's request by the ex-bhikkhu Mahadhamma-thin-gyan, a leading member of the committee appointed by King Bagyidaw to compile the famous *Hman-nan-ya-za-win, The Glass-palace Chronicle,* a secular history of Myanmar. The *Thathana-wun-tha (Sasanavamsa)-lin-ga-ya-kyan* was completed in 1831; and in 1897, it was printed in the form of a modern book for the first time in Yangon. Pannasami based his *Sasanavamsa* on this work. About forty percent of the *Sasanavamsa* is straight translation from the original work, about forty percent summaries and paraphrasing of the latter, and only some twenty percent Pannasami's own work. Pannasami states in his introduction to the *Sasanavamsa* that his treatise is based on the works of the ancients *(porana).* The concept of mental property or copyright had not been born and there was no moral need to refer the reader to sources except to give authority to a statement. The only references that would lend authority to a treatise would be the scriptures, their commentaries, and sub-commentaries, but not a work as recent as the *Thathana-wuntha-lin-ga-ya-kyan*.

The preface to the original work in Myanmar explains the reason for its compilation. The king's representative had many times pleaded with the author to write a history of the succession of [righteous] religious teachers so that the people would not become heretical. Apparently the king felt that the lack of a work recording the history of the pure religion in its entirety left scope for wrong views to arise. But with an authoritative record of the lineage of teachers, bhikkhus could not call on views of shameless bhikkhus of the past anymore in order to support their heresies. This is exactly what had happened again and again through the centuries and especially in the robe-draping dispute. The *ekamsikas,* the one-shoulder-drapers, had repeatedly dug out obscure teachers in order to support their point of view. This was to be made impossible once and for all.

Whether this has been successful is difficult to ascertain without a detailed study of the developments in the Sangha since the publication of this work. However, the fact that the original Myanmar chronicle was revised and translated into Pali for the Fifth Buddhist Council indicates that it was by this time considered a useful tool to put the king's authority behind a well-defined orthodox lineage, thus making it easy to refute heresy by referring to the historical teachers.

Tharrawaddy-Min

King Bagyidaw never overcame his shock over the loss of part of his realm. He was declared insane and was removed from the throne by Tharawaddy-Min (1837-1846), King Mindon's father.

In the reign of Tharrawaddy-Min, another mission from Sri Lanka visited Myanmar and was received by the Sangharaja Neyyadhammabhivamsa. Neyyadhamma instructed the two bhikkhus and the accompanying novice in the teachings and conferred the bhikkhu ordination on the novice. He is known for his critical emendation of the text of the *Saddhammapajjotika* and its translation into Myanmar. He was also the teacher of the later Sangharaja Pannasami, the compiler of the *Sasanavamsa* and one of the most influential theras at the time of King Mindon. Neyyadhamma showed the need for a recension of at least some of the Pali texts by editing the *Saddhammapajjotika*. His disciple, Pannasami, was to preside over the recension of the entire Tipitaka as Sangharaja under King Mindon.

Pagan-Min

Tharrawaddy-Min was himself deposed because of insanity by his son Pagan-Min (1846-52), the brother of Mindon-Min. Pagan-Min appointed Pannajotabhidhaja as his Sangharaja. In his tenure, scholarship received encouragement as the Sangharaja himself wrote a commentary and its sub-commentary in Myanmar on the Anguttara Nikaya. Other works of the time, all in the vernacular, are a translation of the *Saddhammavilasini* and commentaries on the Samyutta Nikaya and the Digha Nikaya. This is also the time when the author of the *Sasanavamsa* appears. He started his scholarly career with the translation into Myanmar of a commentary on the *Saddatthabhedacinta*. His next work was a comparison of the existing versions of the *Abhidhanappadipika* and the translation of his emended text.

In accord with the pre-eminence Myanmar had achieved in the Theravada Buddhist world, the kings of the country became less fierce and wars were fewer. The successors of Bodawpaya seem to have shown a genuine interest in religion as well as in improving the administration of the country. Upper Myanmar moved into a period of peace, which meant improved conditions for the bhikkhus.

The first half of the nineteenth century saw the translation of many Pali texts into the Myanmar language. Almost the whole of the Suttanta was now available in the vernacular and many commentaries and sub-commentaries on Suttanta, Abhidhamma, and the Vinaya were composed in it. This not only made it easier for bhikkhus with limited linguistic skills to study the texts, but also made them readily accessible to the laity. That people in a peaceful country have more time for the study of religion is obvious and soon Myanmar would see the first Buddhist texts printed on modern printing presses. This made it possible for a great number of people to acquire texts relatively cheaply without having to pay a scribe to copy them laboriously onto palm leaves.

Politically Pagan-Min was no luckier than Bagyidaw, as he lost the provinces of Pathein (Bassein) and Yangon (Rangoon) to the British, who were ever ready to create some pretext for war. So, in 1852, the Kingdom of Ava lost access to the sea and became increasingly dependent on the colonial power. Like his father, Pagan-Min was overthrown in a palace revolt. Although not a leader of the uprising, his brother Mindon was placed on the throne. He did not execute the deposed king as was usually the case after a revolt, but allowed him to end his days in dignity.

The Colonial Administration and the Sangha

The occupation by the British forces was of utmost significance for the Sangha as the British administration did not grant the traditional protection afforded it by a Buddhist ruler. In accordance with the colonial policy established in India, that the colonial government should be strictly secular, the new lords refused to take on the role of a Buddhist monarch and accept responsibility for the enforcing of the bhikkhus' discipline. Without this, Buddhism in Lower Myanmar soon suffered and offending bhikkhus went unpunished. The colonial administration would recognise its mistake only much later, when it was too late, and when they were not able to establish control in the Sangha any longer.

King Mindon

Even today King Mindon's reign (1852-1877) is surrounded by the mystique of a golden era in the minds of the Myanmar people. No war occurred during the twenty-five years of his tenure and the king himself is said to have been of gentle disposition and adverse to violence. He even declared a dislike for capital punishment which was customarily inflicted by sovereigns for the slightest disobedience or even disagreement. He was not only held in esteem by his subjects, but even praised by a British envoy.

The colonisers' comments on the Myanmar and their kings were usually dictated by a parochial narrow-mindedness and a simplistic view that was only widened by contact with the conquered. Therefore General Fytche's words describing King Mindon are all the more impressive: "Doubtless one of the most enlightened monarchs that has ever sat on the Burmese throne. He is polished in his manner, has considerable knowledge of the affairs of state and the history and the statistics of his own and other countries. In personal character he is amiable and kind and, according to his light, religious."

King Mindon transferred the capital from Ava to Mandalay, the last royal capital before the British annexation of the whole of Myanmar in 1886. In the early years of his reign, Mindon strove to improve monastic discipline. Although a system of official investigation of complaints relating to bhikkhus' misdemeanours existed, each king had to take his own initiative in re-establishing order in the Sangha.

Mindon found that the attitude of many members of the Sangha to their code of conduct was exceedingly lax. He therefore wanted all bhikkhus of his dominions to take a vow of obedience to the Vinaya rules in front of a Buddha image.

He consulted the Sangharaja who convened an assembly of mahatheras, the Thudhamma Council. As opinions regarding the vow differed, the primate's disciple, Pannasami, had to deliver a religious address in support of the king's views. He reasoned that vows were also taken by the bhikkhus at the time of ordination and that if the king sincerely desired to improve the discipline in the Order, he should be supported. All agreed, and the vow was prescribed.

The greatest challenge King Mindon had to face as a Buddhist monarch was undoubtedly his duty to look after the spiritual welfare of his subjects not only in his own dominions, but also in the parts of Myanmar occupied by the British. Moreover, he and many of the leading sayadaws of his court were increasingly aware that the British were only waiting for an occasion to annex the whole of Myanmar.

Mindon's army clearly would not be able to stand up to the might of the Indian colonial government. Therefore, it was not only important to support religious activities in the occupied territories but it was also essential to prepare the religion for the time when it would have to survive without the support of a Buddhist monarch. The British had made it clear at the outset that they would not take over the traditional role of the Myanmar kings, that of protector of the Sasana. The new masters' religion, Christianity, rapidly gained influence through the missionary schools.

The schools were popular because their education provided much assistance in securing a job and favor with the colonisers. Christian religious education was a compulsory part of their curriculum.

After the conquest of Lower Myanmar, many bhikkhus had fled north in order to remain within the jurisdiction of the Myanmar kings. Many monasteries in British Myanmar were left without an incumbent and whole villages were therefore bereft of the opportunity to receive religious and general education.

King Mindon, aware of this situation, tried to convince bhikkhus to return to Lower Myanmar in order to serve their people. The king's efforts proved successful and many bhikkhus returned to their places of origin. But soon it became clear that without the king's ecclesiastic officials to control the discipline of the Sangha, many bhikkhus developed a careless attitude towards their code of discipline.

The Okpo Sayadaw, from Okpo between Yangon and Pago, had stopped many bhikkhus on their way to Upper Myanmar when the movements of bhikkhus out of the conquered territories was at its peak around 1855. He assembled the bhikkhus around himself teaching that the Sangha needed no protection from the secular power if it observed the rules of the Vinaya strictly. His monastery was the birth place of a movement of strict monastic discipline.

He also emphasised that mental volition was what really mattered in the religion of the Buddha and that acts of worship done with an impure intention were worthless. He obviously felt that much of the Buddhist practice had become a ritual and that the essence had been lost. In addition to this, however, his movement also challenged the authority of the king's Council of Sayadaws, the leaders of the unified Thudhamma sect, when he declared their ordination was invalid due to a technicality.

As a result, he took the higher ordination anew together with his followers.

The Okpo Sayadaw was not the only critic of the Thudhamma sayadaws. In Upper Myanmar, the Ngettwin Sayadaw criticized many religious practices and maintained that a radical reassesment of religious teachings was necessary. The Ngettwin Sayadaw was also a source of inspiration for the Okpo Sayadaw and other reformers.

He had been the teacher of Mindon's chief queen and had also advised the king on many occasions. Interestingly, he was a driving force in a movement in Upper Myanmar that wanted to return to the fundamentals of the religion, but more radically than the Okpo Sayadaw.

The Ngettwin Sayadaw, together with many other bhikkhus, left the royal city and went to live in the forest near Sagaing. He started to preach that meditation was essential for all bhikkhus and he required an aspirant to novicehood to prove that he had practiced meditation before he would ordain him. All the bhikkhus around him had to spend a period of the day in meditation and he emphasised that meditation was of much greater importance than learning.

He advised lay people to stop making offerings of flowers, fruits, and candles to Buddha images, but to meditate regularly on the Uposatha days. Of course, his instructions that offerings to Buddha images were fruitless and merely dirtied the places of worship, caused considerable unhappiness with the traditional Thudhamma Council and presumably with many ordinary people.

However, the Ngettwin Sayadaw never strove to form a different sect by holding a separate ordination as did the Okpo Sayadaw. His reforms were within the community and within a Buddhist society that was presided over by a king. The Okpo Sayadaw had no place for royalty in his view of the world and did not hesitate to confront the system that was still alive, though obviously doomed.

Two other important sayadaws of King Mindon's reign deserve mention: the Shwegyin Sayadaw and the Thingazar Sayadaw. The Shwegyin Sayadawalso tried to reform the

Sangha and his movement is still very much alive and highly respected in Myanmar today. He had studied under the Okpo Sayadaw, but when he returned to his native Shwegyin near Shwebo in Upper Myanmar, he avoided controversy in never rebelling against the Thudhamma Council.

He introduced two new rules for his bhikkhus, that they must not chew betel and consume tobacco after noon. He also maintained that the Sangha must regulate itself without help from the authority, but he never doubted the validity of the traditional ordination ceremony.

The Thingazar Sayadaw was one of the most popular of the great sayadaws of his time. He was also part of the movement to return to the basics of the teachings and greatly emphasised the importance of practice as opposed to mere scholarship. Though he was greatly honored by the king and made a member of the Thudhamma Council, he preferred spending long periods in solitude in the forest. In the numerous monasteries built for him by the royal family and the nobility of the country, he insisted on the practice of the purest of conduct in accordance with the Vinaya. However, he did not involve himself in disputes with the extreme reformers or the Thudhamma council. He became very popular through the humorous tales he told in sermons preached in his frequent travels up and down the country.

King Mindon had no easy task. One section of the Sangha was pressing for far reaching reforms, yet it was the king's duty to maintain a certain continuity of the traditional ways for the benefit of the people in general. What complicated the situation was the fact that the Sangha of Lower Myanmar felt more and more independent of the Buddhist monarch and his Thudhamma council of senior mahatheras.

This is illustrated graphically by the Okpo Sayadaw's declaration that the Sangha needed no regulation by the worldly power. This view gained popularity also in Upper Myanmar. Luckily, King Mindon's devotion to Buddhism was genuine and he was not deterred by the difficulties confronting him. He was determined not to allow the Sangha to split into factions that were openly opposing each other. This he achieved to some extent through careful diplomacy and through the calling of a great Synod, a Sangayana, in the royal city of Mandalay.

The Sangayana, or Buddhist Council, is the most important function of the Buddhist religion. The first Sangayana was held during the first Rains Retreat after the Parinibbana of the Buddha; the texts to be regarded as authentic were determined at this time.

There had been three more Sangayanas since, according to the Theravada tradition. The council convened by the great Emperor Asoka, whose missionaries brought Buddhism to Myanmar, probably provided the most inspiration for Mindon. The Fourth Council, the one prior to Mindon's council, was held in Sri Lanka in the first century BC, at the Aluvihara near Matale, for the purpose of writing down the Tipitaka, which up to that time had been passed on orally.

King Mindon himself presided over the Fifth Buddhist Council, during which all the canonical texts were recited and the correct form was established from among any variant readings. The task took more than three years to accomplish, from 1868 to 1871.

When the bhikkhus had completed their great project, the king had all of the Buddhist scriptures, the Tipitaka, engraved on 729 marble slabs. The slabs were then housed each in a separate small pagoda about three meters high with a roof to protect the inscriptions from the elements. The small shrines were built around a central pagoda, the Kutho-daw Pagoda, the Pagoda of the Noble Merit. To commemorate the great council, King Mindon crowned the Shwedagon Pagoda in Yangon with a new Hti or spire.

The Fifth Buddhist Council and the crowning of the Shwedagon Pagoda reminded all the people of Myanmar of the importance of their religion, as well as of the fact that the king and the Thudhamma Council of senior monks were still the guardians of the Sasana. The authority of the Thudhamma Council was greatly enhanced also in Lower Myanmar through the synod. Although the British had not allowed King Mindon to attend the raising of the new spire onto the Shwedagon, the crowning was a symbol of the religious unity of Myanmar which persisted in spite of the British occupation. The religion was also later to become the rallying point for the Myanmar nationalists who fought for independence from the colonisers.

King Mindon's reign produced a number of scholarly works as well as translations from the Pali. Neyyadhamma, the royal preceptor, himself wrote a sub-commentary on the Majjhima Nikaya, which had been translated by one of his disciples under his guidance. A commentary in Myanmar on the Pali Jatakas was composed by Medhavivamsa and the compiler of the *Sasanavamsa,* Pannasami, put his name to a great number of works.

One of the queens of King Mindon requested Pannasami to write the *Silakatha* and the *Upayakatha*. His teacher asked him to compose the *Voharatthabheda, Vivadavinicchaya, Nagarajuppattikatha.*

He also wrote a commentary on Aggavamsa's *Saddaniti.* Whether all these works were composed by Pannasami or whether they were composed under his supervision and control is difficult to assess. It is interesting to note that a majority of his works were composed in Pali, which was no doubt an attempt to encourage bhikkhus not to forgo Pali scholarship now that Myanmar translations were readily available. The calling of a great Buddhist council to purify the scriptures was part of this movement towards the revival of the study of the original texts.

During King Mindon's reign bhikkhus from Sri Lanka came to Mandalay on several occasions to solve difficult questions of Vinaya and to receive the bhikkhu ordination in Myanmar. After Mindon's death in 1877, his son Thibaw ascended the throne. He was weak and of feeble intellect, and his reign was short. In 1886, he lost his kingdom to the British empire and was exiled to India.

With the complete annexation of Myanmar by the British, a historical era came to an end. Theravada Buddhism developed in Myanmar over more than two millennia. The visits of the Buddha were the first brief illuminations in a country that was shrouded in darkness. The worship of the Buddha that is thought to have resulted from these visits and from the arrival of the hair relics, may have been merely part of a nature religion. The pure religion could not endure for long in a country which was yet on the brink of civilization. Later, however, the teachings of the Buddha were brought repeatedly to those lands by various people.

The visits of the Arahats sent out after Emperor Asoka's council are historically more acceptable than the visits of the Buddha. Their teachings were understood and perpetuated possibly in Indian settlements along the coast and later in communities of people from central Asia such as the Pyu. Through their contact with India, these cultural centers of the Pyu and Mon could remain in contact with Buddhism. At first the important centers of Theravada Buddhism were in northern India and later in South India and then Sri Lanka. Through repeated contact with orthodox bhikkhus abroad, the understanding of Buddhism grew ever stronger in the minds of the people of Myanmar. The religion was distorted dozens of times through ignorance and carelessness, but someone always appeared to correct the teachings with the help of the mainstays of the Sasana abroad. Gradually the role was reversed: instead of traveling abroad for advice, the bhikkhus of Myanmar became the guardians of Theravada Buddhist teaching and their authority was respected by all. Eventually, when Theravada Buddhism had long been lost to India and its future was uncertain in Sri Lanka, it found a secure home in Southeast Asia, especially in Myanmar.

4

BUDDHISM IN SRI LANKA

Buddhism was introduced to Sri Lanka in 236 b.e. (cir. 250 BCE) and became the national religion of the Sinhalese from that date. It is, however, necessary for a proper study of the history of Buddhism in the island to consider the state of the island and its social and political developments and the culture and character of the people immediately preceding this period. This will enable us to get a clear understanding of the manner in which such a far-reaching revolution in the beliefs, manners, customs and character of a people was effected by the introduction of this new religion and the progress in literature, art and culture that has been manifested through its influence.

Early Traditions

According to the early chronicles relating the historical traditions of Sri Lanka, a prince named Vijaya and his followers who came from India and landed in Lanka on the day of the Parinibbaana of the Buddha were the first human inhabitants of this island. When they came the island was occupied by "yakkhas" (sprites, demons). "Yakkhas" and "naagas" are also said to have inhabited Lanka in the time of the Buddha. A legend relating the existence of a great civilization before this time, under a king named Raavana, is also current though the early chronicles make no mention of it.

The Vijaya legend of these chronicles is taken by modern historians as a poetic expression of the actual aryanization of Sri Lanka in about the sixth century BCE The term "yakkhas and naagas" may refer to the aborigines who occupied the island before their arrival. No traces of an advanced civilization, however, have yet been discovered to support the Raavana legend. Archaeologists have discovered chert and quartz implements and tools at various sites, believed to have been used by aborigines of Sri Lanka, and they indicate that these people were a primitive tribe who lived by hunting. These aborigines have not left traces of a strong political organization or an advanced culture. The present Veddas are believed to be their descendants.

Colonization by Prince Vijaya and his Followers

Vijaya and his 700 followers are described in the Lankan chronicles as a set of adventurous young men who, when they were banished from their Indian homeland Laala (or Laata), came in search of new land for settlement. Other legends, some of which are even older, relating how the first aryan inhabitants came to settle down in Lanka are found in several Pali and Sanskrit works. Most of them show that the settlement of early aryan settlers is due to the enterprise of the pioneering merchant mariners who came to this island for pearls and precious stones. Historians thus do not lay much reliance on the details of the Vijayan legend but they accept Vijaya as the first traditional ruler of the newcomers — the Sinhalese.

Vijaya, who was a Kshatriya, landed in Lanka, according to the chronicles, on the day of the Parinibbaana of the Buddha. He allied himself with an aboriginal princess named Kuveni and married her and with her influence soon became the master of the country. Later he drove Kuveni away and obtained a princess from Maduraa whom he made his queen. Maidens of high birth came from the Pandyan kingdom as wives of his followers.

Vijaya ruled from his settlement Tambappanni and his ministers founded other settlements like Anuraadhagaama, Upatissagaama, Ujjeni, Uruvelaa and Vijitapura. Thus the earliest settlements that were founded in the time of King Vijaya were located along the river banks in the northwestern region of Lanka like the Malvatu-oya and the Kalaa-oya.

Political Development and Social Organization after Vijaya

Vijaya died after a rule of 38 years. Since he had no son to succeed him, before his death he sent messengers to his brother Sumitta in Sihapura to come and rule here. Sumitta sent his youngest son Panduvaasudeva, since he himself was king of Sihapura and was also too old. Panduvaasudeva, Vijaya's nephew, arrived one year after Vijaya's death during which period the ministers of Vijaya ruled the country. When Panduvaasudeva came he brought with him 32 sons of ministers.

The early chronicles preserve an episode which connects the Sakka family of the Buddha with the sovereignty of Lanka from the time of King Panduvaasudeva. According to this account, Bhaddakaccaanaa, who also arrived in Lanka with 32 other maidens shortly after Panduvaasudeva arrived, was the daughter of Pandu Sakka, who himself was the son of Amitodana, an uncle of the Buddha.

Panduvaasudeva ruled for 30 years and was succeeded by his eldest son Abhaya, who ruled for 20 years. Abhaya's successor was Pandukaabhaya, the son of his sister Ummaadacitta. Pandukaabhaya was a great ruler in whose reign Anuraadhapura developed into a great city with well-marked boundaries. After a long reign of 70 years, Pandukaabhaya was succeeded by his son Mutasiva who ruled for 60 years. Mutasiva's second son, Devaanampiya Tissa, succeeded him in 250 BCE, that is, 236 years after the accession of Vijaya.

These 236 years could be reckoned as a separate period in the history of Sri Lanka for it formed the background for the offical introduction of Buddhism, which occurred during the opening years of the next ruler, King Devaanampiya Tissa. During this period the aryan colonists founded settlements along the fertile river banks almost throughout the island. They chose the river banks because they were mainly agriculturists. Thus the regions watered by the Malvatu-oya, Kalaa-oya, Valave-ganga, Kirindi-oya, Menik-ganga and Kumbukkan-oya, the Kelani-ganga and some regions around the Mahaveli-ganga soon became populated. Anuraadhapura became a well-organized city with boundaries marked, lakes dug and hospitals and other buildings constructed. In the south, Mahaagaama (Maagama), became the center of activity. The majority of the aboriginal inhabitants were absorbed into the new community through intermarriage while a few withdrew to the Malayadesa, the highlands.

Pre-Buddhist Religion in Sri Lanka

It is evident from the chronicles relating the early history of Sri Lanka that before the introduction of Buddhism in the reign of King Devaanampiya Tissa (250-210 BCE) there was no single religion which was widely accepted as the national religion of the country. Nevertheless, there was a wide range of religious beliefs and practices, different from one another, and each individual seems to have freely observed his religion according to his belief.

A noteworthy feature of the pre-Buddhist religion of Sri Lanka is that it was a mixture of the aboriginal cults and the beliefs of the aryan newcomers.

The worship of yaksas and yaksinis was a widely prevalent aboriginal custom of pre-Buddhist Lanka. King Pandukaabhaya, the grandfather of Devaanampiya Tissa, provided shrines for many of these spirits and also gave them sacrificial offerings annually. Some of these yaksas and yaksinis mentioned by name are Kaalavela, Cittaraaja, Vessavana, Valavaamukhi and Cittaa. Vyaadhadeva, Kammaaradeva and Pacchimaraajini, though not known as yaksas and yaksinis, also belong to the same category of aboriginal spirits. Trees like the banyan and palmyrah were also connected with the cults of these spirits showing that tree-worship was also prevalent.

Many scholars agree that these yaksas and other non-human beings are none but the spirits of the dead relatives and tribal chiefs who, the people believed, were capable of helping friends and harming enemies. This belief, as is widely known, formed one of the main features of the primitive religion and is extant even today.

Accounts relating the pre-Buddhist history of Sri Lanka also show a considerable influence of the religious trends of India on the society of Lanka. Several niganthas (Jainas) such as Giri, Jotiya and Kumbhanda lived in the reign of Pandukaabhaya and hermitages were constructed for them and other ascetics like aajivakas, brahmans and the wandering mendicant monks. Five hundred families of heretical beliefs also lived near the city of Anuraadhapura. The brahmans occupied a high place in society and their religious beliefs were also respected. The worship of Siva too may have been prevalent.

The account in the *Mahaava.msa* of the settling of the adherents of various sects by King Pandukaabhaya does not specifically mention the presence of any adherents of Buddhism among them. But the work refers to three visits of the Buddha to Sri Lanka, a statement which, though not corroborated by other evidence, has not been disproved. Legendary accounts also claim that two stuupas — the Mahiyangana and the Girihandu — were constructed before the introduction of Buddhism. Among the newcomers too there could have been some members who were acquainted with Buddhism, especially as Bhaddakaccaanaa, who arrived with 32 other maidens in the guise of nuns, was a close relative of the Buddha.

Emperor Asoka and Buddhism in India

Buddhism as a form of religious expression gained ascendency in India during this period. Emperor Asoka was crowned, according to the chronicles, in the year 218 of the Buddhist era (i.e., 268 BCE). Like his father Bindusaara and grandfather Candragupta, Asoka was a follower of the brahmanical faith at the beginning of his reign. In the early years of his reign he followed an expansionist policy and in the eighth year of his coronation he conquered Kaalinga, in the course of which 100,000 were slain and 150,000 taken prisoners. But the carnage of the Kaalinga war caused him much grief and the king was attracted towards the humanistic teachings of Buddhism. According to the Sri Lanka chronicles, it was a young novice named Nigrodha who converted Asoka.

After the conversion of this great emperor Buddhism flourished under his patronage. He inculcated the teachings of the Buddha and set up edicts of morality at numerous places of his vast empire so that his subjects would adhere to them and his successors might follow him. He himself followed those morals and set an example to the others. The king is reputed to have built 84,000 stupas. The monks were lavishly provided with their requisites.

The king even permitted his son Mahinda and daughter Sanghamittaa to join the Order when they were twenty and eighteen years of age respectively. These two illustrious disciples became noted for their piety, attainments, learning and profound knowledge of the Dhamma.

Vast numbers joined the Order in the reign of Asoka solely to share the benefits showered on it by the king, and such people were not only lax in their conduct, but also held doctrines counter to the teachings of the Buddha.

It was this dissenting element that led to the holding of the Third Buddhist Council under the patronage of King Asoka in order to purify the Buddhist religion (Saasana). It was at this Council held by a thousand theras (elders) under the leadership of Moggaliputta Tissa, at Paataliputta, that the Pali Canon of the Theravaada, as it exists today, was finally redacted.

At this Council was also taken the important, decision of sending missionaries to different regions to preach Buddhism and establish the Saasana there. Thus the thera Moggaliputta Tissa deputed Majjhantika Thera to Kaasmira-Gandhaara, Mahaadeva Thera to Mahisamandala, Rakkhita Thera to Vanavaasi, Yona-Dhammarakkhita Thera to Aparaantaka, Dhammarakkhita Thera to Mahaarattha, Mahaarakkhita Thera to Yonaloka, Majjhima Thera to Himavanta, theras So.na and Uttara to Suvannabhuumi, and Mahinda Thera with theras Itthiya, Uttiya, Sambala and Bhaddasaala to Lanka, saying unto the five theras: "Establish ye in the delightful land of Lanka the delightful religion of the Vanquisher."

The Mission to Sri Lanka

Mahinda was thirty-two years old when he undertook the mission to Sri Lanka. He had adopted the religious life at the age of twenty, mastered the doctrines and attained the highest spiritual life, i.e., arahantship. Pondering on the fitting time to come to Lanka, he perceived that Mutasiva, the ruler at that time, was in his old age, and hence it was advisable to tarry until his son became ruler. In the meantime Mahinda visited his relatives at Dakkhinaagiri and his mother at Vedisagiri along with his companions. His mother Devi, whom Asoka had married while he was yet a prince, was living at Vedisagiri at that time. Having stayed for six months at Dakkhinaagiri and a month at Vedisagiri, Mahinda perceived that the right time had come, for the old ruler was dead and his son Devaanampiya Tissa had become king.

Devaanampiya Tissa was the second son of Mutasiva. He was a friend of Asoka even before he became king but the two had not seen each other. The first thing that Devaanampiya Tissa did when he became king was to send envoys to Asoka, bearing costly presents. The envoys, when they returned, brought among other things the following message from Asoka:

"Aha.m Buddhañ ca Dhammañ ca Sanghañ ca sara.na.mgato upaasakatta.m vedesi.m Saakyaputtassa saasane tvamp'imaani ratanaani uttamaani naruttama citta.m pasaadayitvaana saddhaaya sara.na.m bhaja."

"I have taken refuge in the Buddha, his Doctrine and his Order, I have declared myself a lay-disciple in the religion of the Saakya son; seek then, O best of men, refuge in these best of gems, converting your mind with believing heart."

This message of Asoka was conveyed to King Devaanampiya Tissa in the month of Vesakha and it was the full-moon day of the following month Jettha (Sinh. Poson) that Mahinda fixed for his arrival in Sri Lanka. Among the companions of Mahinda were the theras Itthiya, Uttiya, Sambala and Bhaddasaala, the saamanera Sumana who was the son of Sanghamittaa, and the lay-disciple Bhanduka who was the son of a daughter of Devi's sister and had become an anaagaami (once-returner) on hearing a sermon of Mahinda preached to Devi.

Arrival of Mahinda

Thus on the full-moon day of the month of Jettha in the year 236 b.e. (i.e., 250 BCE) Mahinda and his companions, departing from Vedisagiri, rose up in the air and alighted on the Silakuuta of the pleasant Missaka hill, presently Mihintale, eight miles east of Anuraadhapura. The thera alighted here for he had perceived that he would meet the king there on that day.

The first meeting of the king of Lanka and the thera Mahinda is graphically described in the chronicles of Sri Lanka. The full-moon day of Jettha was a day of national festival in Lanka. Men and women were engaged in amusing themselves. The king with a large party of followers went to Mihintale hills on a hunting expedition.

There he saw the theras with shaven heads dressed in yellow robes, of dignified mien and distinguished appearance, who faced him and addressed him not as ordinary men addressing a king but as those to whom a king was their inferior. The conversation impressed the king and his immediate surrender to the wisdom and piety displayed by the thera was complete. Mahinda Thera in reply to the king's inquiry as to who they were and whence they had come, said:

"Sama.naa maya.m Mahaaraaja Dhammaraajassa saavakaa tav'eva anukampaaya Jambudiipaa idhaagataa."

"We are the disciples of the Lord of the Dhamma. In compassion towards you, Mahaaraaja, We have come here from India."

When he heard these words of the thera, the king laid aside his bow and arrow, and approaching the thera, exchanged greetings with him and sat down near him. Mahinda then had a conversation with the king, and realizing that the king was intelligent enough to comprehend the Dhamma, preached the Cuulahatthipadopama Sutta.

At the end of the discourse the king and his retinue of forty thousand people embraced the new faith. Having invited the missionaries to the city the king left for his palace. Mahinda spent his first day in Sri Lanka at Mihintale where he solemnized the first ecclesiastical act by admitting to the Order the lay-follower Bhanduka who had accompanied him from India.

Entry into the Capital

On the invitation of the king, Mahinda and the other theras arrived at Anuraadhapura the following day. Going forward to meet the theras, the king respectfully led them into the palace where he himself served them with dainty food. After the meal Mahinda preached the Petavatthu, the Vimaanavatthu and the Sacca-sa.myutta to the royal household.

The people of the city who heard of the theras flocked near the palace-gate to see them and the king prepared a hall outside the palace so that the townspeople could see the theras. On this occasion Mahinda preached the Devaduuta Sutta (Majjhima Nikaaya, No. 130).

This hall too was not spacious enough for the vast gathering and seats were prepared for the theras in the Nandana-garden in the royal park, where Mahinda preached the Baalapandita Sutta, (Majjhima Nikaaya, No. 129).

In the evening the theras expressed their desire to go back to Mihintale. The king, who wished them to stay in his capital, granted to the Sangha the royal park Mahaamegha for their residence. The king himself marked the boundaries by plowing a furrow.

Thus was established the Mahaavihaara which became the earliest celebrated center of the Buddhist religion. Having spent twenty-six days in the Mahaamegha Park, the thera returned to Mihintale for the rain-retreat (*vassa*). This was the beginning of the Cetiyagiri-vihaara, another great monastic institution of early Buddhist Sri Lanka.

Sanghamittaa and Women Disciples

Many women of Sri Lanka, headed by Queen Anulaa, desired to enter the Order of disciples and thus it came about that emissaries led by the king's nephew Arittha were sent to Emperor Asoka to obtain the help of female disciples to enable the women of Lanka to obtain ordination.

Sanghamittaa, the sister of Mahinda Thera, who had entered the Order and had received ordination, was sent out to Lanka at the request of the king and the people and on the recommendation of Mahinda Thera.

The message sent by thera Mahinda to Emperor Asoka pleased him very much, for in it he realized that the mission to Lanka had been eminently successful and the king and the people of Lanka had accepted the new doctrine with enthusiasm.

Arrival of the Sacred Bo-Tree

Emperor Asoka decided on sending a token of the Great and Enlightened One to the land of Lanka and prepared a branch of the Sacred Bodhi Tree under which the Lord attained enlightenment. He planted the branch in a golden vessel and, when it had taken root, conveyed it to the ship, depositing it in the ship. He also sent a large number of attendants to accompany the tree. The chronicles mention that these were selected from the brahmans, nobles and householders and consisted of 64 families. Sanghamittaa Therii and her attendants embarked on the same ship as well as the ambassadors and messengers who came from Lanka.

The ship sailed from Taamralipti (Tamluk) and arrived at the port in Lanka in seven days. The port was known as Jambukola and was situated in the north of the island. The king of Lanka on hearing of the arrival of the ship had the road from Jambukola to the capital city of Anuraadhapura gaily decorated. He arrived in state and himself took charge of the Sacred Bodhi Tree. This tree was planted in the Mahaamegha garden of Anuraadhapura with great festivities and tended with honor and care. Up to this date it flourishes as one of the most sacred objects of veneration and worship for millions of Buddhists.

The Firm Establishment of the Saasana

Arittha, the king's nephew who had obtained the king's permission to enter the Order of monks on his return from India, did so with five hundred other men and all became arahants. With the ordination of Anulaa and the other women both the Bhikkhu-saasana and the Bhikkhuni-saasana were established in the island. Separate residences for monks and nuns were built by the king.

The Thuupaaraama-cetiya enshrining the right collar-bone and other bodily relics of the Buddha was built, and the Sacred Bodhi Tree was planted for the devotion of the laity. When these acts of religious devotion were accomplished, the king asked Mahinda Thera whether the Saasana had been firmly established in the island, to which the latter replied that it had only been planted but would take firm root when a person born in Sri Lanka, of Sinhalese parents, studied the Vinaya in Sri Lanka and expounded it in Sri Lanka.

Arittha Thera had by this time become noted for his piety and his learning and on an appointed day, at a specially constructed preaching hall, in the presence of numerous theras, the king and the chiefs, Arittha Thera was invited to give a discourse on the Vinaya in the presence of the thera Mahaa Mahinda. And his exposition was so correct and pleasing that there was great rejoicing as the condition required for the firm establishment of the Saasana was fulfilled by him.

Progress of Buddhism in Lanka

Devaanampiya Tissa ruled in Sri Lanka for forty years. It was in the first year of his reign that Buddhism was introduced and from that time the king worked for the progress of the new faith with great zeal. Apart from the Mahaavihaara, the Cetiyapabbatavihaara, the Thuuparaama and the Sacred Bodhi Tree, he established numerous other monasteries and several Buddhist monuments. The chronicles mention that he built monasteries a yojana from one another. Among these monuments the Isurumuni-vihaara and the Vessagiri-vihaara are important centers of worship to this day. He is also credited with the construction of the Pathamaka-cetiya, the Jambukola-vihaara and the Hatthaalhaka-vihaara, and the refectory.

Thousands of men and women joined the Order during his reign. The king not only built vihaaras for their residence but also provided them with their requisites. It was not only in the capital city that Buddhism spread in his reign but even in distant regions like Jambukola in the north and Kaajaragaama and Candanagaama in the south.

The remarkable success of Mahinda's mission and the rapid spread of the religion in a very short time were mainly due to the efforts of Mahinda and the unbounded patronage of King Devaanampiya Tissa. Apart from them the people of Lanka too were eminently ripe at this period for receiving and adopting the teachings of the Buddha. The people in the land were prosperous, their wants were few, and these were supplied by the fertile soil. There was prosperous trade, for merchants came from all lands to barter goods; their art was well developed, for in the leisure people enjoyed they were able to build cities and tanks, great and small, and to perform works both of utility and artistic value. Contentment reigned supreme. Where such conditions existed the people were ready to embrace new ideals that had the prospect of helping their culture and elating their thoughts and activities, and as such the new doctrine preached by Mahinda Thera fell on a fertile soil, where it soon rose to its full height. Hundreds of thousands of men and women rose to high spiritual attainments on hearing the new message and thus the Law of the Blessed One was firmly established.

The Passing Away of Mahinda and Sanghamittaa

Both Mahinda and Sanghamitta survived Devaanampiya Tissa. Mahinda lived to the age of 80 years and Sanghamittaa to the age of 79 years. They spent nearly 48 years in the island.

The former died in the eighth year and the latter in the ninth of the reign of King Uttiya, brother and successor of Devaanampiya Tissa. Uttiya performed their funerals with great honor and built stuupas over their relics. The king himself died in the following year, 286 b.e., after a reign of ten years.

The hierarchy of the disciples was continued in pupilary succession. Arittha Thera succeeded Mahinda Thera; he was in turn succeeded by Isidatta, Kaalasumana, Diighanaama and Diighasumana.

Invasion of Tamils and Restoration of the Saasana by King Dutthagaamani

Twenty years after the death of Uttiya foreign usurpers from South India seized Anuraadhapura. Two of them, Sena and Guttika, reigned together for twenty-two years and another Tamil usurper, Elaara, reigned for forty-four years. The lack of interest of these Tamil rulers in the Buddhist faith and the vandalism of their supporters evidently retarded the progress of the religion. Furthermore, the Sinhalese rulers were not free to work for the religion during these periods of political unrest. Nevertheless, the people held strongly to their new religion and showed no signs of laxity.

It was a young prince from Maagama of the southeastern principality of Ruhuna who restored the lost glory of the Sinhalese and their religion. He was Abhaya, known to posterity by a nickname which means "disobedient," Dutthagaamani. He was a descendant of Mahaanaaga, who had established himself at Maagama when his older brother Devaanampiya Tissa was ruling at Anuraadhapura. Kaakavanna Tissa and Vihaaramahaadevi were his parents.

After a thorough preparation for war Dutthagaamani defeated and killed Elaara in battle and became the ruler of Anuraadhapura. Thus the sovereignty of the Sinhalese rulers of Anuraadhapura was once more established.

Dutthagaamani reigned for twenty-four years. The advancement of the Buddhist religion was his main concern. The Ruvanveli-saaya, the most celebrated stupa in Sri Lanka, was his greatest work. The magnificent edifice of nine storeys and nine hundred chambers, called the Lohapaasaada, "the Brazen Palace," was constructed by him for the use of the monks. Mirisaveti-daagaba was another of his works. Dutthagaamani was not only a supporter of Buddhism but was also a zealous follower himself. Many episodes in the Pali commentaries depict him as a pious monarch. Under his patronage there flourished several learned monks during his reign.

Social and Cultural Development due to Buddhism

It is well to find out the social and cultural development of the Sinhalese during the two centuries following their acceptance of the Buddhist religion. We have many incidents and stories in the Sri Lanka chronicles from which a definite idea regarding these conditions can be inferred. For instance, the *Rasavaahinii,* a Pali work composed in the thirteenth century of the Christian era, contains over a hundred stories of the life of the people during this early period. According to these stories, among the Sinhalese there do not appear to have been any caste divisions. Brahmans are mentioned as living apart in their own villages, and they were more or less counted as foreign to the Sinhalese. The members of the royal families were held in a class by themselves, and those of such families who aspired to the kingdom had to marry a member of a royal family or at least from a Brahman family. The rest of the people were grihapatis (householders with settled abodes).

The Candaalas (despised) were those without a fixed abode; they were despised on account of being tramps and vagrants with no fixed residence. In some cases the word Candaala was used in a self-deprecatory manner in order to indicate unworthiness. There is the instance of Prince Saali, son of King Dutthagaamani, who fell in love with a village artisan's daughter, Devi (Asokamaalaa).

In addressing the prince she said that she was a Candaali as she did not belong to a family into which a member of the royal family was allowed to marry. The two divisions of people merely appear to be those who had a fixed abode and those who had no fixed abode. There were at this time no special caste divisions for trades or occupations, for a householder or members of a family were, in general, expected to engage themselves in one of the three occupations, as traders, as artisans or as cultivators.

Prince Dighaabhaya, when appointed as governor of Kasaatota, required attendants and asked each chief family of a village to send one of its sons for service and sent a messenger to Sangha, the chief of the village. The chief called together his seven sons. The elder six asked him to send the youngest to the king's service as he was idling his time at home without engaging in any work. "We six are engaged in such occupations as trade, industries and cultivation and work hard at our occupations." Again, in another story, the father, a chief of a village, addressing his daughter regarding her husband, tells her that her husband is living in idleness, and like her brothers should engage himself in an occupation such as cultivation, industry and commerce. Thus it appears all trades were common, and the same family engaged in work as artisans, tradesmen and cultivators without distinction.

The religion of the Sinhalese during this period was purely and entirely Buddhist and the stories indicate much practical activity in religious affairs, both in endowment and maintenance of religious institutions and the practice of religious principles. The Orders of bhikkhus and bhikkhunis flourished during this period; a very large number of men and women entered the religious Orders. Some of the vihaaras (monasteries) had thousands residing in them.

There were also large numbers who were practicing meditation in forests and rock caves. They were well supported by the laity. There were four classes of disciples: the novices (saamanera), bhikkhus (fully ordained), theras (elders) and mahaatheras (chief elders.) There are no Sangharaajas (heads of the entire Sangha) mentioned in any of the stories and no interference by kings or ministers in appointment or in giving ranks to the members of the Order. The affairs of the Sangha were managed by the monks themselves under well established rules of the Vinaya.

There appear to have been large numbers of disciples who had attained to the state of arahant, i.e., saints who had gained emancipation. In addition practically every man or woman was an upaasaka or upaasikaa, a devotee who regularly performed religious duties. The bhikkhus lived in their vihaaras during the rainy season and at other seasons traveled far and wide in the country, visiting villages, other vihaaras, and as pilgrims worshipping at shrines. Both laymen and bhikkhus are frequently mentioned as going on pilgrimages to Gayaa in India to worship at the sacred Bodhi Tree there. These parties of pilgrims sometimes crossed over to Southern India and walked all the way to Gayaa, taking about six months on the journey; sometimes they went by sea and landed at Taamralipti at the mouth of the Ganges and reached Gayaa in half the time.

The canonical scriptures had not been committed to writing at this time though writing was known. The bhikkhus learned the Dhamma and many committed to memory the scriptures or parts of them, thus preserving the tradition by frequent rehearsal. That the art of writing was probably introduced to Sri Lanka only after the introduction of Buddhism seems deducible from the circumstance that so far, no pre-Buddhist writing, lithic or other, has been identified. The earliest lithic records date back to the time of King Uttiya, successor of Devaanampiya Tissa.

The bhikkhus were the instructors of the people. This was practically a duty. The Dhamma was expounded individually on every occasion and sermons to congregations were also held from time to time. There is mention of the periodical expounding of the Dhamma at a temple. Each temple in a district sometimes took its turn once a year to preach the Ariyava.msa Sutta, which was continued each time for seven days; the gatherings on these occasions appear to be very large as in instances mentioned it is said that the crowds were so great that large numbers usually had to stand outside the hall for the whole night and listen to the Dhamma, the audience including bhikkhus and the laity. There is also mention of discourses by lay preachers well versed in the Dhamma employed by the king at halls of preaching. It is not clearly stated whether brahmans who lived in brahman villages practiced their own religion. Mention is made of sannyaasis or yogis who practiced asceticism and sometimes lived in cemeteries scantily clad, with bodies covered with ashes, and as the story says, pretending to be saints while at the same time they led sinful lives. There is no mention of brahman temples or places of worship.

Women had a very high status in society during this period. Practically in every strata of society the position of women showed no distinction from that of men. They freely took part in every activity of life and their influence is well marked. Their character is depicted in most favorable terms; they were gentle, courteous and good natured, hospitable, tender and intelligent, ever ready to help others, to preserve the honor of their families, devoted to religion and country with untrammelled freedom of action. The position of women is further seen from the fact that monogamy was a definite institution. There is no mention of any other form of marriage. Women had freedom to choose their husbands.

Vattagaamani Abhaya

After the death of King Dutthagaamani his younger brother Saddhaatissa ruled for eight years and did a great deal for Buddhism. He was succeeded by his sons Thuulatthana, Lanjatissa, Khallaata Naaga and Vattagaamani Abhaya, in succession. The period of Vattagaamani Abhaya, also known as Valagambahu, is noteworthy in the history of early Buddhism in Sri Lanka. Five months after his accession to the throne, in 103 BCE a brahman named Tiya (or Tissa) from Ruhuna, South Lanka, revolted against him. At the same time a Tamil army led by seven Tamil chiefs landed at Mahaatittha and waged war against the king. The Tamil army vanquished Tiya and defeated Vattagaamani in battle after which the latter fled and lived in exile for fourteen years.

These fourteen years of Tamil domination were disastrous to the cause of Buddhism, especially because the country was also ravaged by an unprecedented famine during that period. Food was so scarce during that time that even cases of cannibalism are said to have occurred. Many thousands of monks and laymen died of starvation. The monasteries were deserted. The Mahaavihaara of Anuraadhapura was completely abandoned and the Mahaathuupa was neglected. Trees grew in the courtyards of vihaaras. 12,000 arahants from the Tissamahaaraama and another 12,000 from the Cittalapabbata-vihaara passed away in the forest due to lack of food. While thousands of monks died in the country, many left the country and went to India.

As a result of the death of most of the learned monks there was even the fear that some parts of the scriptures would be lost. The Mahaaniddesa of the Sutta Pitaka, for instance, was on the verge of being lost, for this text was known by only one monk at that time. The monks, in their earnestness to preserve the teachings of the Buddha, subsisted on roots and leaves of trees and recited the scriptures, lest they should forget them. When they had the strength they sat down and recited and when they could no longer keep their bodies erect they lay down and continued their recitation. Thus they preserved the texts and the commentaries until the misery was over.

The First Schism

After Vattagaamani Abhaya regained the throne he demolished the monastery of a nigantha (Jain ascetic) named Giri for having mocked him when he was fleeing. He built a Buddhist monastery called the Abhayagiri-vihaara over it, which he presented to a monk named Kupikkala Mahaa Tissa who had helped the king in his exile.

Later, the monks of the Mahaavihaara imposed the punishment of expulsion on Tissa on the charge of improper contact with lay families. Tissa's pupil Bahalamassu Tissa, who resented the punishment imposed upon his teacher, was likewise expelled from the Mahaavihaara.

He then went away with a following of five hundred monks and lived at Abhayagiri-vihaara, refusing to return to the Mahaavihaara. There was thus a group of monks who broke away from the Mahaavihaara and lived separately in the Abhayagiri-vihaara, but they did not yet disagree with each other either in the theory or the practice of the Dhamma.

The actual schism occurred only when monks of the Vajjiputta sect in India came to Sri Lanka and were received at the Abhayagiri, not long after Tissa and his followers occupied that monastery. Tissa and his followers liked the new monks and adopted their doctrines.

Thenceforth they came to be known as the Dhammaruci sect, after the name of the great Indian monk who was the teacher of the newcomers to Abhayagiri. There was no official suppression of the new sect, presumably because the king was in their favor, but the Mahaavihaara monks opposed them as unorthodox and heretical. From this time the Abhayagiri existed as a separate sect opposed to the Mahaavihaara.

Writing of the Sacred Books

It is stated in the early chronicles that after the acceptance of Buddhism by the people in Lanka and after the formation of a hierarchy of disciples who were Sinhalese, a council was held under Mahinda Thera, where all the leading theras were present and the teachings were recited and authoritatively laid down, as was done in the third convocation held in India under the direction of Emperor Asoka. Theravaada was thus established in Sri Lanka and according to tradition and custom the various parts of the Tipitaka were learned by the members of the Order, committed to memory, and preserved as oral traditions. It was seen how, during the famine that broke out in the time of King Vattagaamani Abhaya, a great strain was put on the continuance of this form of preserving the teachings of the Tipitaka. When conditions became normal, the members of the Order considered that they could lose the teachings if any similar calamity or calamities were to occur in the future, and they decided that the time had arrived for committing these teachings to writing so that they might be preserved for future generations. The advent of schisms about this time might also have weighed strongly in favor of this decision.

Thus the members of the Order assembled at the Mahaavihaara at Anuraadhapura, took counsel together, and with the permission and encouragement of the king a convocation was held. The teachings were recited and scribes were engaged to commit to writing, on palm leaves, the Pali canonical texts (the Tipitaka) consisting of Vinaya, Sutta and Abhidhamma, and the Sinhalese commentaries. According to the *Nikaaya Sangraha*, a Sinhalese work of the fourteenth century dealing with the history of the Buddhist order, after the convocation at the Mahaavihaara at Anuraadhapura, the selected number of reciters and scribes, 500 in all, went to Alulena (Aluvihaara) cave temple close to Matale, in the central province. There in retirement they completed the work assigned to them and thus for the first time brought out in book form the teachings of the Buddha.

The Growth of Dissentient Schools

About two centuries after the formation of the Dhammaruci sect at the Abhayagiri-vihaara, in the days of King Vohaarika

Tissa (214-36 a.c.), the monks of the Abhayagiri-vihaara adopted the Vaitulyavaada. Thereupon the monks of the Mahaavihaara, having compared it with their own texts, rejected the Vaitulya doctrines as being opposed to traditional doctrine. The king, who had them examined by a learned minister named Kapila, burnt them and suppressed the Vaitulyavaadins.

Despite the suppression by Vohaarika Tissa, the Vaitulyavaadins began to assert themselves again and a few years later, in the time of King Gothaabhaya (Meghavanna Abhaya, 253-266 a.c.), the Dhammaruci monks of Abhayagiri again accepted Vaitulyavaada. When this happened, about three hundred monks left the Abhayagiri-vihaara to reside at the Dakkhinavihaara, founding a new sect known as Saagaliya. The king, having assembled the bhikkhus of the five great monasteries of the Theriya Nikaaya (Mahaavihaara Nikaaya), had the Vaitulya books examined, ordered the books to be destroyed, and expelled the Vaitulya monks. Sixty of them left for the Chola country in South India.

The struggle did not end here, for the adherents of the new doctrine were firmly established in South India and they planned to undermine the Mahaavihaara Nikaaya in Sri Lanka. With this object a very learned monk by the name of Sanghamitra came to Sri Lanka and obtained the post of tutor to the king's two sons. Sanghamitra gained considerable influence over the young pupil, Mahaasena, and was able to instil into him the new doctrine and make him a follower of his views. When Mahaasena ascended the throne, the opportunity looked forward to by the Vaitulyans came. The new king became a great supporter of his tutor and as such persecuted the Mahaavihaara monks. The king, at the instigation of Sanghamitra Thera, ordered that no one should give food to the monks of the Mahaavihaara. The Mahaavihaara, as a result, had to be abandoned for nine years. The supporters of Sanghamitra destroyed the buildings of the Mahaavihaara and carried away their material to construct new buildings for the Abhayagiri-vihaara.

Two persons, a minister and a queen, came forward this time to suppress Vaitulyavaada and save the Mahaavihaara. The minister, Meghavannaabhaya by name, managed to persuade the king to rebuild the Mahaavihaara. The queen caused Sanghamitra to be put to death and burned the Vaitulya books.

But the king, who was yet favorable towards the followers of Sanghamitra, built and gave the Jetavana-vihaara to a monk named Tissa. Tissa, who was later charged by the Mahaavihaara monks of a grave offense, was expelled from the Order. The monks of the Sagaliya sect at Dakkhina-vihaara then came to reside in the Jetavana-vihaara. In the reign of Silaakaala (522-35) a Vaitulyan book called the *Dharmadhaatu*, which was brought to Sri Lanka from India, was kept at the Jetavana-vihaara and venerated.

Thus from this time the monks of Jetavana-vihaara too became adherents of Vaitulyavaada. In the reign of King Aggabodhi I (575-608) a great monk and teacher named Jotipaala, coming from India, so exposed the fallacies of the Vaitulya doctrines that in his day they fell into disrepute and disappeared from Sri Lanka. Since that time the monks of the Abhayagiri and Jetavana vihaaras who adhered to Vaitulyan doctrines, abandoned their pride and lived in submission to the monks of the Mahaavihaara.

Intercourse with India was so frequent that from time to time other unorthodox doctrines occasionally found favor with certain monks, but these had no marked effect on the general progress or the stability of the Mahaavihaara Nikaaya.

For nearly three centuries after the time of Aggabodhi I the chronicles make no mention of the Vaitulyavaada or any other heretical teaching, until in the reign of King Sena I (833-53) a monk of the Vaajraparvata Nikaaya came to Sri Lanka from India and introduced Vaajiriyavaada, converting the king to his doctrines. It was at this time that teachings like the Ratnakuuta-suutra were also introduced to Sri Lanka and another heresy called Nilapata-darsana appeared. Sena II (853-87), who succeeded Sena I, managed to suppress these new doctrines. From his time until the Chola conquest in the early eleventh century there is no mention of any heretical sect in Sri Lanka. However, a survey of the religious monuments of that period clearly shows that their teachings survived side by side with the teachings of the Theravaada.

The Nature of the New Doctrines

It is opportune here to enquire about the nature of the new doctrines that were mentioned in the previous chapter as having been introduced into Sri Lanka from time to time since the first century a.c. It was the monks of the Vajjiputra sect in India who were the first to introduce a new teaching. The Vajjiputra sect is mentioned in the Sri Lanka chronicles as one of the groups that parted from the Theriya Nikaaya after the Second Buddhist Council to form a new sect. They thus evidently held some views different from those of the orthodox teachings. Buddhaghosa mentions in the Pali commentaries that the Vajjiputrakas held the view that there is a persistent personal entity, which is opposed to the accepted theory of *anattaa* of the Theravaada teachings. They also believed that arahants may fall away from their attainment.

These followers of the Vajjiputraka doctrines, residing at the Abhayagiri-vihaara, became adherents of the Vaitulya doctrines about two centuries afterwards, and until the beginning of the seventh century Vaitulyavaada became closely associated with Abhayagiri-vihaara and Jetavana-vihaara.

Like the Vajjiputra sect the Vaitulyavaada is mentioned in the *Nikaaya Sangraha* as one of the sects that arose in India after the Second Buddhist Council. The *Nikaaya Sangraha* also states that the Vaitulya Pitaka was composed by heretic brahmans called Vaitulyas who entered the Order in the time of King Asoka to destroy Buddhism. It has been noticed that the terms Vaitulya, Vaipulya and Vaidalya are commonly used as a designation for Mahaayaana suutras and hence the term Vaitulyavaada is used in the Sri Lanka chronicles to denote Mahaayaanism in general without having a particular Buddhist school in view.

The Vaitulyavaadins were considered even more heretical than the Vajjiputrakas. The Pali commentaries mention some of their heretical views. They held the view that the Buddha, having been born in the Tusita heaven, lived there and never came down to earth and it was only a created form that appeared among men. This created form and ânanda, who learned from it, preached the doctrine. They also held that nothing whatever given to the Order bears fruit, for the Sangha, which in the ultimate sense of the term meant only the path and fruitions, does not accept anything. According to them any human pair may enter upon sexual intercourse by mutual consent. The *Diipava.msa* used the term Vitandavaada in place of Vaitulyavaada and the Pali commentaries mention them as holding unorthodox views regarding the subtle points in the Dhamma, particularly the Abhidhamma. Buddhaghosa also refers to the Vaitulyavaadins as Mahaasuññavaadins. The philosophy of the Mahaayaana as expounded by the great Mahaayaana teacher Naagaarjuna was Suunyavaada. Thus the fact that the first appearance of Vaitulyavaada in Sri Lanka took place shortly after Naagaarjuna's teachings spread in South India, and that Vaitulyavaada is also identified with Suunyavaada of Naagaarjuna, suggests that it was the teaching of Naagaarjuna that was received by the monks of Abhayagiri-vihaara in the days of Vohaarika Tissa.

The book called *Dharmadhaatu*, which was brought to Lanka in the reign of Silaakaala, is described in the chronicles as a Vaitulyan book. The monks of the Abhayagiri-vihaara and the Jetavana-vihaara are connected with the honors paid to it. It has become evident that a book named *Dharmadhaatu* was known and held in high esteem in the tenth century in Lanka and it is quite probable that this book was a Mahaayaanistic treatise dealing with the doctrine of the three bodies of the Buddha found among the teachings of the Mahaayaana.

Vaajiriyavaada was introduced in the reign of King Sena I by a monk of the Vajraparvata Nikaaya. Scholars have pointed out that the Vaajiriyavaadins are identical with the Vajrayaanists, a school of Buddhism which flourished in eastern India about this time and which was an exponent of the worst phases of Tantrism. The *Nikaaya Sangraha* describes their writings as "secret teachings" and the Guudhavinaya, i.e., the "secret Vinaya," is one of the compositions of the Vajrayaanists.

The *Nikaaya Sangraha* mentions that about this time the Ratnakuuta-suutra was introduced to Sri Lanka. In the Chinese Canon the second of the seven classes of the Mahaayaana-suutras is called the Ratnakuuta. The Niilapata-darsana, which was also introduced about this time, was also an extreme form of Tantrism. Blue has been a color often favored by Tantrists.

The Sacred Tooth Relic

An important event in the early history of Buddhism in Sri Lanka is the arrival of Buddha's Tooth Relic, the left eye-tooth, from India about 805 b.e. (311 a.c.), during the time of King Sirimeghavanna, son and successor of King Mahaasena. Ever since this Sacred Tooth Relic was received in Sri Lanka it has been a national treasure of great value and a tangible token of the attachment of the Sinhalese to the doctrine of the Blessed Tathaagata. King Sirimeghavanna held a great festival for the Tooth Relic and decreed that it should be brought every year to the Abhayagiri-vihaara and the same ceremonial should be observed. Today it is enshrined in golden caskets in the Temple of the Tooth Relic (Daladaa Maaligaawa) in Kandy, which has become the center of devout pilgrims from all over the island and from Buddhist lands elsewhere.

Ancient customs and ceremonies are scrupulously kept up, offerings are made daily, and in honor of the Sacred Relic an annual festival lasting fourteen days is held in Kandy every year during August. The Perahera, or procession, on these occasions is conducted by the temple authorities with elephants, lights, music and dancers, and is witnessed by thousands of devotees. Chiefs in full ancient attire accompany the procession. Large tracts of land have been set apart as fees for services at this temple and the tenants of these lands have various services apportioned to them. The exhibition of the Sacred Relic itself takes place at rare intervals when tens of thousands of pilgrims find their way to the Temple to worship and view the Relic. A medieval chronicle, chiefly of the eastern part of the island, mentions the existence of the right eye-tooth and its enshrinement in Somavati Cetiya in pre-Christian times.

The Sacred Tooth Relic was in the possession of King Guhasiva of Kaalinga before it was brought to Sri Lanka. When he was about to be defeated in battle he entrusted it to his daughter Hemamaalaa: Hemamaalaa with her husband Dantakumaara brought the Sacred Tooth to Lanka and handed it over to King Sirimeghavanna at Anuraadhapura. From this date the Sacred Tooth Relic became the care of the kings of Lanka, who built special temples for it. During the many vicissitudes of the fortunes of the kings of Lanka, the Sacred

Relic was conveyed from place to place where the fortunes of the king happened to take him. Replicas of the Sacred Tooth were made at various times and were owned by princes claiming the throne. About the year 1071 King Anawrahta (Anuruddha) of Burma sent various presents to King Vijayabaahu I of Sri Lanka and in return received a duplicate of the Sacred Tooth Relic, which he received with great veneration, and a shrine was built for it in Burma. The Portuguese, in one of their expeditions to Sri Lanka, claim to have captured the Sacred Tooth Relic at Jaffna in the year 1560. Jaffna was an outlying port away from the strongholds of Sinhalese kings and the relic said to have been found by the Portuguese in a temple at Jaffna appeared to be one of the several duplicates which had been made at various times. On this question Prof. Rhys Davids wrote in the *Academy* of September 1874: "Jaffna is an outlying and unimportant part of the Ceylon kingdom, not often under the power of the Sinhalese monarchs, and for some time before this it had been ruled by a petty chieftain; there is no mention of the Tooth brought by Dantakumaara having been taken there — an event so unlikely and of such importance that it would certainly have been mentioned had it really occurred. We have every reason to believe therefore that the very Tooth referred to in the *Daañhaava.msa* is preserved to this day in Kandy."

In 1815 the British occupied Kandy. As usual the Sacred Tooth Relic had been taken to the mountains for security and one of the earliest tasks of the Agent of the British Government in the Kandyan Province was to arrange for the bringing back of the Relic with due ceremony. The houses and streets of Kandy were decorated, the surface of the streets whitened, and the Relic was brought in a magnificent procession. In 1818 there was a rebellion in the Kandyan provinces and the Sacred Tooth Relic was taken away from Kandy and hidden in a forest. After the suppression of the rebellion the British were able to find the Sacred Tooth Relic and bring it back to Kandy. The Sacred Tooth Relic continued to be in the custody of the British Government till 1853, when by order of the Secretary of State for the Colonies, the charge was given over to the Diyawadana Nilame (lay custodian) and the chief monks of Malwatte and Asgiriya monasteries in Kandy.

Buddhaghosa Thera and the Compilation of the Pali Commentaries

The compilation of the Pali Atthakathaa (commentaries) by Buddhaghosa Thera is another important event in the annals of Sri Lanka, which marks the progress of Buddhism. As has already been stated, the Pitakas or the teachings of the Buddha which were being handed down orally were committed to writing in 397 b.e. (89 BCE) and the commentaries on these, composed in Sinhalese, were also committed to writing at this time. Since this period much by way of exegetical works in Sinhalese was added from time to time and during the next five hundred years literary activity progressed considerably. By about 896 b.e. (410 a.c.), when King Mahaanaama reigned at Anuraadhapura, the fame of Buddhist literature in Sri Lanka was well recognized throughout India and tradition mentions Sinhalese Buddhist monks visiting India, China and other countries and introducing the literature produced in Sri Lanka. Monks from India and China also visited Anuraadhapura during this time to procure Buddhist books.

It was about this time that Buddhaghosa Thera came to Sri Lanka in the reign of King Mahaanaama (410-432). Mahaanaama succeeded to the throne 79 years after the death of King Sirimeghavanna, during whose reign the Sacred Tooth Relic was brought to Sri Lanka, and three rulers, namely Jetthatissa II, Buddhadaasa and Upatissa I, reigned in between. The story of Buddhaghosa is given in detail both in the *Mahaava.msa* and the Sinhalese works composed in later times. According to these sources Buddhaghosa was a brahman youth who was born in the vicinity of Buddha Gayaa and became well known as an exponent of Veda and philosophy. He was such a proficient scholar that in his youth he was able to assert his knowledge among the great scholars of the time. He traveled from place to place, from one seat of learning to another, from one set of teachers to another, triumphantly asserting his knowledge and scholarship.

At a well-known Buddhist monastery at Tamluk, he met Revata Mahaathera, one well versed in the doctrines and philosophy of Buddhism. There he entered into discussions and found not a peer but one superior to him in knowledge and understanding. This made him join the Order of Buddhist monks as a pupil of Revata Mahaathera. At this vihaara he studied Buddhist philosophy diligently and produced a treatise on Buddhism, *¥aa.nodaya*; he also planned to compose commentaries on the Abhidhamma and the suttas. His teacher at this stage advised him to go to Anuraadhapura before undertaking this work, as he said that in Lanka were preserved not only the Tipitaka, the teachings of the Buddha himself, but also the Sinhalese commentaries and various expositions of the teachings which were very valuable and of high repute.

Buddhaghosa Thera proceeded to Sri Lanka and stayed at the Mahaapadhaanaghara of the Mahaavihaara. He then asked the monks at Anuraadhapura for access to books for the compilation of commentaries. The learned theras at Anuraadhapura tested his knowledge and ability by setting him a thesis on which he compiled the well-known *Visuddhimagga*. They were so pleased with this work that he was given facilities for his projected work and books were placed at his disposal for the preparation of Pali commmentaries.

The old Sinhalese commentaries from which Buddhaghosa drew material for the compilation of his Pali commentaries are occasionally named in his works. The Mahaa (or Muula) Atthakathaa occupied the foremost position among them while the Mahaa-paccari Atthakathaa and the Kurundi Atthakathaa were also important. These three major works probably contained exegetical material on all the three Pitakas. Apart from these there were other works like the Sankhepatthakathaa, Vinayatthakathaa, Abhidhammatthakathaa and separate commentaries on the four âgamas or Nikaayas, namely, the Diigha Nikaaya Atthakathaa, Majjhima Nikaaya Atthakathaa, Samyutta Nikaaya Atthakathaa, and the Anguttara Nikaaya Atthakathaa. References to numerous other sources like the Andhakatthakathaa, the âcariyaa (or Teachers), and the Poraanaa (or Ancient Masters) are also found in Buddhaghosa's works.

Utilizing the copious material of these commentaries and other sources, which sometimes contained conflicting views and contradictory assertions, Buddhaghosa compiled his Pali commentaries including all authoritative decisions, sometimes giving his own views but leaving out unnecessary details and repetitions as well as irrelevant matter. The first of such commentaries was the *Samantapaasaadikaa* on the Vinaya Pitaka. The *Kankhaavitaranii* on the Paatimokkha of the Vinaya Pitaka was compiled later. These books were followed by the commentaries on the four Nikaayas, the *Sumangalavilaasinii* on the Diigha Nikaaya, the *Papañca-suudanii* on the Majjhima Nikaaya, the *Saaratthappakaasinii* on the Samyutta Nikaaya, and the *Manorathapuura.nii* on the Anguttara Nikaaya. The *Dhammapadaññhakathaa* on the Dhammapada, the *Jaatakaññhakathaa* on the Jaataka, and the *Paramatthajotikaa* on the Khuddaka Nikaaya, are also ascribed to him. On the books of the Abhidhamma Pitaka, Buddhaghosa compiled the *Aññhasaalinii* on the Dhammasanganii, the *Sammohavinodanii* on the Vibhanga, and the *Pañcappakara.naññhakathaa* on the other five books.

The voluminous literature which Buddhaghosa produced exists to this day and is the basis for the explanation of many crucial points of Buddhist philosophy which without them would have been unintelligible. His commentaries become all the more important since the old Sinhalese commentaries gradually went out of vogue and were completely lost after the tenth century. Buddhaghosa's activities gave an impetus to the learning of Pali in Sri Lanka which resulted in the production of many other Pali commentaries and other literary works, and also established the pre-eminence of Sri Lanka as the home of Theravaada Buddhism.

The Pali Chronicles

Some time before and after the compilation of the Pali commentaries by Buddhaghosa two important literary works of a different type were produced in Sri Lanka. They are the *Diipava.msa* and the *Mahaava.msa*, described in the foregoing pages either as the Sri Lanka chronicles or the Pali chronicles. These two works are the earliest extant literary records giving a continuous history of the activities of the kings of Sri Lanka from pre-Buddhistic times up to the end of the reign of King Mahaasena. Both works are composed in Pali metrical verses.

The *Diipava.msa* is the earlier of these two chronicles. It is not a compilation of one individual author but is the outcome of several previous works to which additions have been made from time to time, taking its present form about the fourth century a.c. The chronicle does not name any author but it has been held by some scholars, from the abundant material it contains about nuns, that the *Diipava.msa* is a work compiled and continued by nuns from time to time.

The *Diipava.msa* consists of 22 chapters. They contain accounts of the three visits of the Buddha to Sri Lanka, the ancestry of the Buddha, the three Buddhist councils and the different Buddhist schools which arose after the Second Council, the activities of King Asoka, the colonization of Sri Lanka by Vijaya, his successors, the introduction of Buddhism in the reign of King Devaanampiya Tissa and the activities of his successors, especially Dutthagaamani, Vattagaamani and Mahaasena. The narrative ends with the reign of Mahaasena (276-303).

The *Diipava.msa* has obtained its material from different sources of which the Sihala *Mahaava.msatthakathaa* (also called the Sihalatthakathaa or Poraanatthakathaa or merely Atthakathaa) was pre-eminent. Besides this there were several other sources like the Uttaravihaara Mahaava.msa, Vinayatthakathaa and the Dipava.msatthakathaa. By these names were known the records collected and preserved in the Mahaavihaara and the other monasteries.

The *Mahaava.msa*, which is the better work in its comprehensiveness, arrangement of facts and high literary standard, was compiled by a thera named Mahaanaama either in the late fifth century or the early sixth century a.c. It also covers the same period of history and its material is drawn from the same sources as the *Diipava.msa*, but it contains much more additional material presented in a better form.

The *Mahaava.msa* contains 37 chapters in all. They deal mainly with the same events as those of the *Diipava.msa*, but there are much longer accounts and greater details of the activities of several kings such as Pandukaabhaya and Dutthagaamani and events like the establishment of Buddhism and the rise of new schools.

These two chronicles contain many myths and legends. Yet they are among the primary sources for the reconstruction of the early history of Sri Lanka for they contain a great deal of historical facts, especially in the narratives dealing with the period after the 2nd century BCE, corroborated by epigraphical, archaeological and other evidence.

The *Mahaava.msa* has been continued in later times, at three stages, giving a connected history of the island up to modern times. This continuation of the chronicle, which is in three parts, is called the *Cuulava.msa*. The first part brings the history down to the twelfth century, the second part to the fourteenth century and the third part to modern times.

Political Unrest and the Decline of Buddhism

The political situation in Sri Lanka from about the middle of the fifth century a.c. until the third quarter of the eleventh century a.c. was not favorable towards the progress of Buddhism. This period of Sri Lankan history is marked with continuous warfare between the reigning king and his rival claimants or the foreign invaders. Often when the reigning king was defeated in battle he fled to India and came back with a Tamil troop to regain his lost throne, and as a result the Tamils who thus settled down in Sri Lanka from time to time also became an important element even powerful enough to seize political power for themselves.

Such a political situation evidently did not give the rulers an opportunity to work for the religion and as a result the community and the monasteries were neglected. Some rulers like Aggabodhi III and Daathopatissa I even resorted to the evil practice of robbing monasteries of their gold images, precious gems and other valuables which had accumulated there for centuries, for the purpose of financing their military operations when the royal treasury had become empty.

Daathopatissa I also removed the gold finial of the Thuupaaraama and the gem-studded umbrella of the cetiya. Relic chambers of stuupas were opened and valuable offerings were removed. Their Tamil soldiers were allowed to burn down monastic buildings like the Sacred Tooth Relic Temple and take away the valuables. The Pandya and the Chola invaders from South India who also attacked Sri Lanka several times during this period ransacked the monasteries and carried away vast treasures. These conditions necessarily worsened when Sri Lanka passed into the hands of the South Indian Cholas in 1017 and remained a part of the Chola empire until 1070.

Amidst this political unrest and the resultant religious decline several events important in the history of Buddhism in Sri Lanka occurred. In the reign of Moggallaana I (495-512) the Sacred Hair Relic of the Buddha was brought to Sri Lanka from India and the king placed it in a crystal casket in an image house and held a great festival. The writing of the *Mahaava.msa* by a Mahaavihaara monk is ascribed to the reign of his successor Kumaara Dhaatusena (512-520). In the reign of Silaakaala (522-535) the Mahaayaana book, the Dharmadhaatu, was brought to Sri Lanka and in the reign of Aggabodhi I (575-608) the monk Jotipaala defeats the Vaitulyavaadins in a public controversy. Apart from these special events several rulers purified the Saasana and repaired the old and neglected monasteries. They also encouraged the recital of Dhamma.

Vijayabaahu I and the Revival of Buddhism

In the year 1070 Vijayabaahu I succeeded in defeating the Cholas and becoming the king of Sri Lanka. Residing at Polonnaruwa, which he made the capital of his kingdom, he turned his mind to the noble task of repairing the damage that had been inflicted upon the national religion by the invaders. The great religious edifices, the pirivenas and the monasteries which were in utter destruction were restored and new ones were built. But the greatest of his tasks was the restoration of ordination of monks.

When he found that the five ordained monks required to carry out an ordination ceremony could not be found in the whole island, he sent an embassy to his friend and ally, King Anuruddha (i.e., Anawrahta) of Burma, soliciting his help in restoring the Saasana in Sri Lanka. King Anuruddha sent a number of eminent theras who re-established the Saasana in Sri Lanka and instructed a large number of monks in the three Pitakas and the commentaries. The king also brought about a reconciliation of the three Nikaayas of the Mahaavihaara, Abhayagiri and Jetavana and restored their ancient monasteries to them. Thousands of laymen joined the Order.

The religious revival inaugurated by King Vijayabaahu led to a great intellectual re-awakening and a large number of religious literary works in Pali and Sanskrit were written. King Vijayabaahu also encouraged learned men to come and settle down in Sri Lanka and also induced his courtiers to engage in literary pursuits. These activities suffered temporarily with his death in 1110, but were revived after the accession of Paraakramabaahu the Great in 1153.

Revival of Buddhism under Paraakramabaahu the Great

King Paraakramabaahu the Great (1153-1186) ascended the throne after a great struggle with rival claimants and even after his accession he had to suppress many rebellions. Being a great leader of men he was able to restore order and even carry his prowess as a conqueror to foreign lands including South India and Burma. He rebuilt the city of Polonnaruwa. King Paraakramabaahu also undertook the restoration of the ancient capital city of Anuraadhapura which had been neglected and abandoned after the Cholas had captured and devastated it about a century and a half earlier. The four great thuupas were overgrown with trees, and bears and panthers dwelt there. The king restored all the important monuments at Anuraadhapura and the entire Mihintale monastery.

But the most important task which the king performed for the establishment of the Saasana was its purification and the unification of the Sangha. In spite of the activities of King Vijayabaahu I there were by this time members of Sangha who were unfit to lead the monastic life. Some of the monks are said to have even supported wives and children. With a learned thera named Mahaa Kassapa of Udumbaragiri Vihaara (Dimbulaagala near Polonnaruwa) at its head, the king convened a Council of the leading monks of the dissentient schools and was convinced that the teachings of the Mahaavihaara were correct and their claims were in keeping with the Dhamma. Consequently with great care and patience, the king made investigations into the members of the schismatic schools. Many of the unworthy monks were persuaded to leave the Order and those who were not open to persuasion were expelled. Some monks were made to return to the status of novices. After that the three fraternities of the Mahaavihaara, the Abhayagiri-vihaara and the Jetavana-vihaara remained united.

Subsequent to this purification of the Sangha the king, with the assistance of the leading monks, proclaimed a code of regulations for the guidance of the bhikkhus. After the proclamation of that code the internal discipline of the Sangha was in the hands of the monks themselves and the king acted only when a necessity arose. The code of regulations enforced by King Paraakramabaahu became a royal proclamation. It gave directions for the proper observance of the Vinaya rules and dealt with the procedure that should be followed by his subjects who had become or who wished to become lay pupils, novices and subsequently ordained monks. The king also caused this proclamation to be engraved on the rock surface of the Uttaraaraama, presently known as Gal-vihaara, which exists to this day. It is now known as Polonnaru-katikaavata or the Paraakramabaahu-katikaavata.

The great interest taken by the king in the affairs of the religion coupled with internal peace and prosperity brought about a revival of Buddhist learning which created a rich literature during this period.

Compilation of Religious Treatises

It has been mentioned earlier that Buddhaghosa Thera compiled the Pali commentaries to many of the texts of the Tipitaka in the early part of the fifth century. Buddhaghosa was, however, not able to compile commentaries to all the books of the Tipitaka due perhaps to the fact that the illness of his teacher Revata in India caused him to leave Sri Lanka before he finished the entire work. Fortunately, there were several other scholars who took up the work left undone by Buddhaghosa, and in the succeeding years they compiled commentaries to the rest of the texts of the Pali Canon.

Thus the commentator Dhammapaala Thera compiled the commentaries to the Udaana, Itivuttaka, Vimaanavatthu, Petavatthu, Theragaathaa, Theriigaathaa and Cariyaapitaka of the Khuddaka Nikaaya; all these commentaries are known by the name *Paramatthadiipanii*: Upasena Thera compiled the *Saddhammappajjotikaa* on the Niddesa. Mahaanama Thera compiled the *Saddhammappakaasinii* on the Patisambhidaa-magga, and Buddhadatta Thera compiled the *Madhuratthavilaasinii* on the Buddhava.msa. The author of the Visuddhajanavilaasinii, which is the commentary on the Apadaana, is not known. Of these commentators Buddhadatta was a contemporary of Buddhaghosa; Upasena and

Mahaanaama flourished about the latter part of the sixth century, and Dhammapaala about the latter part of the tenth century.

The political disturbances from the time of King Dhaatusena until the reign of Vijayabaahu I greatly hampered literary activities and as a result only a few religious works were composed during this period. About the end of the tenth century, a thera named Khema wrote an expository work on the Abhidhamma, called the *Paramatthadiipanii*. To the same period belongs also the Pali *Mahaabodhiva.msa*, which gives primarily the history of the Sacred Bodhi Tree at Anuraadhapura and the ceremonies connected with it. A poem entitled *Anaagatava.msa* on the future Buddha Metteyya is also ascribed to this period. To the tenth or the early part of the eleventh century belongs a Pali poem of 98 stanzas, called the Telakañaahagaathaa, in the form of religious exhortations of a great elder named Kalyaaniya Thera, who was condemned to be cast into a cauldron of boiling oil.

King Vijayabaahu I, in whose reign occurred a great intellectual re-awakening, was himself a great patron of literature and a scholar of high repute. Many Sinhalese works including a Sinhalese translation of the Dhammasanganii are attributed to him but not one of them exists today. About this time a monk named Anuruddha composed the *Anuruddhasataka*, the *Abhidhammattha-sangaha*, the *Naamaruupa-pariccheda* and the *Paramattha-vinicchaya*. The first is a Buddhist devotional poem of 101 stanzas, in elegant Sanskrit. The second work is a compendium on the teachings of the Abhidhamma and is held in high esteem by all Buddhists of the southern school. The third and fourth are two short works in verse on the Abhidhamma, giving the reader a general idea of the subjects dealt with in the Abhidhamma Pitaka.

The reign of King Paraakramabaahu the Great ushered in another great epoch of literary activity. Three great scholarly monks flourished in his reign, namely, Mahaa Kassapa of Dimbulaagala Vihaara, Moggallaana Thera and Saariputta Thera. Mahaa Kassapa was the author of a Sinhalese paraphrase (*sanne*) to the *Samantapaasaadikaa*, which is now lost. He is also reputed to have written a sub-commentary to the *Abhidhammattha-sangaha*. It is probable that he was also the author of several other works such as the *Mohavicchedanii*, which is a treatise on the Abhidhamma, and *Vimativinodanii*, which is a commentary on the Vinaya. Moggallaana, a contemporary of Mahaa Kassapa, was the author of the Pali grammar, *Moggallaana Vyaakara.na*. He is also credited with the authorship of the *Abhidhaanappadiipikaa*, which is the only ancient Pali dictionary in Sri Lanka.

Saariputta was the most prominent scholar of the reign of Paraakramabaahu the Great. A clever Sanskrit scholar as he was, Saariputta compiled two works on Sanskrit grammar. Another work by him, the *Vinayasangaha*, was a summary of the Vinaya Pitaka. This work was known by several titles and was widely known in Burma. On this work Saariputta himself wrote a sub-commentary (*ñiikaa*) and a Sinhalese paraphrase. The most comprehensive and therefore important work of Saariputta is the masterly sub-commentary called the *Saaratthadiipanii*, which he composed on Buddhaghosa's commentary on the Vinaya, the *Samantapaasaadikaa*. The immense and valuable information it contains shows that his knowledge was extensive and profound even as that of the great commentator Buddhaghosa.

He further wrote a Sinhalese paraphrase to the *Abhidhammattha-sangaha* of Anuruddha Thera and this paraphrase is still held in high esteem by modern scholars. Saariputta is also credited with the authorship of two other ñiikaas, the *Saratthamañjuusaa* on the *Manorathapuura.nii* and the *Liinatthappakaasinii* on the *Papañcasuudanii*, which are commentaries on the Anguttara and Majjhima Nikaayas, respectively, by Buddhaghosa. To this period also belong the ñiikaas on the other three Nikaayas of the Sutta Pitaka, collectively known as the *Saratthamañjuusaa-ñiikaa*. It should be mentioned here that the ñiikaas named above formed one of the major groups of Pali literature compiled during this period. As described in the *Saddhamma-sangaha*, a Pali work of the 14th century, Mahaa Kassapa and a large congregation of monks who assembled at the Jetavana Vihaara at Polonnaruwa decided to compose exegetical commentaries since the existing sub-commentaries on the old Atthakathaas were unintelligible. Acting on this decision they compiled ñiikaas, namely, the *Saaratthadiipanii* on the Vinaya Pitaka, the

Saratthamañjuusaa in four parts on the first four Nikaayas of the Sutta Pitaka, and the *Paramatthadiipanii* in three parts on the Abhidhamma Pitaka.

These ñiikaas or sub-commentaries were works containing expositions of points in the Atthakathaas compiled by Buddhaghosa and other commentators, which needed further elucidation for their correct interpretation. There were ñiikaas compiled from time to time subsequent to the compilation of the commentaries, and what the council headed by Mahaa Kassapa performed was the bringing of these various ñiikaas together and making a synthetic summary of them. Though the *Saddhamma-sangaha* does not give any prominence to the part played by Saariputta at this council, it is well known that several ñiikaas were compiled either by him or under his supervision.

Several religious works written in Sinhalese also belong to this period. The Sinhalese exegetical works on which the Pali commentaries were based were preserved in the Mahaavihaara as late as the tenth century. Likewise there were the collections of Jaataka stories and the stories connected with the verses of the Dhammapada, in the Sinhalese language. A collection of stories from which the Pali *Rasavaahinii* drew material and a work called the *Siihalaññhakathaa Mahaava.msa*, on which the Pali chronicles were based, also existed in Sinhalese. None of these works is now extant. Several Sinhalese religio-literary works which were composed in or about the twelfth century are popular even today. Among them are the *Sasadaavata*, which is a poem on the Sasa Jaataka; the *Muvadevdaavata*, which is a poem on the Makhaadeva Jaataka; and the *Kavsilumina*, which is a poem on Kusa Jaataka. Gurulugomi's *Amaavatura* and *Dharmapradiipikaava* and Vidyaacakravarti's *Butsara.na* are also generally ascribed to the twelfth century.

Decline of Buddhism after Paraakramabaahu I and Restoration by Paraakramabaahu II

After the death of Paraakramabaahu the Great there was much internal disturbance in the country caused by rival claimants to the throne and invasions by foreigners. As a result Buddhism was on the decline again. Paraakramabaahu's immediate successor, Vijayabaahu II, promoted trade and religious relations between Burma and Sri Lanka but was slain after a year's rule by a usurper. The usurper was, however, slain five days later by Nissankamalla, who thereafter reigned for nine years (1187-96). Nissankamalla was a great benefactor of Buddhism. He built several notable religious edifices in Polonnaruwa, his capital. Some of these, like the Ruvanveli-daagaba (now called Rankot-vehera), the beautiful Vatadaa-ge, the Sacred Tooth Relic Temple (Hetadaage), and the Nissankalataa-mandapa exist to this day. He made occasional tours in his kingdom, visiting places of religious significance like the Sumanakuuta (Sri Paada, or as called by the English, Adam's Peak) and the Dambulu-vihaara. He built alms-houses at several important places and purified the Saasana by expelling corrupt bhikkhus from the Order.

The period of two decades that followed the death of King Nissankamalla was one of the most disturbed periods in Sri Lanka, during which time occurred several assassinations of rulers and invasions by foreigners. In 1214 a foreigner named Megha invaded, defeated the Sinhalese ruler and reigned for 36 years (1215-51). His reign was one of the most disastrous for Buddhism, for he plundered the monasteries and made them over to his soldiers to dwell in. The people were persecuted by torture and were forced to adopt a different faith. He also destroyed libraries containing many valuable books. The situation was temporarily saved by Paraakramabaahu II, who ruled from Dambadeniya from 1236 while Maagha was still dominating north Lanka. Paraakramabaahu II, who was a ruler of great learning, earned for himself the title Kalikaala Sahitya Sarvajña Pandita. He made efforts to restore the Saasana by bringing over monks from the Chola country in South India and holding a festival to admit monks to the higher ordination. He established several monasteries and pirivenas and encouraged learning. The king also held a great council of monks under the leadership of the great thera Aranyaka Medhankara and purified the Saasana. Subsequently, like Paraakramabaahu I, he formulated rules for the proper conduct of the monks, the code of these rules being known by the name Dambadeni Katikaavata. At Palaabatgala he constructed a great monastery for the hermit-monks who were full of virtue and were able to undergo strict austerities. Two succeeding kings, Vijayabaahu IV (1270-72) and Paraakramabaahu III (1287-93), took much interest in maintaining Buddhism and consolidating the efforts of their predecessor.

The Literary Revival

The religious revival brought about by Paraakramabaahu II continued until about the fifteenth century, though there was not much political stability in the country during that period. The outstanding feature of the period is the compilation of a large number of religio-literary works. Paraakramabaahu II himself obtained teachers from India to teach Lankan monks. He persuaded his younger brother Bhuvanekabaahu to become a scholar and be a teacher to many thousands of elders. The king's minister Devapatiraaja was a great patron of learning. To Paraakramabaahu II is ascribed the authorship of the Sinhalese translations to the *Visuddhimagga* and the *Vinaya Vinicchaya*, the Sinhalese poem *Kavsilumi.na*, the masterpiece of Sinhalese poetry, based on the Kusa Jaataka, and the Sinhalese prose work *Daladaa-sirita*. In the reign of Paraakramabaahu II lived the thera Dharmakirti who was the author of the Pali poem Daathaava.msa and the first part of the *Cuutava.msa*.

The *Thuupava.msa* on the erection of stuupas in Lanka, the *Hattha-vanagalla-vihaara-va.msa* on the history of the ancient vihaara at Attanagalla, the *Rasavaahinii* which is a collection of stories about ancient India and Sri Lanka, the *Samantakuuta-va.n.nanaa* on the Buddha's visit to Sumanakuuta (Adam's Peak), the *Kesadhaatuvamsa* on the history of the hair-relics of the Buddha, the *Paarami-mahaasataka* on the ten perfections (*paraamitaa*), the *Saddhamma-Sangha* which gives an account of the history and development of Buddhism in Lanka, are several of the religious works of merit composed in Pali from the time of Paraakramabaahu II until the fifteenth century.

A large number of Sinhalese works on religious subjects too belongs to this period. The *Saddharmaratnaavalii*, which narrates the stories of the Pali Dhammapadatthakathaa in Sinhalese, the *Puujavalii* which relates the honor and offerings received by the Buddha, the *Pansiya-panas-jaataka* based on the Pali Jaataka commentary, the Sinhala *Bodhiva.msa* on the history of the Bodhi Tree, the *Elu-Attanagaluva.msa* which is a translation of the Pali work, the *Saddharmaalankaara*, based on the Pali *Rasavaahinii*, the *Guttilakaavyaya* based on the Guttila Jaataka, the *Kaavyasekharaya*, based on the Sattubhatta Jaataka, the *Budugu.naalankaaraya*, which narrates the dispelling of the calamity in Vesaali by the Buddha, and the *Loveda-sangaraava*, containing religious instructions for the laity, are the standard works among them.

Embassy from Burma to Obtain Ordination

As a result of this religious revival, the reputation of the Sangha in Sri Lanka became so well established that in the year 1476 King Dhammaceti of Burma decided to send twenty-two selected bhikkhus to Lanka to obtain ordination and bring back to Burma the traditions of Lanka. He sent these bhikkhus with numerous presents in charge of two ministers, Citraduuta and Raamaduuta.

They came in two ships. The first ship with eleven bhikkhus and their attendants, in charge of the minister Citraduuta, arrived in Colombo and the other ship in charge of Raamaduuta with eleven bhikkhus and attendants arrived at Weligama on the southern coast of Lanka. These deputations were received with due ceremony and given a cordial reception by King Buvanekabaahu VI (1470-78), who reigned at Kotte (Jayawardhanapura), six miles from Colombo.

The king of Burma sent the following message to the chief theras of Lanka: "My Lords, I am sending many articles to be offered to the Sacred Tooth Relic, etc. and I request you to make an endeavor to offer these to the Sacred Tooth Relic.

May the noble ones obtain facilities for the twenty-two bhikkhus and their pupils and the two ministers, Citraduuta and Raamaduuta, who are attending on these bhikkhus to assist them in worshiping, honoring and viewing the Sacred Tooth Relic if they are so fortunate as to get an opportunity to do so; after which may the Noble Ones be pleased with their endeavor to enable the twenty-two bhikkhus and their pupils to be ordained in the community of succession from Mahaavihaara fraternity founded by the great thera Mahinda by selecting such bhikkhus who hold an established high reputation and giving the ordination of

Upasampadaa in the Siimaa (ordination hall) in the river Kalyaani, which has been made sacred by its association with our Great Lord."

The request made by the king of Burma was duly granted, the bhikkhus were ordained in the Siimaa in the Kalyaani River. The minister Raamaduuta with twenty bhikkhus and thirty-three pupils, duly ordained, returned to Burma. The other minister, Citraduuta, and his party of bhikkhus were shipwrecked and six of these bhikkhus met with their death. The remaining ones reached their country.

Establishment of Mahaavihaarava.msa in Burma

In Burma King Dhammaceti built an ordination hall, known as Kalyaani Siimaa, and the bhikkhus ordained there went by the name of Kalyaaniva.msa. At a later period ordination of this Nikaaya was carried to Siam from Burma.

The connection with Burma at this period has an important bearing on the fortunes of Buddhism in Sri Lanka, for through these embassies the books that existed in Lanka were taken to Burma, Siam and Cambodia and the Mahaavihaara Nikaaya was established in these countries. This helped Lanka to reobtain the books and the ordination at a subsequent period, when ordination had disappeared in the island and the books were lost.

The Arrival of the Portuguese and the Persecution of Buddhism

The political stability that was maintained by Paraakramabaahu II and his successors until about the fifteenth century began to weaken by the end of that century. At this time the Sinhalese king who ruled at Kotte was the head of a very small territory. The interior regions of the country were in the hands of several petty chiefs who did not care about the religion or the welfare of the people. The Moors on the other hand controlled the trade of the coastal regions. Economically too the country had sunk to such a very low level that by this time Sri Lanka had become dependent on India even for food.

Such was the condition when the Portuguese, who were engaged in discoveries and conquests in the East and were in pursuit of Eastern trade, landed in Lanka in 1505, when Vira

Paraakramabaahu VIII (1484-1508) was ruling at Kotte. The Portuguese promised him military aid against his rivals and great riches from the trade which they proposed to establish. They then gained a foothold in Lanka by erecting a fortress on the rocky beach in Colombo and establishing many trading settlements. Before long the entire coastal region passed into the hands of the Portuguese and the kings of Kotte were entirely at the mercy of their allies. They even made several assaults on the interior of the country in order to become masters of the whole island.

The Portuguese arrived in Colombo in 1505 and, gradually occupying all maritime provinces, remained in their possession up to 1658. The Lanka chronicles as well as the records of their friendly historians describe them as cruel, inhuman, rapacious, bigoted and savage persecutors of Buddhism in their endeavor to impose their own faith — Roman Catholicism — on the people of Sri Lanka.

A few decades after the arrival of the Portuguese, King Bhuvanekabaahu VI (1534-1551), who ruled at Kotte, sought the assistance of his allies, the Portuguese, to ensure the succession of his grandson Dharmapaala to the throne. For this purpose an ivory image of Dharmapaala was sent to Portugal where a coronation of the effigy was held by the Portuguese emperor. When the Sinhalese ambassadors returned they were accompanied by a party of Franciscans who, under the direction of the Portuguese emperor and with the permission of the king of Kotte, preached the Christian Gospel in Lanka. Thus for the first time Christian communities were organized in the maritime provinces of Lanka. Dharmapaala, who had become a baptized Christian under the name of Don Juan Dharmapaala, as an expression of thankfulness to the Portuguese gave them a deed of gift (*sannas*) after his accession, transferring to them the Daladaa Maaligaawa (i.e., the Temple of the Tooth), the temple at Kelaniya and all the temple revenues in the island for the maintenance of the missionary establishments.

Thus there was the necessary assistance given to the Portuguese by the rulers of Kotte to suppress the national religion of the Sinhalese and propagate their own religion — Catholicism. With this support they set about their task. In their conversions they adopted two distinct methods, namely, inducement by offices and other temporal favors, and brutal punishment where inducement failed. People who wished to obtain high offices under them and who wished to earn the goodwill of those in power readily adopted the new faith and took up new Biblical names. Others who hesitated to give up their national faith and showed resistance were brutally punished.

There are lurid accounts of men thrown into rivers to be eaten by crocodiles, babies spitted on the soldiers' pikes and held up before the parents, or crushed between millstones before the eyes of their mothers who later were to be tortured to death. Those who dared to worship in public or wear the yellow robe were put to death. Buddhist monasteries and institutions were destroyed and their treasures looted. Libraries were set on fire. Thus did the period of Portuguese rule become one of the darkest periods of Buddhism in Sri Lanka.

Persecution of Buddhism by Raajasinha I

The Portuguese were not the only enemies of Buddhism at this period. King Raajasinha I (1581-1592), who was the son of Mayaadunne, a brother of Bhuvènekabaahu VI, ruled from Sitawaka when the Portuguese were holding power at Kotte. A gallant leader as he was, Raajasinha succeeded in gaining the confidence of the Sinhalese who opposed the Portuguese rule and winning several battles against the Portuguese, the battle at Mulleriyaawa being the most famous. But, as the chronicles mention, his popularity was shortlived. The foolish king, in his thirst for power, slew his old father with his own hands. Later, being seized with the fear of his crime, Raajasinha sought the advice of the monks for setting himself free from the sin. When the monks explained to him that it was too great a crime to be absolved, the king was provoked to anger.

He then became a follower of the Saivites, in whose advice he took refuge, and became an enemy of Buddhism. The chief Buddhist elder was stoned to death, and many other monks were buried neck-deep in the earth and their heads plowed off. Some others were put to the sword. The sacred edifices and the monasteries were pulled down, and the sacred books were reduced to ashes. The lands which had been endowed in earlier times to the monastic establishments were taken away and Sri

Paada, the Sacred Footprint of the Buddha on Adam's Peak, was handed over to the Saivites. Those monks who managed to escape from the king's wrath disrobed themselves and fled.

Vimala Dharmasuriya's Attempt at Restoring Buddhism

In 1592, the year in which Raajasinha died, a Sinhalese ruler, Vimala Dharmasuriya I, ascended the throne of the hill capital, Kandy, and ruled for twelve years. Though he had been educated by the Portuguese and was originally favored by them, the king soon after his accession turned against them out of his love for the country and the religion.

Vimala Dharmasuriya I was a great patron of Buddhism of that time. After his wars with the Portuguese he set his heart on repairing the damage done by Raajasinha. Several Buddhist monuments were restored. Finding that there was hardly a single monk left in the country who was properly ordained, Vimala Dharmasuriya sent an embassy to the country of Arakan (now part of Burma) to obtain monks to restore ordination in Sri Lanka. The mission was successful; several monks led by the elders Nandicakka and Candavisaala came to Kandy and in the year 1597 an ordination ceremony was held in the Udakukkhepa Siimaa at Getambe, near Kandy, many men of noble families entering the Order on this occasion. The king also built a storeyed pavilion and, bringing back the Sacred Tooth Relic from the Delgamuvihaara where it was hidden, deposited it in the pavilion. The control of Sri Paada was taken from the Saivites and handed over to the Buddhist monks.

Successors of Vimala Dharmasuriya I and the Arrival of the Dutch in Sri Lanka

Vimala Dharmasuriya was succeeded on the throne of Kandy by Senarat, a man zealous in religious works. In his reign the Portuguese invaded Kandy and the king carried away the Sacred Tooth Relic to Mahiyangana for safety. Senarat's son and successor Raajasinha II (1634-1687) was a great warrior but was not zealous. In his reign ended the Portuguese rule in the maritime provinces of Lanka, a feat which the king accomplished with the aid of the Dutch in June 1658.

It was as early as 1602 that the Dutch visited the court of Kandy, in the reign of Vimala Dharmasuriya I, seeking an alliance. In 1612 a treaty was agreed upon between the Dutch and King Senarat, the then king of Kandy, and in accordance with this agreement, in 1638 Raajasinha II sought Dutch assistance against the Portuguese. From that time the two European nations fought each other until in 1658 the Portuguese were expelled from the country and the Dutch came to occupy those regions which formerly were occupied by the Portuguese. They remained in possession until 1796, in which year they were ousted by the British.

The Dutch, whose religion was Protestant Christianity, followed a policy which was in marked contrast to that of the Portuguese. Extension of commerce was their main concern and since peace was essential to achieve this end, they even endured with subdued humbleness and patience whatever insult and provocation came from the Sinhalese. They even assisted the Sinhalese in two embassies to Siam which were sent to obtain monks to establish higher ordination in Sri Lanka.

The Dutch, however, had an established system of education throughout their territories. The school building was both church and school, the schoolmaster was both teacher and representative of the religion. Services were held regularly at these places; births and marriages were registered according to Christian rites. When the agent of the Church was so disposed, he was able to get those who did not attend church punished for the alleged offense. All civil rights and inheritance depended on a person's church affiliation. No person who was not a Christian could hold even a minor office under government, no person who was not a Christian could get married legally or register the birth of a child.

There was, however, one redeeming feature of this system. The organization was so extensive that they had to employ Sinhalese as their teachers and agents of religion. The vast majority of these Protestant agents were at heart Buddhists; they were Christians only in the sense of their office. The people themselves followed this plan: they were Buddhists inwardly but were officially Christians, for the purpose of registering their marriages, the births of their children, for holding office, etc. Thus the efforts of the Dutch in the propagation of their religion did not affect Buddhism much. On the other hand the Portuguese, where they had priests and where they had established churches under the direct control of these priests, were able to look after the congregations and gradually established their religion in such centers. Most of them were zealous and earnest in their duties and took a genuine interest in the welfare of their flocks.

Vimala Dharmasuriya II and his Successors

When the Dutch were occupying the maritime provinces, several Sinhalese rulers of the Kandyan kingdom made attempts to restore Buddhism. One of them was Vimala Dharmasuriya II (1687-1706), son and successor of Raajasinha II. He constructed a three-storeyed pavilion for the Sacred Tooth Relic. The king also made a pilgrimage to Sumanakuuta (Adam's Peak) on foot. Seeing that the state of the Order of monks was unsatisfactory again to such an extent that not more than five ordained monks were found in the whole country, the king sent an embassy to Arakan and obtained monks for an ordination ceremony. With the help of these monks an ordination ceremony was held at Getambe, at the place where a similar ceremony had been held formerly in the reign of Vimala Dharmasuriya I. At this ceremony thirty-three novices were given higher ordination and another one hundred and twenty persons were admitted to the Order.

Vimala Dharmasuriya II was succeeded by his son Sri Viraparaakrama Narendrasinha (1706-1739), a just ruler, mindful of the welfare of the religion. He constructed a two-storeyed building for the Sacred Tooth Relic, provided the monks with their requisites, and induced several members of the laity to enter the Order. However, during his reign many a monk had resorted to scandalous practices.

His successor Sri Vijaya Raajasinha (1739-1747), also a pious ruler, induced many a young person to join the Order and also held several religious festivals. He spent money on getting religious books written, caused preaching halls to be constructed at several places, and took measures to educate the people in the doctrine. Discovering that the Order of the Sangha was almost extinct in the island, he sent two missions to Siam, with the help of the Dutch who lent a ship for the voyage. The first expedition proved disastrous due to shipwreck, and before the second mission returned the king died. Thus his attempt to restore higher ordination failed.

The Reign of Kirti Sri Raajasinha

Sri Vijaya Raajasinha was succeeded by King Kirti Sri Raajasinha, whose reign proved to be one of the most inspiring periods for Buddhism in that century. At the time of his accession the Order of monks had sunk to very low levels of degeneracy. There was not a single monk in the whole island who had received the higher ordination. There were plenty of novices (i.e., saamaneras), but apart from a few skillful and pious ones among them the majority were leading a life unbecoming to monks. They set aside the study of Dhamma and Vinaya and resorted to the study of astrology, medicine and devil worship, led scandalous lives and engaged in cultivation of land and in trade. The older saamaneras ordained only the sons of their relatives so that they could obtain the immense wealth which the generations of kings and ministers had dedicated to the service of the Order. Kirti Sri Raajasinha was determined to set right this state of affairs. With the aid of the Dutch who gave a vessel for the voyage, the king sent an embassy to King Dhammika of Siam and re-established the higher ordination in Sri Lanka. Several hundreds were ordained and education was fostered. The king also proclaimed a code of conduct (*katikaavata*) for the guidance of the monks.

Velivita Sri Saranankara

In all these religious activities of King Kirti Sri Raajasinha he was inspired and guided by a great personality, a saamanera who was distinguished for his piety, enthusiasm, learning and determination. He was Velivita Pindapaatika Sri Saranankara. Born in 1698 at Velivita, a village near Kandy, he became a novice at the age of sixteen as a pupil of an elder saamanera called Suuriyagoda. With great effort and devotion he studied the Pali language and the doctrine, for which purpose he traveled from place to place in search of books and tutors. Later he went about preaching the Dhamma, thus encouraging others to rise up for the welfare of the religion. These activities of Saranankara Saamanera soon made him popular as a teacher of great renown who devoted his life to his own welfare and that of others, a poet, preacher and controversialist.

Apart from his skill as a scholar he was also known for his austere practices. When he went round the country learning or preaching, he depended for his sustenance on the ancient practice of a bhikkhu, called *pi.n.napaata*, gathering his food from house to house in his almsbowl. For this he became known as Pindapaatika Saranankara. When King Vimala Dharmasuriya II reigned he was a saamanera, but his sincere devotion had pleased the king so much that he made a gilt casket set with seven hundred gems and presented it to Saranankara Saamanera, with many books. This king also provided the monk with the requisites and induced him to write several literary works.

When King Sri Vijaya Raajasinha came to the throne it was at the request of Saranankara Saamanera that the king sent two embassies to Siam. In the reign of King Kirti Sri Raajasinha, Saranankara Saamanera offered his fullest cooperation in his activities in the revival of Buddhism and the king depended upon the saamanera for guidance, advice and inspiration. He urged the king to send the embassy to Siam and himself wrote the messages that were taken to the Siamese king and the Sangharaaja of that country. The king's ministers who constituted the embassy were chosen on his advice and this mission was successful mainly due to his exertions. After the return of the embassy Saranankara Saamanera was given higher ordination and was appointed Sangharaaja of Sri Lanka, the highest office conferred on a monk.

The activities of Saranankara Thera not only restored the higher ordination and the purity of the Sangha but also brought about a literary revival as a result of the impetus given by him to the study of the Pali language and the Buddha's teachings.

Saranankara Thera himself compiled several important religious works such as the *Munigu.naalankaara*, a Sinhalese poem in praise of the Buddha, the *Saaraartha Sangraha*, a treatise on various doctrinal teachings in Buddhism. *Abhisambodhi-alankaara*, a Pali poem in a hundred stanzas on the life of the Buddha from the time of Dipankara up to his enlightenment, the *Madhuraartha Prakaasanii*, which is a Sinhalese commentarial paraphrase to the Pali *Mahaabodhiva.msa*, and the *Ruupamaalaa*, a work on Pali grammar. Several others who were pupils of Saranankara Thera also composed many literary works. The great monk died in 1778 a.c. at the age of 81.

The successors of Sri Saranankara Thera are known as belonging to the Syaamopaali Nikaaya, now popularly called the Siyam (Syaama) Nikaaya. Only those who belonged to what was regarded as the highest caste could obtain higher ordination in that Nikaaya. In the year 1799 a saamanera named Ambagahapitiya ¥aanavimalatissa, who did not belong to that caste, went to Amarapura in Burma to obtain higher ordination and on his return he established the Amarapura Nikaaya in 1803. Subsequently, in 1863 Ambagahawatte Sri Saranankara Thera established the Raamañña Nikaaya. These three Nikaayas exist up to this day, with no doctrinal differences between them.

The Arrival of the British and the End of Sinhalese Rule in Sri Lanka

King Kirti Sri Raajasinha, whose reign, as was seen above, was one of the most fruitful for the cause of Buddhism, was succeeded by his brother Raajaadhi Raajasinha. A scholar of Pali, Sanskrit and Sinhalese as he was, the king himself composed the beautiful Sinhalese poem *Asadisa-daa-kava* and worked for the religion by taking necessary steps to preserve the purity of the Saasana. His nephew, Sri Vikrama Raajasinha, was the next and last king of Lanka. This ruler, who was in constant fear of the intrigues of his Adigar Pilima Talawe and his allies, had recourse to intoxicating drinks, hoping thus to forget his sorrows, and tortured all his enemies with appalling cruelty. There was general unrest in the kingdom and these conditions were evidently not conducive to the progress of Buddhism.

It was in 1796, during the reign of Raajaadhi Raajasinha, that the Dutch, who were defeated in battle, surrendered their territories to the British colony and Sir Frederick North was sent as the first British governor.

Before long North realized that the opportunity would come soon for them to possess the whole island, for Pilima Talawe, the Adigar of King Sri Vikrama Raajasinha of Kandy, disclosed his plans to ruin the king to the British governor himself. However, this plan of Pilima Talawe was revealed to the king, and the Adigar was beheaded in 1812. Ehelepola, who became the next Adigar, was detected in an attempt to organize a general rebellion against the king, and as punishment, the king tortured his wife and children cruelly. Subsequently the king punished all whom he suspected and as a result, unrest and disorder became the order of the day.

In these circumstances, Ehelepola appealed to the British for help. In January 1815 a British army marched to the capital city of Kandy and took the Sinhalese king captive. On the 2nd of March 1815, at a solemn assembly of the Kandyan chiefs and the monks, the king was deposed and his dominions were vested in the British Crown. Thus ended the glamour of the Kingdom of Kandy which had withstood the invasions and attacks of the Portuguese and the Dutch and for some time the English. Thus ended too the line of the Buddhist kings of Lanka who for 2301 years, from the accession of Vijaya in 486 BCE, brought glory and fame to their country and religion.

The British Attitude towards Buddhism

It was seen in the previous chapter how the British occupied the low-country of Lanka in 1796 and the Kandyan territories in 1815. These territories remained in their hands until 1948, in which year Sri Lanka regained her independence.

Mention has already been made of the solemn assembly of the 2nd of March 1815 held in Kandy. At this assembly a treaty was signed between the British rulers and the Kandyan chiefs, by which the chiefs handed over the country to the British and the British promised to safeguard Buddhism, declaring its rites and ceremonies sacred and inviolate.

The inclusion of this clause referring to Buddhism in the very treaty by which the chiefs handed over the country to the British is very significant. On the one hand, it indicates how concerned the Sinhalese leaders were about the future of Buddhism even in the hour of their misfortune. On the other hand, the British had obviously considered that its omission would bring disastrous results.

However, the British attitude towards Buddhism soon caused dissatisfaction among the Sinhalese chiefs. The chiefs and the Buddhist monks realized that the British had no desire to respect the clause of the treaty relating to Buddhism, and that they were keen to convert the people to their own faith.

During the early years after the signing of the treaty the British governor took part in the annual ceremonies connected with the Sacred Tooth Relic and appointed the chief theras, as had been done by the Sinhalese kings in former times. This created resentment on the part of the Christian missionaries in Sri Lanka and the Christian authorities in England, and soon both practices were dropped, severing whatever connection they had with Buddhism.

From 1847 the bhikkhus were required to elect and appoint their own chiefs and in 1853 the British government handed over the Tooth Relic from their custody to the Diyawadana Nilame and the chief monks of the Malwatte and the Asgiriya monasteries.

While thus violating the treaty of 1815 the British rulers even prohibited the Buddhists from enjoying some of the privileges that were granted to the followers of the Christian faith. Thus, for instance, even as late as 1805 no child could be legally registered without previous baptism by a Christian minister, and the clergy did not solemnize the marriage of unbaptized individuals.

Further, only those who adopted the Christian faith were favored with government employment. This attitude of the British made vast numbers of Buddhists adopt the new faith without any understanding of its teachings. These people saw in Christianity "not only happiness in the world which is to come, but, what was more important to them, the promise of this life as well!"

Some of the British governors in their attempt to disrupt the Buddhist organization even tried to bring about disunity between the monks and the laity and also to win over some of the leading Buddhist monks to their side. For they realized that the monks were the main obstacle to their conversions and that as long as the monks and the laity remained united their attempts would not meet with great success.

Lastly, the British rulers gave all possible support to the Christian missionaries to carry out their educational and missionary activities. How these missionary bodies attempted the Christianization of Lanka will be discussed in the next chapter.

The Christian Missionary Activities

From the beginning of the period of British rule several Christian missionary bodies engaged themselves actively in missionary activities in Sri Lanka. The Baptists had already started their activities in 1792. They were followed by the Wesleyan Methodists in 1814, the Americans in 1816, and the Church of England in 1818. These missionary bodies received every encouragement and assistance from the government.

The establishment of missionary schools in various parts of the island was one of the principal undertakings of these missionary bodies. These schools were manned and managed by the missionary societies with the assistance of the British government and were partly financed by public funds. The schools attracted large numbers of Buddhist children because they were the centers where young men were trained for high government offices. Hitherto the temple had been the village school and the monks were the instructors of the village children in secular learning as well as in spiritual wisdom. But under the British government temple education could not provide the learning necessary for government employment. Thus the Buddhist parents who wished to see their children in high government offices willingly sent them to the new missionary schools.

In these schools the children were molded according to the requirements of the missionary bodies. The authorities did not insist that one should become a Christian before admission, but each student was required to learn the Christian religion and to participate in the morning and evening religious services in the school. They had no opportunity of participating in their own religious observances. Almost every school had its own church. The lessons imparted to these children were arranged with a view to undermining their Buddhist religion. The teaching of the Buddha was criticized and condemned and the Buddhist practices were ridiculed. Buddhism was held up as a religion of the vulgar masses as opposed to the Christianity of civilized people.

This disparagement in course of time naturally had its expected result. People gradually began to give up their national faith for the new faith which they were trained to think of as more refined and cultured. It now became the fashion to adopt the Christian faith and Christian names and customs. Even those who did not embrace Christianity became indifferent to their own religion. When they grew up they did not even mind their conversion to any religion.

The missionaries also did not neglect the education of the girls. Convents were opened up with boarding facilities and in them the girls were brought up and educated with the utmost care until they were married in due time, with the sanction of the Christian guardians.

Mohottiwatte Gunaananda Thera and the Buddhist Reawakening

When the Christian missionaries were thus active in towns and villages propagating their gospel and converting the Buddhists to their faith, the Buddhist monks were not able enough to offer much resistance. When the villagers assembled in the temple on Poya (*uposatha*) days, they attempted to refute the arguments of the Christian preachers in the course of their sermons, but this method was not very effective. It was at this time, about 1860, that a young Buddhist saamanera named Mohottiwatte Gunaananda appeared on the scene and challenged the Christian missionaries to meet him in open-debate. This young novice had obtained his early education in Christian schools and had thus studied the Christian scriptures and was also well versed in the Buddha's teachings. He went from village to village making public speeches and held meetings in several Christian strongholds, often challenging the Christian clergy to face him in open debate. Soon he earned a great reputation for his eloquence and people flocked in thousands to hear him.

The Christian clergy at first took no notice of the challenge of this monk, but later, quite confident of their success they accepted the challenge. This resulted in three public controversies, one at Udanvita in 1866, another at Gampola in 1871 and the last at Panadura in 1873.

The Panadura controversy, which lasted for a week, was the most important of them all. It was the culmination of his efforts and it led to a Buddhist reawakening. The controversy was to take place in the presence of leading Sinhalese Christians and Buddhists. Rules were laid down so that the meeting could be held in a fair manner. The leading English newspaper of the time, *The Ceylon Times*, sent a special representative to report the proceedings. A complete report of all the speeches corrected by the speakers themselves was published in English day by day. The controversy ended with victory for the Buddhists. The Buddhist orator not only replied effectively to the fallacies of the Christian speakers, but also enlightened them on the principles and tenets of the Buddhist doctrine. When the Christians retired from the debate defeated, the Buddhists were overjoyed. Festivities were held in every temple to mark their triumph and the effigy of Gunaananda Thera was carried in procession in every village.

The triumph of the Buddhists over their Christian adversaries at the Panadura controversy flushed into their veins vigor and enthusiasm to work for the recovery of their lost glory.

Colonel Olcott and Buddhist Activities

An American scholar named Dr. Peebles, who happened to be in Sri Lanka on a visit about the time of this Panadura controversy, was so impressed with it that he published its proceedings in book form on his return to America. The attention of Colonel Henry Steele Olcott was first drawn towards Buddhism by this report of the controversy which he happened to read in a public library in America. Olcott was an American by birth who had spent his early life as a very successful farmer and a colonel of both the army and the navy. At an early age of 43 years in 1875 he gave up all worldly fortunes and together with Madame Blavatsky formed the Theosophical Society for the quest of truth in all religions. Having read the reports of the Panadura controversy, he realized the importance of the teachings of the Buddha and in 1880 he came over to Lanka along with Madame Blavatsky to gain a first-hand knowledge of Buddhism. When his studies soon convinced him of the teachings of the Buddha, he embraced Buddhism and worked for the upliftment of the Buddhists in Lanka.

Olcott showed the Buddhist leaders of Sri Lanka that if Buddhism was to raise its head against the Christian missionary activities, they should open up Buddhist schools to educate their children. Under his guidance and leadership, and with the support of all the leading Buddhist monks, the lay Buddhist leaders in Sri Lanka at that time founded the Buddhist Theosophical Society on 17th June 1880. The primary objects of the society were the establishment of Buddhist schools, and the bringing together of Buddhist workers in a cooperative body without distinction of caste or position for the purpose of promoting the welfare of the Buddhists of Lanka.

At the time of Olcott's arrival there were only three Buddhist schools in Sri Lanka which obtained government grants, one at Dodanduwa, another at Panadura, and the third at Bandaragama. In 1897, twelve years after the establishment of the society, there were 25 boys' schools, 11 girls' schools, and 10 mixed schools founded by the society. In 1903 there were 174 schools under the management of the society with an attendance of about 30,000 children. In 1940 the number of schools had risen to 429. Olcott and his supporters went from village to village appealing to the people to donate subscriptions for the maintenance of these schools, and funds were readily forthcoming. Several leading educationists of his day made his educational plans a great success. Mention should be made among them of C. W. Leadbeater, Bowles Daly, F. L. Woodward, A. E. Bultjens and Mrs. M. M. Higgins. Mrs. Higgins was particularly responsible for the successful education of the Buddhist girls. The leading Buddhist schools of the present day such as Ananda and Nalanda Colleges in Colombo, Dharmaraja in Kandy, Mahinda in Galle, Dharmasoka in Ambalangoda, Visakha in Bambalapitiya, and Museus in Colombo are outstanding examples of the success of his efforts.

Olcott pointed out to the Sinhalese Buddhist leaders of his time that they should have their own publications to give publicity to Buddhist and national opinion. For this purpose the Buddhist Theosophical Society started the Sinhalese newspaper, *Sarasavisandarasa*, in December 1880, and later its English supplement, *The Buddhist*, now a monthly of the YMBA, Colombo. Colonel Olcott worked hard to win back for the Sinhalese their lost rights. It was as a result of his efforts that the Buddhists of Lanka gained freedom to hold their Buddhist processions and that the full-moon day of Vesak was declared a public holiday. The present Buddhist flag is also a creation of Olcott which he appealed to the Buddhists to hoist on all important Buddhist occasions. His efforts also resulted in the appointment of Buddhist registrars of marriages.

Of the Panadura controversy and the consequent arrival of Colonel Olcott, it could justly be said that these two events jointly closed down a dark period in Lankan Buddhism and ushered in a new bright era.

This noble personality who awakened the Sinhalese Buddhists and showed them the path on which they should proceed passed away in 1907 while he was in India.

Other Activities of the Buddhist Renaissance Movement

Apart from meeting the Christian opponents in open debate, Mohottivatte Gunaananda Thera and his companions had planned other devices to counteract the anti-Buddhist propaganda of the Christian missionaries and revive the Buddhist faith in the country. One of these devices was the establishment of a printing press whereby they could reply to the criticisms of the Christians and also publish books for the study of Buddhism.

Thus the first press, controlled by Sinhalese Buddhists, was established in 1862 under the name of Lankopakaara Press. It was a donation by the king of Siam. In the same year Mohottivatte Gunaananda Thera established the Sarvajña-saasanaabhivurddhi-daayaka Press at Kotahena, near Colombo. Consequently the Lakrivikirana Press was established in 1863 and the Lankabhinavavisruta Press in 1864.

In the meantime learned monks of the period, with the assistance of lay followers, brought about a revival of Buddhist learning. Pioneers among them were the venerable Hikkaduve Sri Sumangala, who founded the Vidyodaya Pirivena of Maligakanda in Colombo in 1874 and the venerable Ratmalaane Sri Dhammaaloka, who founded the Vidyaalankara Pirivena of Peliyagoda in Colombo in 1875. In these two great centers of learning a vast number of monks and lay people received education and in a short time the fame of these two pirivenas spread even in foreign countries.

The scholars whom these two centers produced opened up other pirivenas in different parts of the country and also contributed to Buddhistic studies by compiling and editing numerous books. It was also about this time that devoted scholars from foreign countries who happened to be in Sri Lanka evinced a great interest in Buddhism, its culture and literature, and created an interest in their kinsmen in the West through their valuable treatises. Turner, Tennant, Childers, Rhys Davids and Geiger were but a few among them.

Anagaarika Dharmapaala and the Buddhist Cultural Revival

A different type of revivalistic activity was carried out by a group of lay Buddhist leaders just at this time, the foremost of this group being Anagaarika Dharmapaala. The fame of this great personality lies in his successful effort of reforming the Buddhist society in Sri Lanka, which had fallen into a very low moral state, and also in his activities in India for the purpose of reviving Buddhism in that country and for winning back the Buddhist sacred places there for their rightful owners, the Buddhists. We are presently concerned only with his social reformation in Sri Lanka.

Anagaarika Dharmapaala, formerly known as David Hewavitarana, was born in 1864 as the eldest son of a leading businessman in Colombo who had migrated to the capital city from Matara in south Lanka. The father, mother and the grandfather of the child were devoted Buddhists who were close associates of the venerable Hikkaduve Sri Sumangala Thera. At home the child was thus brought up in a Buddhist environment though he received his education in Christian schools. Those were the days when Mohottiwatte Gunaananda Thera was engaged in verbal battles against the Christian missionary activities, and young Dharmapaala had not only listened to the orations of the great speaker with much inspiration, but also had become a favorite of the monks by his constant visits to the temple at Kotahena. When Colonel Olcott and Madame Blavatsky arrived in Lanka in 1880, Dharmapaala, then a youth of 16 years, naturally became a great favorite of the two foreigners through his association with Gunaananda Thera.

The speeches and activities of Colonel Olcott greatly inspired the young enthusiast. In 1883, consequent upon a brutal assault on a Buddhist procession by a Catholic mob at Kotahena, Dharmapaala left his Catholic school and in the following year became a member of the Buddhist Theosophical Society in Colombo, of which his grandfather was the president. At the age of 20 Dharmapaala obtained permission from his father to leave home and lead a celibate life as he wished to devote all his time to the welfare of the Saasana. From that time he stayed at the headquarters of the Buddhist Theosophical Society.

In 1886 when Colonel Olcott returned to Sri Lanka after a short stay abroad and planned to go round the country addressing public gatherings and collecting money for the Buddhist Educational Fund, Anagaarika Dharmapaala joined him as his interpreter. For this purpose he obtained leave from the Education Department where he was working as a junior clerk and subsequently vacated his post in order to dedicate all his life to the good of the religion.

As the interpreter of Colonel Olcott, Dharmapaala gained immense experience as a speaker. He now traveled throughout the country with or without his companion, Olcott.

Those were the days when the Buddhists of Lanka were reluctant to declare themselves Buddhists, for Buddhism was considered to be the faith of the unurbanized masses. It was the fashion at that time to become a Christian, to study English and other allied subjects, to adopt a foreign name and to imitate the dress of the foreigners and their customs and manners. Buddhism and Buddhist culture were subjected to ridicule and were the heritage of villagers in the interior.

Anagaarika Dharmapaala was the foremost among those who rose against this mentality of the Buddhists. Through his public speeches and numerous articles in newspapers and journals he vehemently opposed the habit of imitating foreigners in religion, names and customs. He emphatically pointed out that this tendency to imitate was a clear manifestation of a lack of the primary element of self-esteem. In keeping with his preaching he himself changed his name from David to Dharmapaala. The people listened to his sermons and attentively read his articles in journals and newspapers and were convinced of the truth of his philosophy. Gradually there came about a cultural revival. The people began to take pride in their religion, their language and their customs. Above all, several younger men of his time joined the Buddhist forward movement to guide the destinies of future generations of Buddhists in Sri Lanka.

This great personality, who indefatigably gave his services for the revival of Buddhism in Lanka, India and other parts of the world, in his last days entered the Order as the venerable Devamitta Dhammapaala Thera. He passed away in the year 1933, while he was in India. To perpetuate his memory Sri Lanka and India celebrated his birth centenary in 1964-65.

Buddhism in Sri Lanka in the First Half of the Twentieth Century

The leading men in the Buddhist community at the beginning of the twentieth century were inspired by the activities of Anagaarika Dharmapaala and they formed into organized bodies for the promotion of the Buddhist revivalistic movement. Among them were great personalities such as Sir D. B. Jayatillake, F. R. Somnayake, Valisinha Harishchandra and W. A. de Silva. To them the Buddhist revival was the national revival.

These prominent men, whose names have gone into history, became active members of leading Buddhist associations like the Buddhist Theosophical Society (founded 1880), the Colombo Young Men's Buddhist Association (1898), the Maha Bodhi Society (1891), and the Ceylon Buddhist Congress (1918), and worked with remarkable success to achieve the aims and objects of those organizations. Through such organizations these Buddhist leaders were able to unite and bring together all Buddhists in Sri Lanka, to inspire them to be active, to collect funds for educational and other religious purposes, to give the Buddhist children a sound religious and secular education, to do a great deal of social work and to raise the spiritual and moral standard of the people.

A great deal of literary work was produced during this period. The Vidyodaya and the Vidyaalankaara Pirivenas and their affiliated institutions, which numbered about 200, had produced many scholars who edited several canonical and commentarial works in the early twentieth century. Simon Hewavitarana, the youngest brother of Anagaarika

Dharmapaala, had left a large legacy which was to be used for the printing and publishing of Pali books, and this greatly facilitated the production of books at this time. From about 1930 many modern scholars, both monks and laymen, have edited and published many more texts of Pali Buddhism and have also compiled several secondary works on the different aspects of Buddhism. To name these scholars and their publications is not necessary since they and their works are very well known.

A great enthusiasm was also created for the rebuilding of ancient Buddhist shrines in the old capitals of Sri Lanka. The Ruwanveli Daagaba was the first to receive attention. The other shrines too were renovated one by one and today the old city of Anuraadhapura has once more become a sacred city with the Catholic Church and the commercial sites which were in the city being moved to other places.

Sri Lanka has not only reorganized her Buddhist activities within the country but has also taken a leading part in sending *Dhammaduutas*, "messengers of the Dhamma," abroad. In 1950 the World Fellowship of Buddhists was set up in order to bring all Buddhist countries together, and several conferences were held in the subsequent years.

It is a very significant fact that this revival of Buddhism in the twentieth century was accelerated towards the middle of that century as a result of the Sinhalese Buddhist leaders of the time gaining control of the reins of government. Ultimately in 1948 Sri Lanka regained its independence after a period of British rule of 133 years. The Buddhist leaders who worked indefatigably for the cause of Buddhism were also the Sinhalese national leaders who led the struggle for liberation from foreign rule. It was therefore to be expected that when these leaders gained national freedom and took over the reins of government from the British rulers, they were mindful of their national faith and its culture and therefore took the necessary steps to set things right so that Buddhism would once more receive its rightful place.

The Buddha Jayanti and After

In the year 1956, on the 23rd of May, which was the Vesak full-moon day of that year, the Buddhists in Sri Lanka and other parts of the world celebrated the Buddha Jayanti. That was the 2500th anniversary of the Buddha's Parinibbaana, a day specially significant to the Buddhists the world over on account of the tradition that it constitutes half the life-span of the Saasana and that from that year the Dhamma would flourish and spread far and wide.

The history of Buddhism in Sri Lanka from the closing years of the last century has clear indications that the prophecy, as far as Lanka is concerned, is coming true. In other parts of the world too it is seen that more and more people who were not Buddhists by birth are becoming interested in Buddhism.

The government of Sri Lanka, on its part, undertook numerous activities in commemoration of the Buddha Jayanti. A committee of leading Buddhist monks and laymen was appointed to advise the government on all matters relating to the Buddha Jayanti celebrations. Arrangements were made to translate the Tripitaka into Sinhalese and compile an *Encyclopaedia of Buddhism* in English and one in Sinhalese as well. It was also decided to compile other books dealing with the biography of the Buddha, his teachings and the history of Buddhism. The completion of the renovation of the Daladaa Maaligawa (the Temple of the Tooth) in Kandy, before the Buddha Jayanti and to aid the reconstruction of the Mahiyangana Thupa were among its other undertakings. A substantial grant was also given to the organization which was handling the construction work of a Sanghaaraama for the Buddhist monks at the University of Ceylon, Peradeniya. Arrangements were made to hold a World Buddhist Conference in Colombo in the following year.

From the Buddha Jayanti year it was noticeable that the Buddhists in Lanka applied themselves more keenly to the practice of morality taught in Buddhism while showing interest in the celebration of Buddhist festivals. More and more people observe the eight precepts on the Poya days and young children are given a sound religious education. The government on its part has given the necessary encouragement for this religious re-establishment. In January 1959 the Vidyodaya and the Vidyaalankaara Pirivenas were made two universities. The private Buddhist and Christian schools were taken over in December 1960 and are now managed by the government. The four Poya days of the month (i.e., full and new moon, and the two quarter moon days) were made the weekend holidays in 1966, instead of Sundays as in previous times. It has also been planned to start a new Bhikkhu University in Anuraadhapura.

Sri Lanka has today about 6.5 million Buddhists, which is about sixty-five percent of her total population. There are nearly 6,000 Buddhist monasteries all over the island with approximately 15,000 monks. Almost all the monasteries in the island have their Dhamma schools where Buddhist children are given religious instruction on the Poya days (previously on Sundays). The Colombo Young Men's Buddhist Association conducts an island-wide examination annually for the pupils of these Dhamma schools. The children are provided with free books, by the Ministry of Cultural Affairs and prizes are given to those who pass these examinations, including one on the Dhammapada, and this association spends annually a large sum of money on the religious education of children. In 1956-57, 163,180 children sat for the Dhamma examination.

The foregoing account will tell the reader of the vicissitudes that this great religion, Buddhism, had to face during its history of over 2,000 years in this isle of Sri Lanka. It had its tidal ebb and flow. During the four centuries of foreign domination Buddhism withstood all the assaults that almost crushed it.

Since Sri Lanka gained its independence in 1948, there has been a revival of the Buddhist religion and culture in the country, and this reawakening was particularly noticeable when the Buddha Jayanti was celebrated in 1956.

The progress achieved since the eighties of the last century may well be called remarkable. Yet, to the Buddhists of Lanka, this should not be a cause of complacency, for which there is no room in a world of change. It remains the duty of the present generation and the coming ones to preserve and strengthen these achievements against the corrosive forces of a materialist age, and to work devotedly so that the Buddha's message of Wisdom and Compassion may take still firmer and deeper roots in Lanka and also spread its beneficial influence over the world.

5

Buddhism in Thailand

People all over the world who are interested in Buddhism and keep in touch with its news and activities must have heard of the Buddha Jayanti celebrations held a few years ago in all Buddhist countries, including India and Japan. It was in 1957 or, according to the reckoning of some Buddhist countries, in 1956, that Buddhism, as founded by Gotama the Buddha, had completed its 2,500th year of existence. The Buddhist tradition, especially of the Theravada or Southern School such as now prevails in Burma, Ceylon, Cambodia, Laos and Thailand, has it that on the completion of 2,500 years from its foundation, Buddhism would undergo a great revival, resulting in its all-round progress, in both the fields of study and practice. Buddhists throughout the world, therefore, commemorated the occasion in 1956-57 by various kinds of activities such as meetings, symposia, exhibitions and the publication of Buddhist texts and literature.

As to whether or not the tradition mentioned above has any truth behind it, the future alone will testify. However, judging from news received from all corners of the globe, it is no exaggeration to say that mankind is taking an ever-increasing interest in Buddhism. As a matter of fact, since the end of the Second World War interest in Buddhism as evinced by people in Europe, America, and Australia has reached a scale unheard of before. Any casual perusal of journals on Buddhism in any of these continents will convince the readers of this statement. It is a matter worth noticing that after the end of the First World War also, Buddhism made great headway in Europe and elsewhere. This phenomenon can perhaps be best explained by the fact that mankind's spiritual thirst is more sharpened by calamities like war, and that in times of distress mankind realizes Truth better.

The Land of Yellow Robes

Thailand is perhaps the only country in the world where the king is constitutionally stipulated to be a Buddhist and the upholder of the Faith. For centuries Buddhism has established itself in Thailand and has enriched the lives of the Thais in all their aspects. Indeed, without Buddhism, Thailand would not be what it is today. Owing to the tremendous influence Buddhism exerts on the lives of its people, Thailand is called by many foreigners "The Land of Yellow Robes," for yellow robes are the garments of Buddhist monks. In view of the increasing interest the world is taking in Buddhism and in view of the fact that Thailand is one of the countries where Buddhism still exists as a living force it will not, perhaps, be out of place to know something of the story of how this great faith reached that country.

BUDDHISM IN THAILAND: ITS PAST

Different opinions exist about when, exactly, Buddhism reached that part of the world now officially known as Thailand. Some scholars say that Buddhism was introduced to Thailand during the reign of Asoka, the great Indian emperor who sent Buddhist missionaries to various parts of the then known world. Others are of the view that Thailand received Buddhism much later.

Judging from archaeological finds and other historical evidence, however, it is safe to say that Buddhism first reached Thailand when the country was inhabited by a racial stock of people known as the Mon-Khmer who then had their capital, Dvaravati, at a city now known as Nakon Pathom (Sanskrit: Nagara Prathama), about 50 kilometers to the west of Bangkok. The great pagoda at Nakon Pathom, Phra Pathom Chedi (Prathama cetiya), and other historical findings in other parts of the country testify to this fact as well as to the fact that Buddhism, in its varied forms, reached Thailand at four different periods, namely:

I. Theravada or Southern Buddhism

II. Mahayana or Northern Buddhism

III. Burma (Pagan) Buddhism

IV. Ceylon (Lankavamsa) Buddhism

We shall now proceed to study each of these periods in detail.

Theravada or Southern Buddhism

That the first form of Buddhism introduced to Thailand was that of Theravada (The Doctrine of the Elders) School is proved by various archaeological remains unearthed in the excavations at Nakon Pathom, such as the Dharma Chakra (Wheel of Law), the Buddha footprints and seats, and the inscriptions in the Pali language, all of which are in rocks. Such objects of Buddhistic veneration existed in India before the introduction of the Buddha image, which appeared later as a result of Greek influence. Buddhism, therefore, must have reached Thailand during the 3rd century B.C., and it must have been more or less the same form of Buddhism as was propagated by the great Buddhist Emperor Asoka. This form of Buddhism was known as Theravada or Hinayana (The Lower Vehicle) in contradistinction to the term Mahayana (The Higher Vehicle), the two schools having sprung up soon after the passing away of the Buddha. When worship of the Buddha image became popular in India, it also spread to other countries where Buddhism had already been introduced. This is borne out by the fact that many Buddha images, especially those of the Gupta style, had been found in the ruins of Nakon Pathom and the neighboring cities. Judging from the style of the Buddha images found, it can also be assumed that the early Buddhist missionaries to Thailand went from Magadha (in Bihar state, India).

To support the view that the first form of Buddhism introduced to Thailand was that of the Theravada School as propagated by Emperor Asoka, we have evidence from the Mahavamsa, the ancient chronicle of Ceylon. In one of its passages dealing with the propagation of the Dhamma, the Mahavamsa records that Asoka sent missionaries headed by Buddhist elders to as many as nine territories. One of these territories was known as Suvarnabhumi where two Theras (elder monks), Sona and Uttara, were said to have proceeded.

Now opinions differ as to where exactly this land of Suvarnabhumi is. Thai scholars express the opinion that it is in Thailand and that its capital was at Nakon Pathom, while scholars of Burma say that Suvarnabhumi is in Burma, the capital being at Thaton, a Mon (Peguan) town in eastern Burma near the Gulf of Martaban. Still other scholars of Laos and Cambodia claim that the territory of Suvarnabhumi is in their lands. Historical records in this connection being meager as they are, it would perhaps be of no avail to argue as to the exact demarcation of Suvarnabhumi. Taking all points into consideration, one thing, however, seems clear beyond dispute. That is Suvarnabhumi was a term broadly used in ancient times to denote that part of Southeast Asia which now includes Southern Burma, Thailand, Laos, Cambodia and Malaya. The term Suvarnabhumi is a combination of the words *suvarna* and *bhumi*. Both are Sanskrit words; the former means gold and the latter stands for land. Suvarnabhumi therefore literally means Golden Land or Land of Gold. Keeping in view the abundance of nature in that part of Asia just referred to, the term seems but appropriate.

The reason why scholars of Thailand express the view that the capital of Suvarnabhumi was at Nakon Pathom was because of the archaeological finds unearthed in the area surrounding that town. Nowhere in any of the countries mentioned above, not even at Thaton in Burma, could one find such a large and varied number of ancient relics as were found at Nakon Pathom. By age and style these archaeological objects belong to the times of Emperor Asoka and the later Guptas. Even the Great Stupa (Phra Pathom Chedi) at Nakon Pathom itself is basically identical with the famous Sañchi Stupa in India, built by Asoka, especially if one were to remove the *shikhara* or upper portion. Many Thai archaeologists are of the opinion that the shikhara was a later addition to the pagoda, a result, so to say, of the blending of the Thai aesthetic sense with Indian architectural art. Moreover, the name Pathom Chedi (Pali: Pathama Cetiya) means "First Pagoda" which, in all probability, signifies that it was the first pagoda built in Suvarnabhumi. This would easily fit in with the record of the Mahavamsa — that Theras Sona and Uttara went and established Buddhism in the territory of Suvarnabhumi at the injunction of Emperor Asoka. Taking cognizance of the fact that Asoka reigned from 269 to 237 B.C., we can reasonably conclude that Buddhism first spread to Thailand during the 3rd century B.C. It is interesting to note in this connection that the history of the penetration of Indian culture to Southeast Asia also started more or less during the same period.

Mahayana or Northern Buddhism

With the growth of Mahayana Buddhism in India, especially during the reign of King Kanishka who ruled over Northern India during the second half of the first century A.D., the sect also spread to the neighboring countries, such as Sumatra, Java, and Kambuja (Cambodia). It is probable that Mahayana Buddhism was introduced to Burma, Pegu (Lower Burma) and Dvaravati (now Nakon Pathom in Western Thailand) from Magadha (in Bihar, India) at the same time as it went to the Malay Archipelago. But probably it did not have any stronghold there at that time; hence no spectacular trace was left of it.

Starting from the beginning of the fifth century A.D. Mahayana Buddhist missionaries from Kashmir in Northern India began to go to Sumatra in succession. From Sumatra the faith spread to Java and Cambodia. By about 757 A.D. (Buddhist Era: 1300) the Srivijaya king with his capital in Sumatra rose in power and his empire spread throughout the Malay Peninsula and Archipelago. Part of South Thailand (from Surasthani downwards) came under the rule of the Srivijaya king. Being Mahayanists, the rulers of Srivijaya gave much encouragement and support to the propagation of Mahayana Buddhism. In South Thailand today we have much evidence to substantiate that Mahayana Buddhism was once prevalent there. This evidence is in the form of stupas or chetiyas and images, including votive tablets of the Buddhas and Bodhisattas (Phra Phim), which were found in large number, all of the same type as those discovered in Java and Sumatra. The chetiyas in Chaiya (Jaya) and Nakon Sri Thammarath (Nagara Sri Dharmaraja), both in South Thailand, clearly indicate Mahayana influence.

From 1002 to 1182 A.D. kings belonging to the Suryavarman dynasty ruled supreme in Cambodia. Their empire extended over the whole of present-day Thailand. Being adherents of Mahayana Buddhism with a strong mixture of Brahmanism, the Suryavarman rulers did much to propagate and establish the tenets of the Northern School. There is an interesting stone inscription, now preserved in the National Museum at Bangkok, which tells us that in about 1017 A.D. (B.E. 1550) there ruled in Lopburi, in central Thailand and once a capital city, a king from Nakon Sri Thammarath who traced his ancestry to Srivijaya rulers. The king had a son who later became the ruler of Kambuja (Cambodia) and who, more or less, kept Thailand under the suzerainty of Cambodia for a long time. During this period there was much amalgamation of the two countries' religions and cultures. The stone inscription under consideration probably refers to one of the Suryavarman kings who had blood relationship with the Srivijaya rulers.

From the inscription just referred to we also learn that at that period the form of Buddhism prevalent in Lopburi was that of Theravada, and that Mahayana Buddhism, already established in Cambodia, became popularized in Thailand only after Thailand had come under the sway of Cambodia. There are no indications, however, that the Mahayana School superseded the Theravada in any way. This was due to the fact that Theravada Buddhism was already on a firm basis in Thailand when the Mahayana School was introduced there. That there were monks of both schools, Theravada and Mahayana, in Lopburi during those days, is indicated in a stone inscription in the Cambodian language, found in a Brahmanic Temple within the vicinity of Lopburi city itself.

Much of the Brahmanic culture which survives in Thailand till today could be traced to its origin from Cambodia during this period. Many of the Cambodian kings themselves were zealous adherents of Brahmanism and its ways of life. This period, therefore, can be termed Mahayana Period. Sanskrit, the sacred language of the Hindus, took its root deep in Thailand during these times.

Burma (Pagan) Buddhism

In 1057 A.D. King Anuruddha (Anawratha) became powerful in the whole of Burma, having his capital at Pagan (Central Burma). Anuruddha extended his kingdom right up to Thailand, especially the Northern and Central parts, covering areas now known as Chiengmai, Lopburi, and Nakon Pathom. Being a Theravada Buddhist, Anuruddha ardently supported the cause of Theravada which Burma, like Thailand, at first received directly from India through missionaries sent by Emperor Asoka. However, at the time under consideration, Buddhism in India was already in a state of decline, and as contact between Burma and India was then faint, Theravada Buddhism, as prevalent in Burma at that time, underwent some changes and assumed a form somewhat different from the original doctrine. This, at a later stage, became what is known in Thailand as Burma (Pagan) Buddhism. During the period of King Anuruddha's suzerainty over Thailand, Burmese Buddhism exercised great influence over the country, especially in the North where, owing to proximity, the impact from Burma was more felt.

It is significant that Buddhist relics found in North Thailand bear a striking Theravada influence, whereas those found in the South clearly show their Mahayana connections dating back from Srivijaya days. To a great extent this is due to the fact that, in their heyday of suzerainty over Thailand, the Burmese under Anuruddha were content with Upper Thailand only, while leaving the South practically to be ruled by their Khmer (Cambodian) vassals whose capital was at Lopburi.

From the beginning of the 2nd century B.C. the Thai people, whose original homeland was in the valleys between the Huang Ho and the Yangtze Kiang in China, began to migrate southwards as a result of constant friction with the neighboring tribes. In the course of their migration which lasted for several centuries, they became separated into two main groups. One group went and settled in the plains of the Salween River, Shan States, and other areas and spread on as far as Assam. This group of Thais is called Thai Yai (Big Thai). The other main group moved further South and finally settled in what is today termed Thailand. The latter group of Thais is called Thai Noi (Small Thai). The Thais in present-day Thailand are actually the descendants of these migrant Thais. Of course, in the course of their migration which, as said above, continued off and on for a long time, there had been a great deal of mixture of blood through intermarriage which was only natural. We should always bear in mind that there are several ethnic groups scattered through the length and breadth of Southeast Asia from times immemorial. But even today we can trace the language affinity of the Thais living in widely scattered areas such as Assam, Upper Burma, Southern China, Shan States, Laos, North Vietnam, and Thailand.

After struggling hard for a long time the Thais were able to establish their independent state at Sukhothai (Sukhodaya) in North Thailand. This was probably about 1257 A.D. (B.E. 1800). It was during the period of their movement southwards that the Thais came into contact with the form of Buddhism as practiced in Burma and propagated under the royal patronage of King Anuruddha.

Some scholars are of the opinion that as Mahayana Buddhism had spread to China as early as the beginning of the Christian Era, the Thais, while still in their original home in China, must have already been acquainted with some general features of Buddhism.

As the Thai migrants grew in strength their territory extended and finally they became the masters of the land in succession to Anuruddha, whose kingdom declined after his death. During the succeeding period, the Thais were able to exert themselves even more prominently in their southward drive. Thus they came into close contact with the Khmers, the erstwhile power, and became acquainted with both Mahayana Buddhism and Brahmanism as adopted and practiced in Kambuja (Cambodia). Much of the Brahmanic influence, such as religious and cultural rites, especially in the court circles, passed on from Cambodia to the Thais during this period, for Hinduism was already firmly established in Cambodia at that time. Even the Thai scripts, based on Cambodian scripts which, in turn, derived their origin from India, were invented by King Ram Kamhaeng of Sukhothai during the period under consideration. Of the period under discussion it may be observed in passing that Northern Thailand, from Sukhothai District upwards, came much under the influence of Burma (Pagan) Buddhism, while in the central and southern parts of the country many Mahayana beliefs and practices, inherited from the days of the Suryavarmans and the Srivijayas, still persisted.

Ceylon (Lankavamsa) Buddhism

This is the most important period in the history of the spread of Buddhism to Thailand, for it witnessed the introduction to that country of that form of Buddhism which remains dominant there until today.

About 1153 A.D. (B.E. 1696) Parakramabahu the Great (1153-1186 A.D.) became king of Ceylon, known in ancient days as Lanka. A powerful monarch and a great supporter of Theravada Buddhism, Parakramabahu did much to spread and consolidate the Dhamma of the Lord in his island kingdom. He it was who caused (according to some scholars of Southern Buddhism) the Seventh Buddhist Council to be held under the chairmanship of Kassapa Thera, of Dimbulagala in order to revise and strengthen the Doctrine and the Discipline (Dhamma and Vinaya).

As a result of the efforts of King Parakramabahu the Great, Buddhism was much consolidated in Ceylon and the news spread to neighboring lands. Buddhist monks from various countries, such as Burma, Pegu (Lower Burma), Kambuja, Lanna (North Thailand) and Lanchang (Laos) flocked to Ceylon in order to acquaint themselves with the pure form of the Dhamma. Thailand also sent her Bhikkhus to Ceylon and thereby obtained the *upasampada vidhi* (ordination rite) from Ceylon, which later became known in Thailand as Lankavamsa. This was about 1257 A.D. (B.E. 1800).

Apparently the early batches of Bhikkhus, who returned from Ceylon after studies, often accompanied by Ceylonese monks, established themselves first in Nakon Sri Thammarath (South Thailand), for many of the Buddhist relics bearing definitely Ceylonese influence, such as stupas and Buddha images, were found there. Some of these relics are still in existence today. News of the meritorious activities of these monks soon spread to Sukhothai, then the capital of Thailand, and King Ram Kamhaeng who was ruling at the time, invited those monks to his capital and gave them his royal support in propagating the Doctrine. This fact is recorded in one of the King's rock inscriptions, dated about 1277 A.D. Since then Ceylon (Sinhala) Buddhism became very popular and was widely practiced in Thailand. Some of the Thai kings, such as King

Maha Dharmaraja Lithai of Sukhothai dynasty and King Borom Trai Lokanath of the early Ayudhya Period, even entered the Holy Order or Bhikkhu Sangha according to the ordination rite of Lankavamsa Buddhism by inviting a patriarch from Ceylon, Maha Sami Sangharaja Sumana by name, to be the presiding monk over his upasampada (ordination) ceremony. Many monasteries, stupas, Buddha images and even Buddha footprints, such as the well-known one at Sraburi in central Thailand, were built in accordance with the usage popular in Ceylon. The study of Pali, the language of Theravada or Southern Buddhism, also made great progress, and in all matters dealing with the Dhamma the impact of Ceylon was perceptibly felt.

However, there had been no antagonism between the different forms of Buddhism already in existence in Thailand and the Lankavamsa which had been introduced later from Ceylon. On the contrary they seemed to have amalgamated peacefully, and all had adjusted themselves to one another's benefit. This is evident in all religious rites and ceremonies of Thailand. Indeed, somewhat characteristic of the Buddhists, there had been a spirit of forbearance in all matters. For instance, even today Brahmanic rites thrive side by side with Buddhistic ceremonies in Thailand and Cambodia, especially in the royal courts.

History repeats itself. Years after, when in Ceylon under King Kirtisri (1747-1781 A.D.) the upasampada ordination was lost due to a decline of Buddhism and upheavals in the country, Thailand (during the reign of King Boromkot, 1733-1758 A.D.) was able to repay the debt by sending a batch of Buddhist monks, under the leadership of Upali and Ariyamuni Theras, who in the course of time established in Ceylon what is known as the *Siyamopali Vamsa* or *Siyam Nikaya,* or Siamese Sect, which still is a major sect in that country. Upali worked and died in Sri Lanka, the country he loved no less than his own.

Today, for all purposes, Thailand can be termed a Theravada Buddhist country. There are, of course, a few Mahayana monks and monasteries, but they are mostly confined to foreign communities, chiefly the Chinese. All, however, live at peace and cooperate with one another.

So much for the past of Buddhism in Thailand.

BUDDHISM IN THAILAND: ITS PRESENT

According to the census taken in 1960 the population of Thailand numbers 25,519,965. Of this number 94% are Buddhists (the rest are mostly Muslims and Christians). This fact itself demonstrates more than anything else how influential Buddhism is in Thailand. In their long history of existence the Thais seem to have been predominantly Buddhists, at least ever since they came into contact with the tenets of Buddhism. All the Thai kings in the recorded history of present-day Thailand have been adherents of Buddhism. The country's constitution specifies that the King of Thailand must be a Buddhist and the Upholder of Buddhism.

The term "The Land of Yellow Robes" has not been inappropriately applied to Thailand, for two things strike most foreigners as soon as they set foot in that country. One is the Buddhist temple with its characteristic architecture, and the other is the sight of yellow-clad Buddhist monks and novices who are to be seen everywhere, especially in the early hours of dawn when they go out in great numbers for alms. The two sights inevitably remind the foreigners that here is a country where Buddhism is a dominant force in the people's life. Indeed, to the Thai nation as a whole, Buddhism has been the main spring from which flow its culture and philosophy, its art and literature, its ethics and morality, and many of its folkways and festivals.

For clarity and convenience we shall divide the study of the present state of Buddhism in Thailand into two parts, namely the Bhikkhu Sangha or the Holy Order, and the Laity.

The Bhikkhu Sangha or the Holy Order

The Bhikkhu Sangha or the Holy Order of Buddhist monks has been in existence in Thailand ever since Buddhism was introduced there. According to the 1958 census there were in the whole kingdom of Thailand 159,648 monks; 73,311 novices; and 20,944 monasteries or temples. These are scattered throughout the country, particularly more numerous in the thickly populated areas. The Bhikkhu Sangha of Thailand, being of Theravada or Southern School, observes the same set of discipline (Vinaya) as the Bhikkhu Sanghas in other Theravada countries such as Ceylon, Burma, Laos, and

Cambodia. In spite of the fact that the government allots a yearly budget for the maintenance and repair of important temples and as stipends for high ranking monks, almost the entire burden for the support of the Sangha and the upkeep of the temples rests with the public. A survey entitled "Thailand Economic Farm Survey" made in 1953 by the Ministry of Agriculture of the Government of Thailand gives the religious cash expenses of the average Thai rural family per year as ranging from 5 to 10 per cent of its total annual cash income. It may be added here that the report concerns the average Thai rural family, and not the urban dwellers, the majority of whom, in Thailand as elsewhere, are less inclined to religion than the country folks.

Two Sects or Nikayas

There are two sects or Nikayas of the Buddhist Order in Thailand. One is the Mahanikaya, and the other is the Dhammayuttika Nikaya. The Mahanikaya is the older and by far the more numerous one, the ratio in the number of monks of the two sects being 35 to 1. The Dhammayuttika Nikaya was founded in 1833 A.D. by King Mongkut, the fourth ruler of the present Chakri Dynasty who ruled Thailand from 1851 to 1868 A.D. Having himself spent 27 years as a Bhikkhu, the King was well versed in the Dhamma, besides many other branches of knowledge, including Pali, the canonical language of Theravada Buddhism. The express desire of the King in founding the Dhammayuttika sect was to enable monks to lead a more disciplined and scholarly life in accordance with the pristine teachings of the Buddha. The differences between the two Nikayas are, however, not great; at most they concern only matters of discipline, and never of the Doctrine. Monks of both sects follow the same 227 Vinaya rules as laid down in the Patimokkha of the Vinaya Pitaka (the Basket of the Discipline), and both receive the same esteem from the public. In their general appearance and daily routine of life too, except for the slight difference in the manners of putting on the yellow robes, monks of the two Nikayas differ very little from one another.

Organization of the Sangha

Formerly, and in accordance with the Administration of the Bhikkhu Sangha Act (B.E. 2484, A.D. 1943), the organization of the Sangha in Thailand was on a line similar to that of the State. The Sangharaja or the Supreme Patriarch is the highest Buddhist dignitary of the Kingdom. He is chosen by the King, in consultation with the Government, from among the most senior and qualified members of the Sangha. The Sangharaja appoints a council of Ecclesiastical Ministers headed by the *Sangha Nayaka*, whose position is analogous to that of the Prime Minister of the State. Under the Sangha Nayaka there function four ecclesiastical boards, namely the Board of Ecclesiastical Administration, the Board of Education, the Board of Propagation and the Board of Public Works.

Each of the boards has a Sangha Mantri (equivalent to a minister in the secular administration) with his assistants. The four boards or ministries are supposed to look after the affairs of the entire Sangha. The Ecclesiastical Ministerial Council which, by the way, corresponds to the Cabinet, consists of ten members, all senior monks of the Sangha. In addition to this, there is a Consultative Assembly (*Sangha Sabha*), equivalent to the National Assembly, the members of which number 45, selected from various important monasteries. The Sangha Sabha acts as an Advisory Body to the Ecclesiastical Ministerial Council. Below the Sangha Sabha the administration of the Sangha continues to correspond to the secular administration of the country. All monks and novices (*samaneras*) have to live in monasteries which are scattered throughout the country. Each monastery has its abbot appointed by the Ecclesiastical Ministerial Council in consultation with local people. It may be pointed out here that all religious appointments in Thailand are based on scholarly achievements, seniority, personal conduct and popularity, and contacts with monks further up in the Sangha.

There is a Department of Religious Affairs in the Ministry of Education which acts as a liaison office between the Government and the Sangha. In general the Department of Religious Affairs works in cooperation with the Ecclesiastical Ministerial Council on all matters affecting the Sangha. For instance, it issues all legal directives concerning the entire community of monks; it keeps record of the Sangha's property, such as lands etc.; it maintains facts and figures with respect to monks and monasteries. The Religious Affairs Department also prepares the annual budget for the upkeep of the Sangha functionaries and the maintenance and repair of temples etc. It may be added here that all temples and monasteries are State property.

In 1962, the Administration of the Bhikkhu Sangha Act of 1943 was abolished; a new one was enacted instead. By virtue of the new act, the posts of Sangha Nayaka, Sangha Mantris, and Sangha Sabha were abolished. In place of these there is a *Mahathera Samagama* (Council of the Elders) headed by the Sangharaja himself and consisting of not less than four and not more than eight senior monks (*mahatheras*) of the two sects (*nikayas*). The Mahathera Samagama, in collaboration with the Department of Religious Affairs, directly governs the entire Sangha.

Education of Monks

As is well known, the original idea of men's entering monkhood during the Buddha's time or shortly later, was to attain liberation from worldly existence in accordance with the teaching of the Master. Such an idea, of course, springs from man's feeling of aversion to things mundane. In other words, in those far-off days, men entered monkhood with the sole intention of ridding themselves of life's miseries and of obtaining spiritual freedom or Nirvana. Instances of such self-renunciation are found in the holy books of the Buddhists. With the passage of time, as is only natural, many of the ideals and practices of the early followers of the Buddha underwent modifications. Today, over 2,500 years after the passing away of the Buddha, though the ideal of becoming a Bhikkhu still remains very lofty among Buddhists of all lands, in practice it must be admitted that there have been many deviations from the Master's original admonitions with regard to the whys and wherefores of man's entering monkhood. Generalization of any subject matter is often dangerous but it will not be far from truth to say that today, in Thailand as in other Buddhist countries, the practice of Buddhist males entering monkhood is to a considerable extent prompted rather by the dictation of custom, the wish for education and other external considerations than by the desire to attain emancipation. Yet there are also many who join the Sangha through genuine love for a religious life and religious studies, or out of the wish to be of service to Buddhism and their country. Finally, in the Thai Sangha also those are not entirely lacking whose life is vigorously devoted to the aim of ultimate emancipation and to the guidance of others towards that goal. There have been, and still are, saintly and able meditation masters in Thailand, with a fair number of devoted disciples in Sangha and laity. There are also still monks — the so-called *thudong* bhikkhus — who follow the ancient way of austere living embodied in the "strict observances" or *dhutangas*.

In view of the above facts, there are two categories of Buddhist monks in Thailand. One comprises those who become monks for long periods, sometimes for life, and the other those who enter the Order temporarily. To serve in the monkhood even for a short period is considered a great merit-earning attainment by the Thai Buddhists. Even kings follow this age-old custom. For instance, the present ruler, H.M. King Bhumibol Adulyadej, also observed the custom for a period of half a month some time ago. Government officials are allowed leave with full pay for a period of four months in order to serve in monkhood. The idea is to enable young men to gain knowledge of Buddhism and thereby to become good citizens. Life as a monk gives them practical experience of how an ideal Buddhist life should be. In rural districts the general tendency is still to give more deference to those who have already served in monkhood. Such people are supposed to be more "mature" than those who have not undergone the monk's life. Moreover, in Thailand *wats* (monasteries and temples) used to be and are still regarded as seats of learning where all men, irrespective of life's position, could go and avail themselves of education benefits. This is especially so in the case of economically handicapped males of the countryside. Instances are not lacking in which people have climbed high up on life's status ladder after obtaining education while in monkhood. There are neither religious restrictions nor social disapproval against monks' returning to lay life if and when they find themselves unable to discharge their duties as monks.

Cases exist in which, for some reason or the other, men have entered monkhood more than once, although such practice cannot be said to be in the esteem of the public. Looked at from this viewpoint, the institution of entering monkhood in Thailand, apart from being a way of gaining moral and spiritual enlightenment, is a social uplift method by which those not so fortunately placed in life could benefit. Judged from the ideal of adopting a monk's life as enunciated by the Buddha, whether or not such practice is commendable, is a different story. The fact is that even today when modernism has penetrated deep into Thailand, about one half of the primary schools of the country are still situated in wats. With sex and crimes on the increase in the country, the cry for living a better Buddhist life is being heard more and more distinctly in Thailand today.

The traditional education of monks and novices in Thailand centers mainly on the studies of the Buddhist Doctrine (Dhamma) and Pali, the language in which the Theravada scriptures are written. Of the former, the study of the Doctrine, there are three grades with examinations open to both monks and laymen. Those passing such examinations are termed *Nak Dhamm,* literally meaning one who knows the Dhamma. The latter, i.e., the study of Pali, has seven grades, starting with the third and ending with the ninth grade. Students passing Pali examinations are called *parian* (Pali: *pariñña* = penetrative knowledge); in the Thai language the word *parinna* is used to mean academic degree. For example, monks and novices passing the first Pali examination are entitled to write "P. 3" after their names.

Generally the Dhamma and the Pali studies go hand in hand and take at least seven years to complete. The stiffness of the two courses, especially that of the Pali language, can be guessed from the fact that very few students are able to pass the highest grade, the Parian 9, in any annual examination. In the good old days when living was less competitive than now, passing of even the lower Dhamma and Pali examinations used to be of much value in securing good government posts. But now things are quite different; even those successful in the highest Pali examination, the 9th Grade, find it difficult to get suitable employment.

Of late there has developed a new outlook in the education of monks in Thailand. With the rapid progress of science and with the shrinking of the world, Buddhist leaders of Thailand, monks as well as laymen, are awakened to the necessity of imparting broader education to members of the Sangha, if the

Sangha is to serve the cause of Buddhism well, "for the gain of the many, for the welfare of the many." As a result of the new outlook there now function in Bangkok two higher institutes of learning exclusively for monks and novices. One is the Mahachulalongkorn Rajvidyalaya, and the other is the Mahamongkut Rajvidyalaya. Both are organized on a modern university footing and both seem to be making satisfactory progress towards that direction. Inclusion in the curriculum of some secular subjects not incompatible with monks' discipline (Vinaya) is among the notable features of these two institutes; the aim is to give an all-round education to monks in order to enable them to be of better service to the cause of Buddhism amidst modern conditions.

So much for the education of 'long-term' monks. As for those who enter the Order temporarily, mostly for a period of three rainy months during the Vassa, or Buddhist Lent, the education is brief and devoted to the main tenets and features of Buddhism only. As pointed out above, such people enter monkhood either by their own genuine desire for knowledge of the Dhamma, by the dictum of custom or, as generally is the case, by the two reasons combined. Monks of this category return to lay life again as soon as the Lent is over. This is the reason why accommodations in monasteries (wats) are usually full during the Lenten period. Nowadays, owing to the pressure of modern life, the custom of temporarily entering monkhood is not so rigorously observed by people living in urban areas as by those in the countryside. The custom has its parallel in Burma, Cambodia, and Laos where Theravada Buddhism prevails.

Wats and Monks

The word "wat" means monastery and temple combined. It is the residence of monks and novices. There are about 21,000 wats in the whole of Thailand. In Bangkok alone there are nearly two hundred wats. Some big wats in Bangkok have as many as 600 resident monks and novices. Wats are centers of Thai art and architecture. Thai culture, to a considerable extent, flows from wats. Wat-lands and constructions thereon are donated by royalty, wealthy people and the public in general. The wat is the most important institution in Thai rural life.

The social life of the rural community revolves around the wat. Besides carrying out the obvious religious activities, a wat serves the community as a recreation center, dispensary, school, community center, home for the aged and destitute, social work and welfare agency, village clock, rest-house, news agency, and information center. A wat is headed by a *Chao Avas* (the abbot) who is responsible for the maintenance of the wat discipline, the proper performance of religious services and rituals, and the general welfare of the inmates. Besides monks and novices, there are also the "temple boys" in wats, who assist monks and novices in various ways, such as bringing and arranging food, cleaning dormitories, washing yellow robes, etc. Usually these boys are related to resident monks in one way or another, and their stay is free of charge.

Most of them are students whose homes are far away and who would, otherwise, find it impracticable to get education. This is especially so in Bangkok where accommodation is difficult to get and where all higher seats of learning of the country are situated. The census taken in 1954 reveals that there are as many as 119,044 temple boys in Thailand, which indeed is not a small figure. The institution of the wat, in itself a gift of Buddhism, therefore contributes in no small measure to the social welfare and progress of the Thai Buddhists. The benefits in this respect, of course, are more apparent among the lower strata of society than in the case of the fortunate few on the top.

Apart from engaging themselves in doctrinal studies and observing disciplinary rules (Vinaya) in general, monks are expected to be "friends, philosophers, and guides" of the people. Preaching to masses face to face or over the radio is one of the commonest ways by which monks help the promotion of moral stability among various members of the society. It may not be out of place to reiterate the fact that Buddhism lays great stress on the necessity of leading a morally good life in order to obtain happiness in life here and hereafter. In most of the ceremonies and rituals, whether private or public, monks' cooperation and benediction are indispensable. Indeed, in the life of the average Thai Buddhists, from the cradle to the grave, monks are persons to whom they constantly turn for moral support.

The role of monks in rural districts is even more important, for there the local wat is not only the religious but also the social center of the community. It is at the wat that people come together and experience a sense of comradeship. Religious rituals and ceremonies held at wats are always accompanied by social activities: they are occasions for people, especially the young, to enjoy themselves in feast, fun and festivities. This aspect of the religious service helps the common folks to relax and satisfies their needs for recreation. Not a few matrimonial alliances started from contacts at wat premises. Acting as a moral and ethical example, monks are the most venerated persons in the countryside Thai society, remaining very close to the hearts of the people. In times of crisis, it is to monks that people bring their problems for counsel and encouragement. With few exceptions, the Sangha has well justified this attitude of respect and honor shown to it on the part of the laity and, on the whole, has lived up to the dignity of the Faith.

The Laity

Throughout its over 2,500 years of existence Buddhism has been closely connected with the lay community. In Pali the word for a male lay devotee is *upasaka*; *upasika* is its female equivalent. In the history of Buddhism, right from the time of its founder, there had been numerous upasakas and upasikas whose faith in the Teachings of the Master had contributed largely to the dissemination of the Doctrine. Names of the Buddha's munificent followers like Anathapindika, Visakha, Asoka, Kanishka, etc., are on the lips of Buddhists even today. Without the patronage of Emperor Asoka, Buddhism probably could not have spread so far and the course of its history might have been different. In India, the land of its birth, as well as in most of the countries where its Message has been accepted, Buddhism has received unstinted support from people of all classes, especially the ruling class. History of the movements of Buddhism in China, Japan, Burma, Ceylon, Tibet, etc., amply justifies this statement. In the case of Thailand too, ever since its introduction to that country, Buddhism has been warmly received and patronized by kings and commoners alike. It is well-known that many of the Thai rulers, not satisfied with being mere lay-devotees, got themselves ordained into monkhood and became famous for their erudition in the Dhamma. King

Mongkut, Rama IV, probably stands out as most distinguished among this class of royal devotees. The custom of Thai males entering the Sangha also contributes much to the better understanding and cooperation between the lay community and the monkhood. After all, personal experience is better than mere theoretical knowledge.

The Buddha himself, in one of his discourses, exhorted his followers to discharge their duties well so as to enable the Dhamma to endure long in the world. One of the duties of the lay followers, as taught by the Master, is to look after the needs of monks. Hence it is the traditional practice with lay followers in all Buddhist countries, especially those following Theravada Buddhism, to see that monks do not suffer from lack of the four requisites, namely food, clothing, shelter, and medicine. Although in the present age of competitive economy, when life in any field is not so easy, nobody can say in fairness that monk-life in Thailand suffers greatly from shortage of the above four requisites. As Bhikkhus are not allowed to follow any occupational activities, it is clear that they entirely depend on the laity for their existence. In return for this spontaneous support offered them by the public, monks are expected to live exemplary lives for the benefit of themselves as well as of those who look to them as teachers and guides. We have already seen what moral influence monks have upon the people.

Cooperation between the laity and the Bhikkhu Sangha in Thailand is close and spontaneous. To a very great extent this is due to the fact that in an average Thai family some of its members are certain to be found who have for some time served in the Sangha. To the masses yellow robes are symbol of the Master, and Bhikkhus are upholders of the Dhamma, to be deferred to in all circumstances. It is interesting to note that Bhikkhus or Samaneras found guilty of committing crimes are formally divested of their yellow robes before legal action is taken against them by the State, and this is done invariably under permission of the chief monk or the abbot.

"To do good" (*kusala kamma*) is a cardinal point in the teachings of Buddhism. Consequently the idea of performing meritorious deeds is very deeply ingrained in the minds of Buddhists. Ways of doing good or making merit (*puñña*) among the Thai Buddhists are numerous. A man gains merit each time he gives alms to monks or contributes to any religious rituals. To get ordination into monkhood even for a short period, of course, brings much merit. Besides, there are other ways of merit-earning, such as releasing caged birds or freeing caught fishes, plastering gold leaf on Buddha statues or religious monuments, contributing to the construction of a new temple or the repair of an old one, etc. "The Law of Karma" that each action has its corresponding result and the belief in rebirth are two important factors in molding such attitude towards life among the Buddhists. Though *Nibbana* (Sanskrit: Nirvana), the highest bliss in Buddhism, is aspired to by all good Buddhists, the vast majority of them still think it is not so easy to reach and that they will be reborn again in this world, in heaven or some other world, or — at the very worst — in hell. Hence, as long as they live they must try to do good in order to ensure good results in this very life as well as in the life to come.

"Be a light unto yourself. Each man must strive for his own salvation"— these were the Master's words. In view of this, Theravada Buddhism is often said to have individualistic temper. Nevertheless, it is very tolerant, as the long history of its existence will prove. Indeed, the characteristic tolerance of Buddhism, for instance in Thailand, has always permitted the absorption of many beliefs and practices from other sources which have often served to supplement or expand its concepts or to fill gaps. Animism and Brahmanism may be cited in this connection; the two being important supplements of popular Buddhism in Thailand. A foreign writer has rightly observed that the attitude of the Thai masses towards their religion is of an easy-going nature. They do not bother to distinguish among the various components of their religion; for them it is all of a piece. Only the sophisticated few are concerned with doctrinal logic and purity. Of course, they too know much about its legends, its festivals, its ideals, and its general message that "good will render good." On the whole it can be said that the Thais enjoy their religion. Religious observances are to them as social and recreational as sacred occasions. And for the vast majority, Buddhism suffices in that it enables them to feel and believe and enjoy.

Bibliography

Barua, Dipak Kumar: *Viharas in Ancient India: A Survey of Buddhist Monasteries,* Indian Publications, Calcutta, 1969.

Berkson, Carmel: *The Caves at Aurangabad: Early Buddhist Tantric Art in India,* Mapin Publishing, Ahmedabad, 1986.

Chihara, D.: *Hindu-Buddhist Architecture in Southeast Asia,* E.J. Brill, Leiden, 1996.

Dutt, Nalinaksha: *Aspects of Mahayana Buddhism,* Luzac, London, 1930.

Gethin, R. M. L.: *The Buddhist Path to Awakening: A Study of the Bodhi-Pakkhiya Dhamma,* E. J. Brill, Leiden, 1992.

Haldar, J. R.: *Early Buddhist Mythology,* Manohar, New Delhi, 1977.

Jacobson, Nolan Pliny: *Buddhism, the Religion of Analysis,* Feffer & Simons, London, 1974.

Keown, Damien: *The Nature of Buddhist Ethics,* St. Martin's Press, New York, 1992.

Mishra, V. B.: *Religious Beliefs and Practices of North India during the Early Mediaeval Period,* Brill, Leiden, 1973.

Olivelle, Patrick: *The Origin and Early Development of Buddhist Monachism,* Gunasena, Colombo, 1974.

Rahula, Walpola: *History of Buddhism in Ceylon,* M. D. Gunasena, Colombo, 1956.

Sullivan, Michael: *The Cave Temples of Maichishan,* University of California Press, Berkeley, 2001.

Wagle, Narendra: *Society at the Time of Buddha,* Humanities Press, New York, 1967.

Yang, C. K.: *Religion in Chinese Society,* University of California Press, Berkeley, 1961.

INDEX

R

S

T

U

V

W

□□□